The
FURMAN
BISHER
Collection

ALSO BY FURMAN BISHER

With a Southern Exposure
Miracle in Atlanta
Strange but True Baseball Stories
Arnold Palmer: The Golden Years
Atlanta Falcons: Victory and Violence
The Masters: Augusta Revisited
Aaron
The Best of Bisher

Series Editor, Carlton Stowers

The
FURMAN
BISHER
Collection

Introduction by
LEWIS GRIZZARD

TAYLOR PUBLISHING COMPANY
Dallas, Texas

Published by Taylor Publishing Company
1550 West Mockingbird Lane
Dallas, Texas 75235

The columns included in this collection
originally appeared in *The Atlanta Journal-Constitution,*
Sport Magazine, and *Sky Magazine.*
Reprinted by permission. All rights reserved.

Library of Congress Cataloging-in-Publication Data

Bisher, Furman.
    The Furman Bisher collection / introduction by Lewis Grizzard.
        p.   cm. — (The Sportswriter's eye)
    Includes index.
    ISBN 0-87833-629-X : $14.95
    1. Sports—United States.   2. Sports. 3. Newspapers—Sections, columns,
etc.—Sports. I. Title. II. Series.
GV583.B53 1989   88-28632
070.4'49796'0973—dc19   CIP

Printed in the United States of America

0   9   8   7   6   5   4   3   2   1

To a dog named Dean, who could do everything but write and outrun automobiles; to a hick town named Denton (North Carolina, not Texas), where this seed was planted—and long may it remain hick; to Miss Rebecca Gray, loyal and true blue all these years she has kept order in my house; and to all those willing to invest in literary charleyhorses and hamstring pulls.

Introduction

They taught me to read back in 1952. At first, I thought reading was an awful waste of time.

But a couple of years later—let's say when I was eight or nine—I discovered the sports pages of *The Atlanta Journal.*

I always turned directly to Sports. The adults could read of Ike and then spend the rest of the day cursing him because he was at Augusta National playing golf when, in the words of my grandfather, his butt ought to be in Washington running the country.

I wanted the paper because I wanted to know how the Atlanta Crackers, once known as the "Yankees of the Minors," had fared against the Memphis Chicks.

I wanted to know if Duke Snider had hit another homer for the Dodgers. And I wanted to read Sports Editor Furman Bisher's column. Furman was a way out of my hometown—little Moreland, Georgia, 40 miles southwest of Atlanta.

He took me on train rides to Little Rock with the Crackers. He took me to Georgia Tech football games. He took me to US Open golf tournaments. To world championship boxing matches and to the World Series.

One day, it occurred to me, "They are paying this man to go to all these places and write about what he sees and hears."

After that realization, I had only one ambition. I wanted to be a sportswriter. I wanted to grow up to be Furman Bisher.

It would be some years before I began to notice not only what Furman Bisher wrote, but how he wrote it.

He was profoundly different from most of the other sportswriters I read. He had a way. A style. He stood back from the tumult and the shouting and found truths and real meanings.

The words from other writers marched drone-like. Furman's danced.

Young people have asked me, "How do I learn to be a writer?"

And I answer them, "Find somebody whose writing you admire, steal his or her style, and use it until you can come up with one of your own."

That is how I began as a writer. I attempted to write just like

Furman Bisher, and when I realized I couldn't, I wandered over somewhere else.

I wound up working for Furman at *The Atlanta Journal.* We had our difficulties. I was 24 and knew everything. And when he tried to offer me advice such as, "This ain't a magazine we're putting out, it's a goddamn newspaper," I pouted. But years later, I would say to another graduate of the Bisher School of Sports Journalism, "Remember all that stuff Bisher used to tell us we were doing wrong? He was right."

You hold in your hands a long overdue collection of the best of Furman Bisher. His passion for and understanding of life, its participants, and the games they play are evident in each word. Being asked by the author to write this introduction is as fine an honor as I've ever received. I simply hope these warblings of mine are fit to trumpet what follows.

So, I leave you quickly by saying simply this: You are about to read journalism at its best. Cherish each word as I have for nearly all of my life.

Lewis Grizzard

Contents

Fore! / 73

Two Men and Some Horses / 105

Tennis, With Love / 119

Louis, Ali, Frazier, & The Warriors / 131

Politicians, Politics, & Other Games / 157

The Aaron/Williams File / 177

Some Dear, Departed Friends & Others / 201

CONTENTS

Preface

It is good form in such compositions as a preface to his own book that the author—ahem, being me, or I, or he—take a self-effacing posture, especially if it's a collection of old works. God knows, you wouldn't want anybody out there to really think you're serious, beyond the exhilaration that comes from being able to find use for a few old columns that otherwise would have lined a garbage pail, caught paint drippings, or kindled a fire. There is no attempt to reestablish history here, nor to give a course in journalism. Along that line, let me tell you how much better I turned out than I ever expected. All I ever wanted to do was ride trains and cover baseball teams, and here I am being recycled.

An old acquaintance looked longingly at me the other day and said, "I've always thought you had the best of all worlds. Who else can do the things you do and get paid for it?"

It reminded me of another time when he asked me what I was doing the next week.

"I've got to go to the World Series," I said.

"Gotta go, ho, ho, ho. Somebody got a gun at your head. Talk to me about some more of your hardships."

He has a picture of me trudging out of the stadium at 1:30 in the morning. Weary. Beat. Hungry. Cold or sweaty, depending on whether it's Minneapolis or Cincinnati. Hoping I can find a cab back to the hotel, where the bar and the restaurant are closed. Good citizens are in bed at that hour, and I'm walking the street like a derelict. But he'd never understand.

Writing has never really satisfied my taste for sports. I wanted to play right field in Yankee Stadium. I wanted to come into the eighteenth hole at Augusta National needing only a bogey to win. I wanted to play Centre Court at Wimbledon. I wanted to play Bobby Riggs. I wanted to own a racehorse that won.

The truth is, I've done some of these. I've played tennis while Gene Tunney, the old heavyweight, watched and cheered. I've had Gary Player pounding me on the back after sinking a birdie putt. I've stormed at Norm Van Brocklin because he missed one, Stormin' Norman himself. I've played golf on national television, but nobody knew who I was, or cared. I once beat Ted Turner on the high seas, yacht racing. The difference was he owned his yacht; I was only a lowly crewman.

But none of it was as much fun after it was over as writing about it. I could always go back to the old Royal the next day and do it over again in type. All those other things were a now-and-then thing. I could never get a streak going. Writing I could do every day.

There will be no attempt here to rave about the good old days. Good old days are now because we're living them. Tomorrow's column is the future. Yesterday's column is the past. They're that perishable. There is a mixture here of good old days, bad old days, and days of wine and roses, and the bottom line is, you're no better than the last column you just wrote.

I haven't tried to play to any audience here. What is here is some of the best that other people have helped me to remember. I've never known if they were good or bad, and they were neither until the people out there called it.

I have no idea what the title of this thing is going to be, but titles don't sell books, despite *Gone With the Wind* and *For Whom the Bell Tolls*.

They really knew how to write titles back then. Think of what the title *With a Southern Exposure* would do. Catchy, isn't it? Boffo. That was the title of my first book of columns, a few copies still on hand. That was twenty-seven years ago. You can't rush these things, but here we go again. Forget time. Just pick out a page and start reading.

Furman Bisher

The Grand Old Game

THE GAFFER'S LAST GAFFE

AUGUST 31, 1984

The sign was still out front long after the proprietor had pulled stakes and the joint had gone dark. It hung under the marquee on the Ponce de Leon side of the Georgian Terrace Hotel, the neon tubing empty of color.

"Gaffer's" was the name Denny McLain put on his lounge, tavern, bistro—call it what you would. Another watering hole. It was located on the lower level of a once-ornate hotel desperately trying to hold onto the last vestige of flossier times.

So, in a sense, was Denny McLain. His vestiges were threadbare even then, but you had to say this for the guy—he never saw a cloud in his sky. There was a pot of gold out there somewhere, if he could only find the rainbow.

Denny was the kind of guy who always figured he had the world by the tail, even when it was the other way around. He figured nothing could get at Big Denny. He was too smart. He had too much on the ball. He was Dennis Dale McLain, world's greatest baseball pitcher.

It didn't matter that his fastball was gone, he was ingloriously out of condition, his earned-run average was about the size of his waistline, and he was unemployed. Denny had the conviction that once a king, always a king. Once the greatest, always the greatest.

He didn't realize it then, but he had pitched and won his last major-league game in Atlanta on August 8, 1972. He would never make it into another season. "Gaffer's" was his next act.

He would become the world's next great nightclub operator. (His choice of a name for the place was out of character. A "gaffer" is an old man.)

Denny had developed another talent, playing the organ above hobby level. He would have made it in our average Holiday Inn cocktail lounge. So it was expected that he would play in his own parlor, offering himself as his star attraction. After all, he had produced one album.

During the World Series in 1968, he had played wildly into the night for kicks in the lounge of the St. Louis hotel where the Detroit Tigers put up.

No organ playing for him, he said to an interviewer. He would be the Toots Shor of the place, not the organ-grinder.

I don't know when "Gaffer's" took the gas, but I drove past one day and it was shut tight. Denny was gone. He would have one more spring training, a halfhearted appearance. The Braves invited him, the courteous thing to do for the once-greatest pitcher. It was an exercise in futility, considering his condition. Even in his myopic state, that was one thing he could see clearly.

What he couldn't see was what a baseball derelict he was becoming. He'd been working at it since he was at his very peak. He bought jet planes he couldn't pay for. He had this brief vision of himself as an airline entrepreneur. He bought automobiles he couldn't pay for. He bought real estate he couldn't pay for. He tried to pay off his debts with his signature, which was worth something only on a baseball.

A classic pitching arm had come attached to a totally undisciplined character. Not since Lefty Grove had gone 31-4 in 1931 had there been such a season pitched in the major leagues as McLain's 1968, when he was 31-6. Three seasons later, he was 10-22.

In between, he had had one season of 3-5, but that was the season he did time in Bowie Kuhn's cooler. He'd run into trouble with the mob, he'd doused a reporter with a bucket of water, he'd been caught carrying a gat, but otherwise checked out as an exemplary citizen.

Atlanta was his last stop in uniform. Eddie Robinson gave up Orlando Cepeda to get him, and McLain paid for himself in one day. About 50,000 paid to watch him make his first start, which didn't last long. The three games he won for the Braves were strugglesome. He was through, washed up, and he wasn't thirty yet.

After life with "Gaffer's," McLain turned up in Memphis running a minor-league team. The problem there involved missing funds, and he hit the road again. He managed to stay out of major print until the big storm broke over his head.

This time, he was hit with the book: extortion, bookmaking,

drug smuggling, and a few coattail charges. He was hauled in for indictment, which wasn't easy. In 1968, he weighed 186 pounds. In 1984, he had filled out, as they say, to 300 pounds. He could play the blimp at the county fair. He is tragic, pathetic, grotesque, all three. His is a textbook case of self-destruction.

His pitching companion in Detroit was Mickey Lolich, who picked up the Tigers and turned them around in the World Series of 1968. He was of rather rotund construction even then, but he kept his pitching condition long enough to win 217 games. When retirement time came, Lolich exited gracefully, went back to Detroit, and opened a doughnut shop.

One morning last week, Mickey Lolich arose before dawn, as usual, and went to the shop to see that the doughnuts were properly prepared for the day. That same day in Tampa, Florida, the jury was picked to try Denny McLain. Seven women and five men.

A ROSE BY ANY NAME IS STILL A ROSE

JULY 24, 1983

Sometimes when he scrooches up his face, Peter Edward Rose looks as if he may have been made up to play "The Hunchback of Notre Dame." Time has left some tread marks on his features, a face that would stand well behind a bar in Belfast—homely enough, tough enough, yet noble enough to bring out the good nature in another.

He is a Tom Sawyer spirit captured in a 1941-model chassis. He never looked on baseball as an occupation. He arrived in a dirty uniform and ten minutes after it was cleaned, it was dirty again. He played for the love of it.

It came as a shock when the economy turned and he found out baseball could make him wealthy. There was enough money out there to make him leave Cincinnati, though he always says it wouldn't have taken nearly as much to have kept him there as he got to go to Philadelphia, where they used to boo him sinfully.

He'd grown up in Cincinnati, a high-school football star and a sandlot baseball hero. Heaven to Pete Rose was old Crosley Field, a ramshackle piece of tumbledown architecture that seemed to have been put together in one afterthought after another. There was only one team he would ever play for, the Reds. He didn't expect to become a chapter in baseball's history. He only wanted to be a name on the sports pages of the *Post* and the *Enquirer*.

He could hardly believe it when they gave him $7,000 to play his first season. The year before, he had played for peanuts in the stifling summer of Macon, Georgia, on a Reds farm club. Four years later, he led the National League in hits and his salary jumped to an astronomical $24,000.

"I'd rather have played my whole career in Cincinnati, but once I convinced myself they no longer wanted me, leaving was easy," he said.

He had just come in from posing by the Ty Cobb sculpture on the Capitol Avenue side of Atlanta Stadium. "The Georgia Peach," he said, gently, "he was great, but he was a mean player, they tell me."

When Tyrus Raymond Cobb was forty-two, he made his 4,191st hit, batted .323 in ninety-five games, and retired. At the same age, Pete Rose will have his 4,000th hit and be looking forward to being forty-three and making his 4,192nd hit. There has been suspicion that he is playing for the record, otherwise he would be retired and living on his luxury.

He stiffened slightly. "I'm playing for three reasons," he said. "I'm playing because I can still play. I'm playing because the enthusiasm is still there, and the other one is I think I've got a chance to play in another World Series. I'm not playing for the record.

"But I want it."

When he was a Rose bud, forty-two must have looked like the Neanderthal age. "Nannh, forty-two never looked old to me. I got to see my father pay football when he was forty-two. He was a halfback. He was good and he was tough; you had to be to play in that kind of league. I'm sort of a copy of my father in the next generation, with an opportunity."

He still slides into bases head first. He still calls on his guile when the play is close, as when he rolled over Brett Butler trying to pin him off the bag in a pickoff play at first. The speed isn't Olympic stuff, but he never was a sprinter.

"I had quickness. Never had great speed. I knew how to run the bases, and I still do," he said. The most bases he ever stole in the majors was twenty. He was thirty-eight.

Whatever offensive record Henry Aaron doesn't hold in the league, Rose does. The Braves have been his most useful target. He has more hits off Phil Niekro than any other pitcher, mainly because they've been going at it for twenty years, and more hits off the Braves than any other team.

He remembers his first hit. It was off Bob Friend of the Pirates, a triple.

Condition is something Rose is always in. Doesn't drink and doesn't smoke. He laughs. "I never saw my father take a drink or smoke or argue with my mother. My kids never saw me take a drink or smoke a cigarette, but I miss on the third." He was divorced two years ago from Karolyn, and what he misses most about Cincinnati is watching his thirteen-year-old son grow into another Rose off the old bush.

"He is some hitter. Tough. I never saw a kid hit that good. The only good thing about the strike last year was that I got to watch him play," Rose said.

So this is the man who would replace Ty Cobb at the top of the heap. He had never seen the Felix deWeldon sculpture of the sliding "Georgia Peach" before. He looked at it with a peculiar air of respect, then put his voice of approval on it.

"Pretty darn good slide," he said.

GET THIS—
BRAVES AND
PADRES PLAY
CRUCIAL SERIES

JULY 28, 1982

You want a good laugh? This'll kill you. I can hardly see through the tears in my eyes from laughing myself.

But get this: The Atlanta Braves and the San Diego Padres opened a crucial series last night at the Stadium. The Braves and the Padres!

The Dodgers and the Reds play "crucial" series, or the Phillies and the Cards, not the Braves and the Padres. They're usually standing around the kitchen door waiting for the scraps.

The key word is "crucial," as in "crooshil," which is what it used to be in Brooklyn before the Dodgers took a walk. The Braves and the Padres were the deckhands of the Western Division. The Ritz Brothers of the National League. The only thing crucial that ever happened to them was when the pilot told them to take a crash position.

They lead the league in defeat. They've lost 2,418 games between them since they opened for business at their present locations. The rest of the league used to treat them like servants. Here they are playing for first place and August is upon us.

It's a different neighborhood down where they used to live and try to scrape out a living. The Reds and the Astros are in residence now and times are hard for them. The hoity-toity Dodgers were eight games back and feeling pretty left out. The Padres figured they had five players who should have been on the All-Star squad and Tommy Lasorda took only one out of spite.

8

"We've been making the Dodgers look bad and Lasorda doesn't like that," Dick Williams, the manager, said.

The Dodgers aren't used to being out of it, and somebody else attracting the beauties and the swells that arrived in long limousines. The Crucial Series had the big-timers coming out of their castles and their executive towers. Even Roger Angell, the author—sort of the curator of baseball's more refined moments. NBC had a crew in here with Byron Day practicing for the weekend, when the Dodgers do get stage time.

This was two for the price of one. A twin bill. Double dip. Pick the cliché of your choice.

Bob Walk, an incriminating name for a pitcher, and Tim Lollar, another of the Yankees' trading miscalculations, were starting. Lollar is the slugger. He leads National League pitchers in home runs. Walk is your typical hitting pitcher, a hit a month. Not this time. He kept Lollar off the bases, but Lollar couldn't keep him off. Walk singled twice and drove in a run just like he was Red Ruffing.

In the third inning, Glenn Hubbard walks. Dale Murphy is the next batter and a conference is called on the pitching mound. Norm Sherry, the Padres coach, goes out, and this leads to one of life's embarrassing moments. Obviously they're deciding how to pitch Murphy, who almost knocked the fence down with a double the first time up. Sherry goes back to the dugout, Lollar throws two pitches. The first is a strike, the second lands on top of the stack of football seats over the left-field fence, delivered by a classic home-run swing. A hurricane fence won't stop a hurricane, nor pitching conferences Murphy.

This was a game of its own peculiar rarities. Rafael Ramirez finishes off an unassisted double play at first base. The Padres make a triple play, the old third-to-home-to-first route, but it doesn't count. Terry Kennedy steps on home plate instead of putting the tag on Bob Horner, just the way Aaron Robinson cost the Tigers a pennant one year.

Horner is having himself a weird night, like the kid at the dunk tank at the carnival. Padres pitchers are either nailing him solid or missing him a mile. He walks, he's a hit batter, he walks, he's a hit batter and he walks, and his line in the box score is one of those strange ones—0200.

It's a winner for the Braves and Joe Torre's all-right-handed batting order, 9-2, so easy they carelessly squander ten runners on the bases. Both managers are moving players in and out like it's a march across a desert when it's only eighteen innings of baseball, saving them for God-knows-what. You never saw Ty Cobb or Pete Rose sit out a game of a doubleheader to save himself.

Williams was starting his man from the bull pen, Eric Show (as in "Howston" Street), a show (as in picture "show") in himself, I read, as some kind of intellectual freak. Baseball gets nervous around intellects, suspects them of something seditious. Torre started Ken Dayley. That didn't last long. Both were soon gone.

Larry Whisenton gave the Padres a run misjudging a drive, amid it back with a home run, and they went threshing on into the night, tied 6-6.

They're keeping 32,151 devotees of the change-up up past their bedtime. But this is museum stuff, something to put on public display, like James Watt's steam engine or Napoleon's carriage. The Braves and the Padres playing a "crooshil." Hubbard rings the bell at midnight with a two-run homer, and the most people who ever paid to see San Diego play in Atlanta can go home with the happiness of small children who've just had a fairy tale read to them.

WILLIE'S LAST FLING, A LA JOLSON

OCTOBER 15, 1973

A-ha. Now we're getting around to what a World Series ought to be. Too much the old dirty-britches kind of game had gotten away from us. There was the striving for the kind you'd get out of a computer. Smooth execution, perfect timing. Two-to-one scores and play it in two hours thirty minutes. Besides, it pleases television. The networks can move on to Disneyland or Sunday Night at the Movies.

This is World Series like we all remember World Series. Back when the players were Gionfriddo, Lavagetto, Robinson, Martin, Mazeroski, and Amoros. This was one even Snodgrass and Merkle would have loved.

Sloppy. Full of errors. Pratfalls. Wild plays. Outfielders losing flies in the sun. Bases on balls. Hit batters. Haggling and protests and near-brawls. Even Willie Mays down on his knees at home plate pleading with umpire Augie Donatelli. I can't read lips, but I'd have sworn he was doing his old Al Jolson act for the crowd.

That's another thing—Willie Mays in a World Series.

It was the twelfth inning in Oakland Coliseum Sunday afternoon. Just about the time everybody had decided that God had abandoned the New York Mets, who had their quota of miracles—one to a customer, please—in 1969, Willie shows up with His proxy. The Mets had been ahead once, 6-3, but the Athletics tied it and Mays is not to be denied his fair share in the credits. With him playing center field like an old dog who'd lost his smell for the hunt, the Athletics tied it 6-6 in the ninth inning.

The twelfth inning comes up. Bud Harrelson, who is about

to become the motivating figure in this series, hits a double. The pitcher, Tug McGraw, is at bat. You got to remember this is the middle of October and Tug McGraw has had four hits since April.

The Athletics are Banzai players. If this were war, they'd all be Kamikaze pilots or bazooka gunners. They come at you like they've been mixing booze and gasoline. So Sal Bando, their third baseman who looks like a Mexican bandit, is charging.

All McGraw wants to do is (give his life for his team) bunt the ball. Give Harrelson transportation to third base.

The pitcher pops the bunt over Bando's head. Harrelson gets third and McGraw gets a base hit and Willie Mays gets what Willie Mays likes. Stage lights up. Strong background music. Everybody's attention.

It wasn't as if he didn't owe the rest of the Mets something. He'd come in as a pinch-runner for Rusty Staub. That's like asking A.J. Foyt to drive a cab. And if it had been, A.J. would have wrecked it. Mays slipped and fell rounding second. Later he fell flat chasing a ball hit by Deron Johnson and played it into two bases. Then let another hit by Reggie Jackson hit the fence, but gave a very detailed explanation of his strategy on this play after the game

"You don't go out and kill yourself. We're four runs ahead at the time. We've got several more games to play and I want to be a part of it. We already got two outfielders hurt and we don't want another."

So with all these thoughts clicking off in his head, Willie Mays, the indomitable center fielder, "lets" a firmly struck fly ball fly free in the twelfth inning, which came to a nail-biting end with three Athletics on base.

"I don't think I play so bad," Mays said.

Wait'll you see the films, Willie.

Anyway, we got Mays at the plate in the Mets' twelfth and Harrelson on third again and two out. This place was already looking like it was no kind of refuge for aging immortals, but Mays plays the part like Barrymore with a bat.

It wasn't a classic in the vernacular of legendary Mays classics. Only an unheroic bounder through the middle of the infield, carefully struck so as to avoid the clutches of Campaneris and Andrews—poor Mike Andrews, no immortal he with his most mortal glove—and the winning run scores. It is followed by three others before Andrews can finally make peace with his recalcitrant leather and the score is 10-6.

When George Stone arrived in the twelfth inning he tied a World Series record. He was the eleventh pitcher. Only once before have two teams ever used as many as eleven pitchers in a World Series game.

The clock confirmed another record. No other World Series game has required four hours and thirteen minutes to reach a decision. Now, the Mets were positive they had it won earlier, when Harrelson, that annoying little devil, was ruled out at the plate trying to score on a fly Felix Millan hit to Joe Rudi in the tenth. This was when Mays, waiting to bat, fell to his knees in supplication to the hard-hearted Signor Donatelli.

Which made that banner hanging along the fence in right field appear a bit territorially inane as the crowd moved out, sobered by defeat and quieted by the sudden realization that the pitching that once had been the home team's wealth was now on the verge of bankruptcy. Said the banner: WE LOVE WILLIE MAYS.

THE PITCHER FROM OTWELL INSURANCE

APRIL 25, 1965

He walked through the mouth of the tunnel under Atlanta Stadium into the Cracker dugout, and he walked past everybody on the bench like a man tying to get lost, and he sat down and without prompting or introductory, made a grave indictment of himself.

"Whit, I found out I made a big mistake," he said. "I quit. I wasn't ready to quit, but I quit. Lord, how I'd like to be out there."

Taylor Phillips's face was drawn. His eyes were glazed with a kind of film that comes from a late-developing foresight.

Ten years ago, Taylor Phillips was on the way to the big leagues. Now he was on the way to the post office, where he works sorting mail.

He wore a gray sport shirt and a gray golf sweater with shafts of gay color splashed across the front.

"They had to cut the uniform off and put fire to me to make me quit," Whitlow Wyatt said.

This is true. When nothing else would work on Wyatt's failing arm in 1945, they "fired" his shoulder, the way a trainer "fires" a horse's leg.

"That's real fire, I mean to tell you," Whitlow said. "All it did was hurt. It didn't do any good."

"I wasn't ready to quit," Taylor said, "but I didn't get a contract from anybody. I didn't write anybody. I just left it that way.

"I went to work in the post office last October, and I'm still working there, putting up mail. I don't like the hours. It makes a long day from 4:30 in the afternoon until 3 o'clock the next morning."

Phillips came out of Douglas County and got a job with the

Crackers. In less than four seasons of minor-league pitching, he found himself wearing the clothes of the Milwaukee Braves and earning a big-league salary at the age of twenty-two.

A year later, he was in a World Series, drawing a full-sized cut of the champion's share. It was a gift. The Braves didn't need him against the Yankees. He was a spectator with a bull-pen view.

Maybe it didn't matter to him, not getting a call. He probably figured there would be plenty more World Series for him.

That winter, John Quinn traded him to the Cubs. He was the key man in the deal, and it looked like this was his big move. It's better to be a big man in Chicago than a figure dimly seen in the bull-pen in Milwaukee.

He didn't dazzle 'em in Chicago. Maybe it had all come too rich and too fast. When he lost, it didn't turn him into a restless sleeper. He was young. There would always be another day and another game. He'd win that one.

The next thing he knew, he was a Philadelphia Philly, traded in the middle of 1959. Here was he, twenty-six years old and on the treadmill. He pitched one complete game that season, won it, and never won again in the big leagues.

From the Phillies to Buffalo, back to the Phillies, back to Buffalo, then to Dallas–Fort Worth, to Indianapolis, up to the White Sox for an audition, and back to Indianapolis—passed around like a counterfeit bill.

"Then I go to the ballpark one morning last summer," he said. "The man meets me at the door and says I'm out of work.

"A nice guy, Max Shoemaker, but he can't use me any longer. I was making good pay. The White Sox need the place on the Indianapolis roster for a prospect.

"Thirty-one years old and you're through. Nobody knows how bad I want to pitch again. I just need seventy-two days to be a five-year man in the majors."

That's pension talk. What it means is $50 a month for the rest of his life after fifty-five, or a little more.

What went wrong? Where would you start over again? What would you do the second time that you didn't do the first?

"Just say this," he said. "Just say I didn't mature until I was back in the minor leagues.

"For the next three years, nobody ever worked any harder than I did. I didn't seem to be getting anywhere.

"The White Sox took me to spring training twice. I looked good the first time, but there wasn't any room for me. They kept me around the second time, but I didn't get the job done. I pitched something like ten innings in ninety days. My earned-run average looked like the national debt.

"Back to Indianapolis."

The end came as a Cracker last season, a desolate finish with a desolate team in the desolate remains of Ponce de Leon Park.

Now he pitches twice a week for the Otwell Insurance team, people sitting on the grass or in parked cars to watch, mostly relatives. At least he's still got hope. Look at some of the other Braves pitchers of his day—Ray Crone, God-knows-where; Red Murff, scouting; Gene Conley, living in that trailer somewhere; and Dave Jolly, dead. He would have been forty.

It ain't like a World Series, pitching for Otwell Insurance, but it's pitching. And the Braves are coming to his town. Just think, thirty-one years old; ought to be at the rise of a good career. Maybe the left-hander who took Spahn's place. Pitching for Otwell Insurance twice a week.

A TRIBUTE TURNS TO ASHES

APRIL 15, 1987

Al Campanis is so devoid of bias he once traded his own son for a player to be named later. This calls for a kind of courage not generally found among menfolk who must go home and eat at the table of the mother of their offspring.

Campanis is well educated, an athlete who earned his way through New York University, but not given to calling attention to it, as Roger Kahn once coarsely accused him. "He had earned a master's degree from New York University, and you could not know Al Campanis ten minutes without hearing about it," Kahn wrote.

This could be explained by a sharp exchange that had taken place. In disbelief, Campanis asked Kahn, "What the hell are you doing wearing a beard?" Kahn with a beard looked like an impersonation of something you catch with a trap.

For all of his education, Campanis is less than spellbinding on his feet. He can let the air out of the most humorous anecdote. It is not an indictable offense. Some people can catch fish, some people can't.

When Campanis was asked to appear on a late-night ABC telecast last week, he thought he would be participating in a tribute to Jackie Robinson. He didn't expect to be treated like carrion by vultures. He was a logical choice to speak well of Robinson. Campanis had played beside him in the infield at Montreal in 1946, and he's now vice president of the Los Angeles Dodgers.

Campanis knows the plight of minorities. He was born on

17

the island of Kos in Greece and came to this country on a boat. He can sing you a chorus on the American way.

That he ever would have agreed to appear on the same air with Roger Kahn, long an O'Malley antagonist, surprises. Kahn's one prize work, *The Boys of Summer*, did not treat Walter O'Malley and family kindly.

Kahn is one of these writing people caught up in his own trance. He fancied himself as a thwarted infielder, but only in his own mind. He threw like a girl. Yet he wrote of playing catch and his on-field experiences without a blush.

When the *Saturday Evening Post* suffered public putrification for its treatment of the Wally Butts–Bear Bryant case several years ago, the real culprit was not Frank Graham, Jr., whose byline appeared on the article, but Roger Kahn, freshly appointed sports editor of the *Post* and determined to make a big splash. He did. His hand was engaged in the rewriting and the graphics, but his face was out of sight.

Kahn operated a minor-league baseball team at Utica, New York for a season to develop another book. His manager was not black, nor was any of his office staff.

Yet, caught in the squeeze between these two professional baiters, Kahn and Ted Koppel, Campanis found himself faced with questions they could not themselves answer for those they represent. He was the pathetic prey, reaching for answers to questions that have no answers. Being asked by two gloating interrogators who smelled blood and bored in.

To fire a man for speaking to a practice that his club has followed all these years is heartless. Campanis has been a loyal contributor to the health of the Dodgers. If firing him gave Peter O'Malley the feeling that he was cleansed, he has another cleansing coming.

Kahn once tried to draw Robinson into one of his smears of Campanis, belittling Campanis as a .100 hitter in his seven-game career as a Dodger in his youth. Robinson would have no part of it.

"Al Campanis is a good guy," Robinson said. "He was very good on integration when it counted."

Strange, on the "Nightline" massacre, Kahn never introduced such a statement from his own writing.

Poor Campanis fell into a defense of confused logic, while around him rose the sounds of braying. Don't answer, let it lie there, you kept wanting to cry out at him. Excuse yourself, tell them you suddenly remembered another appointment, and get out of there.

"You generally have to go to the minor leagues, and the pay is low," Campanis said when asked why there are not black managers in the big leagues.

"Is there still that much prejudice?" Koppel asked.

Prejudice? Somebody seems to have prejudice confused with economics.

TED TURNER STEPS FORTH

JANUARY 15, 1976

Resplendent in his Henry Aaron cravat and his tattersall vest, everything that's dapper down to the neatly tonsured mustache, Robert Edward Turner III bestowed local ownership upon the Atlanta Braves Tuesday. For a price, which by the time the debt is closed will come to something like $12 million, I'm told.

He's buying the franchise permitting him to operate in the National League the same way you bought your car, or the new bedroom furniture. A little bit down and so much per month.

Somebody once said that if you have to buy a Rolls-Royce on the installment plan, you not only don't need it, you can't afford it. Ted Turner has decided that he can afford it and Atlanta needs it.

"There's a civic side to my interest in the Braves," he said. "Economically, you know it's not a wise move in these times, but money is not the prime motivation."

At last he doesn't have to listen again to the sermon about if you're trying to make money, don't buy a sports franchise. And I hope he has noticed that owning a franchise looks even less profitable now that a man named Peter Seitz has just taken target practice with the reserve clause and shot it full of holes. There is the chance, you see, that Turner and his communications empire have bought rights to forty guys who'll be packing up and leaving town next October.

Emancipated "slaves."

But, that's just part of the routine of learning to be the owner of a sports franchise. Way the dice roll. The cookie crumbles. Tough stuff, kid.

Somehow, it isn't easy accustoming my vision to Ted Turner sitting between Dan Donahue and Bill Bartholomay, wearing dress-up clothes and looking dullishly executive. He has always played with boats, not ballplayers and bubble-gum cards. I'm accustomed to him at the helm, wearing his yachtsman's cap, salt spray tinging the gold leaf with a Silas Marner hue of green. Shouting order. Secure the poop deck and ready about, mate!

He has sailed in everything from the Swiss Navy to the Chattahoochee fleet. Anything that'll float and have a chance to win a race. He is, fellow Americans, our society's true-blue twenty-four carat version of A Sportsman. That is, you win, you get paid off with a jug or a plaque.

This is a different tack. You get paid off with a bottom line, red or black. You don't have a grandstand floating along at sea. Your cheers are the self-satisfaction you get from leaving your wake for some lubber to follow.

That works two ways. Neither do you get the boos and the accursed letters to the editor.

Turner's ownership of the Braves creates a unique condition— a man in the communications business depending on rivals to spread the word of his product, and his good works, or otherwise, in baseball. New York was vast enough to swallow and digest CBS's ownership of the Yankees without a burp. Atlanta is still smalltown enough that a small claw can make a large scratch. The rivalries carry some heat. How does the Channel 5 editorial voice come on the air ripping the Channel 17 owner's operation of the Braves?

Not to be neglected in this hour of transition is the retreating ownership. Trying to put a handle on terms to describe the tenure of the Chicago Twelve in the city isn't easy. Perhaps it's best that they sign out. Ten years of winning 797 and losing 815 hasn't endeared them to the territory.

They came in a heat wave of affection. They bow out in a wave of apathy. They tried. They really tried. They tried to be "local," but it never took. To the public, they were still the spoiled kids from the estates and private schools of northwest Chicago, silver spoons still in their mouths. They did some things in such a way, well-meaning notwithstanding, that would make a panhandler throw a $5 handout back in their faces.

Of course, their worst sin was losing. They tried three general managers and six managers and were still losing in the end. They tried to be charitable and recipients asked, "Is that all?"

Strange I should think of this, but fresh in mind is the memory of Paul Richards, deposed, sitting in the Stadium Club at lunch suddenly blurting out, "I don't know the meaning of the word *fired*! I don't know the meaning of it!"

He'd been fired, but they'd tried to be humane about it and instead they were amputating his pride an inch at a time.

No back door in this arrangement. Ted Turner is now chief operating officer of the Braves, and all he has to do is mail in his monthly payments on time or The Seller will send out and pick up his franchise. The least we can do as he casts off and moves away from he dock is wish him smooth sailing. Bon voyage. And don't take any wooden Indians.

ANATOMY OF A WINNING STREAK

APRIL 22, 1982

Come with me now to the alfresco theater called Atlanta Stadium and it shall be illustrated for you, the kind of stuff of which winning streaks are made. It is the last of the ninth inning. The world's all-time-longest-undefeated major-league team behind by a run The Atlanta Braves have their last time at bat. The streak dies at twelve, or it becomes thirteen. The latter seems unlikely. The Braves will send up a reserve catcher, Matt Sinatro, for his thirty-third time at bat in the major leagues. Then Rafael Ramirez, enjoying early resurrection, followed by a pinch-hitter, certain to be his fellow Dominican countryman, Rufino Linares. This is the tag end of the batting order.

Sinatro cleverly accepts a walk. He hasn't been to bat before in the season. Ramirez's mission is to sacrifice Sinatro to second base, but his quick bunt runs under the glove of the pitcher, Bob Shirley. Miraculously, two runners are on base and nobody is out. Linares, who swings at anything within reach and hits it at a rate of .409, pops a fly to the outfield.

Now the Braves are visited by their fairy godmother—or godfather, if you insist on equal rights. The leadoff man, Brett Butler, slashes a hopping drive to the left of second, and it is sure to be double play once the ball is in the sure hands of David Concepcion. But hold it. The ball doesn't reach Concepcion. It bounds off the right foot of Sinatro, who is trying to head for third and bounds into center field. Instead of the end of the game, only Sinatro is out and two men are still on base.

It is here, though, that the 22,153 show the ugliness that makes you ashamed of Atlanta. I shall never again be able to view a Yankee Stadium crowd with disdain. They yowl in protest, and call on a barnyard chant characteristic of football. Some idiot throws a transistor in the direction of the first base umpire, joining three bottles and a can of beer in the night's box score of objects thrown from the stands.

If you know baseball, the rule is basic: Batted ball hits base runner, base runner is automatically out, batter gets a hit, and all hands advance one base. There are no grounds for aggravation.

Out trudges Bill Fischer, Cincinnati pitching coach. Shirley is dismissed. Jim Kern walks Hubbard. Bases loaded. Crowd afire. Out comes Kern, in comes Joe Price, big as a redwood and left-handed, to pitch to Claudell Washington, also left-handed. The old percentage game, you see.

Washington takes a pitch inside. The Cincinnati theory is that you jam him. They'd done it the night before and he'd hit the next pitch out of the park off Frank Pastore. Price's next pitch is like tenderloin, Washington returns it up the middle, Ramirez scores, followed by Butler, who can sprint, Braves win 4-3, crowd loses mind one more time, meaning they're down to their last mind. Heaven knows what it would be if this were the seventh game of the World Series.

Along that line, it does take historians back to the Braves of 1957, and the shoeshine pitch that turned the World Series around. The pitch struck the foot of a fading veteran named Nippy Jones, who called it to the attention of the umpire as the ball rebounded off the wall and rolled back to the plate, clearly marked by the black polish off Jones's shoe. Jones takes first, Braves start a rally, turn a losing game into a winner, and go on to take the Yankees.

Most Valuable Foot of the Year is an award that goes to the plucky Sinatro, who happened to be unable to get his hoof out of the way of the batted ball, and thus saved the streak for one more day. By this time, the gallery of the celebrated had emptied. Gone were most of the itinerant journalists who had swept into the city for the record-setting, the politicians, the spotlight grabbers, even Ted Turner, who had turned his head to Philadelphia, where his brood of Hawks performed.

It is safe to predict, methinks, that the Braves shall lose this season. But don't go jumping ship just yet. This party may not be over until Mother's Day. There is no virtue in baseball, somebody surely must have said, like a fast getaway.

YOU NEVER SAW SUCH AN ARM

MAY 10, 1983

Just the mention of the name Steve Dalkowski to Billy Demars is like the opening scene of an old horror movie. Baseball men who saw him pitch like to try to top one Steve Dalkowski with another. Some who didn't see him pitch, but have heard the tales, speak of him in awe, listen slack-jawed, and ask for more.

He never threw a pitch in the big leagues. He was washed up before he was twenty-seven. Through. Gene Michael batted against Sandy Koufax in the big leagues. Dalkowski threw harder, he said. Cal Ripken the Senior saw Dalkowski and later saw Nolan Ryan.

"Ryan couldn't compare with him," Ripken said.

Billy Demars hit town this week with the Montreal Expos, for whom he directs traffic at third base. Billy is a career coach who paid his dues managing in the bush leagues, riding buses through the night, trying to break maverick players—some who came his way and some who couldn't be broken—and trying to salvage something out of the greatest pitching arm he ever saw. It was the left arm of Steve Dalkowski.

"I had him three times," Billy said, "and he was already a legend by the time I got to him and he was barely twenty-one."

Dalkowski was average size, five feet ten and about 180 pounds, making him even more an object of fascination. He could throw a baseball through a wooden fence, and once did on a $20 bet. He could throw a baseball 456 feet over a grandstand, and once did, without warming up.

He came from a sorry background in the industrial town of New Britain, Connecticut. The Baltimore Orioles gave him a car and $40,000 when he graduated from high school in 1957, and set him out on a road that led to nowhere. He was an alcoholic, he had mental and emotional problems, and, as a combination, these are blamed for the tragedy that became of the greatest arm some men ever saw in baseball, also the wildest.

He came to Bill Demars at Stockton, California, in his fourth season. "I had him during his best times," Billy said. "He struck out 262 batters that season and walked 262."

Let that soak in for a moment. Do you realize what walking 262 batters in 170 innings comes out to? An average of thirteen a game.

"The first game he pitched for me he struck out twenty and didn't walk but five," Billy said. "I thought he was about to shape up.

"My wife is Polish, and I told him, 'Pitch a good game and I'll take you home for a good Polish dinner.' He struck out sixteen the next time and won. I really thought he was turning the corner."

But every game became a reason to hit the bars. After a bad game he had to go drink away his misery. After a good game he had to drink in celebration. It seemed he went deeper into the stew after winning than losing. One of his teammates once said, "Steve can't stand good times."

"I took him to a psychiatrist, and I took him to a hypnotist," Billy said. "Nothing helped."

He had his only winning season with Earl Weaver at Elmira. He struck out 192 and walked only 114, but he hated Weaver. Now he has a picture of Weaver on his wall. He was put through an intelligence test at the time and finished in the bottom percentile.

"That means," Weaver said, "if you were trying to teach 100 people, Steve would be the last to learn."

Dalkowski walked out on baseball and vanished. An old teammate, Ray Youngdahl, came upon him—broken down, filthy, a defeated wino not far from death. He dried him out, got him a job in San Mateo, California, and for a while he went straight. Then empty wine bottles began showing up, and Youngdahl, by then a probation officer, had to turn him out before he broke up his home.

Dalkowski had drifted around after baseball working at odd jobs until sinking to the pits of vagrancy. He joined the sordid army of fruit and vegetable pickers, drinking his cheap wine, which is more ether than wine.

"I had my dog in the field with me, and my bottle of wine. I was happy."

It was probably going to happen to Steve Dalkowski, whatever course he took. He happened to have the arm God gave him, and he happened to be noticed, otherwise he'd have been just another faceless, nameless derelict they keep the missions open for.

"Why the hell do ballplayers drink so much?" he asked himself. "I can't find it. I had it all together once and then I forgot. It starts out, you know, after the game with a pizza and beer, then you hit the broads."

He's forty years old now, beaten and fragile, such a human wreck he can no longer work in the fields. In between his trips to the detoxification center, he works with a broom and a rake in city parks around Bakersfield, California. The biggest strikeout in his life has been his own.

"Sometimes you just sit and wonder what he might have been," Billy Demars said.

HYPOCRISY RIDES AGAIN AT COOPERSTOWN

MARCH 12, 1982

You will have noticed, perhaps, that A.B. "Happy" Chandler, Kentucky's eternal mascot and former commissioner of our national pastime, was accepted for membership in the Baseball Hall of Fame. It was sort of like getting in on a pass. The Old-Timers Committee did it.

Most of the time I'm concerned about those who don't make it. This time I'm concerned with one who did. My God, my immediate reaction was, have they forgotten they fired him at the St. Petersburg meetings in 1950? Have they forgotten this man was the author of an article entitled, "How I Jumped from Clean Politics into Dirty Baseball"?

This will soften only slightly the hammer blow of what follows to say that Happy Chandler is a perfectly delightful man, gregarious, eager to be liked. He would give a touch of conviviality to any picnic or barbecue. He could deliver a sermon or toss a bourbon with equal facility.

As a commissioner of baseball, he was a fan who wanted to please everybody and wound up pleasing few. It was Red Smith, the columnist, who probably put him where he belonged when Red described him as "the greatest commissioner since Judge Kenesaw Mountain Landis." The judge was the man he succeeded.

The New York press was without compassion toward the man who gave up the U.S. Senate to be commissioner because, as the islanders of Manhattan put it, "His major credentials for the job were that he could give a good rendition of 'My Old Kentucky Home,' and said, 'Ah love baseball.'"

Another of my immediate reactions was that it might be just as well that Red Smith passed on this year. If he hadn't, this news would have finished him off. It was Red who called Chandler "Laughing Boy," a "clown and a mountebank."

Here is a man the club owners almost bought out of his contract his first year in office now being elected to the Hall of Fame. It's nothing that should be held against Happy, the fact, as it is written in *The History of Baseball*, that "it was a matter of lack of aptitude for the job." The question is, Why the hell is this necessary in the first place? Why not let the man rest in living peace?

He had not served six years when he was terminated. He wanted so passionately to hold his job that he stood and sobbed and pleaded before his employers at his "last supper" in St. Petersburg. Now, some of the same people who helped to can him sit in a meeting and vote him a ticket to Cooperstown. It's like applying a poultice to cancer.

On the surface it was suggested that Chandler goes into the hall because he stood with Branch Rickey in breaking the color line. There is no mention of Chandler in connection with Jackie Robinson in Rickey's biography, or in Robinson's, or in any major literary work on baseball that I can find.

He happened to be the commissioner at the time, if that counts. His chief supporter for the job was Larry MacPhail, who was in bitter conflict with Rickey at the time. That would pretty much cover that.

Chandler did have his good points. He managed to develop an owner-player relationship that might have forgone the comedy we have today. He put the player pension fund on solid ground. He signed the first big television contract, a million a year for World Series rights. This was a "lame duck" move, probably in the hope that it would restore him to good standing with the owners. It didn't.

He suspended Leo Durocher, objected to Del Webb's ownership of gambling casinos, fought Fred Saigh on Sunday night baseball, and threw Dan Topping out of his office. The next thing we know we'll have Spike Eckert in the Hall of Fame because he played a nice game of tennis and never had a World Series dumped in his time.

Bowie Kuhn was a leading force in the Chandler-for-Cooperstown movement. Discussion in committee wasn't lengthy or heated. The ballot came up and magically Chandler had the twelve votes he needed. If this is a hint of things to come, Kuhn might stand to be lectured on the premise that the Hall of Fame is public, not his private toy.

Since Judge Landis, baseball commissioners have been little more than watch fobs. Chandler was cosmetically appealing at the time, a cornpone figure with a flashing smile *and* Washington connections.

But he took himself seriously. Too seriously, some owners thought, and out he went on the toe of their boot. Now some of them, and their successors, dust him off and install him in the Hall of Fame.

My conclusion is that they should stick to judging players and managers for immortality, and leave it at that.

A CURSE
AND AN
ABOMINATION

SEPTEMBER 13, 1982

You'll pardon me if I confess that I was left somewhat bemused by the recent flurry in "Voice of the Fan" about my expressions on the tenth man in the baseball lineup, otherwise referred to as the designated hitter. They came just short of demanding that I submit to urinalysis.

"The Big Snooze Award," I also confess, draws a blank with me. So far I haven't received it, as promised by its creator, a Mr. VanDercar—hopefully not an import. Assuming that it relates to Rip van Winkle or Susan Anton, of the mattress commercials, and that I have a choice in the matter, I cheerfully choose the latter.

Disenchantment with the DH rule almost always is charged to advancing age and unwillingness to let go of the past. There is no question that I prefer the complete baseball player, not lineups of nine players who bat and nine players who play defense. Curiously enough, the column in question began not as an advocacy of the nine-man lineup, including the pitcher who takes his turn at bat. It was intended to be a report of an interesting occasion spent with Tim Lollar, a pitcher who hits well.

It was the pitcher himself who introduced the subject of the DH, how he deplores it, and how it had turned American League games into slugfests. He applauded his trade from the Yankees to San Diego because now, happily, he is able to take his turn at bat again.

Tim Lollar is twenty-six, not a trace of gray or a wrinkle, a bright-eyed, handsome young man who has a healthy attitude toward baseball as it was designed to be played. No "yesterday's" pitcher there, as one letter writer suggested.

Once Lollar had spoken up on the DH rule, I was impressed with what he had to say and used the occasion to join in and make it a duet. It pleased me to hear him say it, and I found nothing tiring in his denunciation of it. The DH has, in my eyes, made a kind of carnival baseball in the American League.

If you're going to be consistent with the intent of the rule, then the big lummox who can hit a ton but fields with an iron glove should never have to play defense. The catcher with the low-caliber arm should have a strong arm standing nearby to make his throws to second. The lumbering runner who clogs the bases should be replaced by a designated sprinter once he gets on.

If you're going to replace all the weak hitters in your lineup, then there go some of the slickest fielders of all time. Dal Maxvill, Bobby Wine, Eddie Brinkman, and Mark Belanger, to name a few, would never have gotten to bat.

If all the fans want, as suggested by Michael F. Alberlich, is a sky full of base hits, then eliminate the pitcher, crank up the pitching machine, and turn it on.

Surely in these times of advancing idiocy we haven't lost appreciation for the classic pitching duel. Nor for the pitcher who can break up his own game with the bat.

The fact that an athlete has a strong arm shouldn't mean that he should also have been created offenseless. And if pitchers are going to be excused from hitting because of hard labor, what about the catcher? He hits every day. The pitcher only has to hit every fourth day.

Managing in a DH league is like running an elevator. Strategy, thank heaven, has not been wiped out in the National League. The curse of the damnable DH is that kids who pitch grow up never having a chance to hit from high school age through college. We'll never know what monumental hitters may have been lost to us by such folly.

While we're changing things, why not take a bite out of base-stealing? Kids grow up with more speed, smarter, profit by better coaching. They're turning the base paths into a hotbed of thievery, especially in the American League. Why not lengthen the base paths? Ninety feet is too short for the present generation.

Move the pitcher's mound back. They're striking out too many batters, even without the soft-touch pitcher to pick on in the American League.

Move the fences in. They're not hitting enough home runs. If they want a real slugfest, give them one every night. Put a real rabbit inside the ball.

Do you want athletes or one-tracked robots? Do you want to turn baseball into a carbon of platoon football, of the faceless players who lose their identity milling on and off the field like subway passengers?

The game is losing enough of its classicism by expansion, watering down the talent, by defrocking the minor leagues, and by the virtual absence of baseball at the grass roots, where the potential star once had a chance to develop. Gaylord Perry and Nolan Ryan are chasing strikeout records. If Walter Johnson had had a chance to pitch against these donkeys, he'd have fanned 5,000. If Ty Cobb had had a chance to run against these catchers with the popgun arms, he'd have stolen 1,500 bases.

One of the deep-rooted attractions of baseball has been its consistency. Rules haven't been changed because there has been no cause for change. What was sound when Bucky Harris managed is still sound while Dick Williams manages. The "book" has hardly changed a paragraph. The character of the game is focused on the number nine—nine innings, nine men, three outs times nine makes a game.

Then they introduced the tenth man, the batter who never plays, but spends his time between appearances on the field with mustard on his face and dozing on the trainer's table. That's baseball?

A WEIGH-IN, BUT NO HORSE

JANUARY 27, 1983

Now let me see. The way I get it, Bob Horner, who plays third base for the Atlanta Braves when in good health, merely has to present himself to the clerk of the scales thirteen times during the 1983 baseball season, and each time he establishes his weight at 215 pounds or less, he collects $7,692.31. Which converts into $100,000 over the whole season, or $400,000 over the term of his four-year contract, which is about to go into force. Right?

Does he weigh in in the raw? In his lingerie? Is he required to wear sandals, combating the deadly threat of athlete's foot, or his robe, in the interest of common decency?

No contract of such a dramatic nature should be without such specific clauses. To the public, knowing a little isn't enough. The patron who invests in the performance of such a body should be supplied with minute details.

Another thing, do they weigh him at home plate, or will he be granted privacy? If the Braves are to get full value for their money, they should be able to turn it into a spectacle, like a sack race or a greased-pole climb.

Such an embarrassment—of being weighed in like a porker at a stockyard—should encourage a public figure such as an athlete to keep his appetite and his guzzling under control.

Fatty Fothergill, Blimp Phelps, Fat Pat Seerey, and Shanty Hogan, where are you now? You lived too soon.

Tubby Walton, a portly fellow who cut quite a swath as a player and a scout in these parts before he became wealthy and thin, said being fat never bothered him until he got so big they had to take him down to the cotton gin to weigh him. That was humiliation enough to make him keep his weight under 300.

It never occurred to many that suet was Horner's problem. Until last season, he had never played in more than 124 games.

Most of the time, the reason he didn't was that he pulled or twisted something, or had a nosebleed, not fat.

There are athletes who are just naturally better performers fat. No manager ever tried to remove any of the 230 pounds of the aforementioned Fothergill, who spent twelve seasons in the big leagues batting .326. When Ron Northey was the leading pinch-hitter in the majors, he looked as if he should have been delivered to home plate in a wheelbarrow. Bill Casper, the golfer, lost weight and lost his swing.

If they're counting on Horner becoming a niftier fielder, they can forget it. He has the range of a St. Bernard, his arm is adequate, but what they've been getting from him in the field is what they'll continue to get.

What strikes me as peculiar is this: If a professional performer approaching the age of twenty-six, and having had his salary increased to $1,125,000 per season, has to be coaxed by such showbiz to stay in shape, then a $100,000 tip isn't the answer. Money can't buy pride.

Now if he's a jockey, that's another thing. You don't get the horse if you don't make the weight. Willie Shoemaker would stand in line to make a deal like Horner's. With his pockets full of bricks, Willie couldn't make the scales hit 215.

It is a reflection on the insanity that's running rampant in baseball, in the first place, that a .261 hitter should be rewarded with a $5 million contract after such a season. While the Braves were making their stretch drive through California on the way to the division championship, Jerry Royster was on third base and Horner was on the bench. This prompted Ted Turner to decide to put him on the market.

A month ago the Braves are trying to make a deal for him. Now they make him a millionaire. Who's running the joint, the Ritz Brothers?

Taking a random year out of the record book, a look at 1951, when there were eight teams in each major league, Horner would have ranked seventh among full-time third basemen in the National League. There were some power hitters among them, and the pitching wasn't Kitty League. Willie Jones hit 190 home runs in a short career, Bob Elliott hit 170 in a career interrupted by war, and Billy Cox, who was a craftsman with the glove, also managed to hit .279 that season.

Now a .261 hitter breaks the bank at Turner Communications,

an investment in the suspicion that he might be great. Then a dealer in ballyhoo tacks on this carnival clause. "Guess how much the fat lady weighs and win a genuine fuzzy doll! Step right up!"

Some skeptics have sneakily suggested that what this amounted to was an unofficial out-of-court settlement in the suit of Bucky Woy, Horner's agent, against Turner for slander. The trial was scheduled to begin last week but was postponed.

One thing is sure—if they ever start weighing agent Woy instead of the client, there goes the $7,692.31 per weigh-in. There even goes the thirty-one cents.

TWELVE-CYLINDER INSANITY

OCTOBER 15, 1984

If the world had come to an end Sunday night, Detroit wouldn't have known it until Monday. Motor City was busy going insane.

What did come to an end was the World Series, #81, and down below this press box, from which I write, what remains of the grassy surface of Tiger Stadium is the ripped and torn evidence pointing the finger at the suspected champions. The "greatest team in baseball" lived up to its accusation.

Champions of the world, or at least this hemisphere, are the Detroit Tigers. A championship run from April to October, out of the gate in the lead and never behind, down through American League playoffs into the telephone booth where manager Sparky Anderson took his call from President Reagan, who is running up quite a phone bill these days.

It will be noted historically that the San Diego Padres came in second.

There were 51,901 here in person, including Vice President George Bush, who came to deliver his encomiums in person, going through their variety of routines, their "waves," their chants, their insults, their tiddly little hand exercises, some behavior not uncommon among English soccer crowds. Outside this grand old house of baseball there must have been just as many waiting to celebrate the hour. As early as the seventh inning, they began gathering on Michigan and Trumbull, marching down both streets like a mob marching on the palace. Hours later, thousands were still there, and others, wild and unbridled, had distributed the insanity throughout the province.

It was fitting and proper that the decisive blow in this five-game autumnal exercise should have been a pop fly delivered by a twenty-nine-year-old utilityman. A Russell J. Kuntz, known as "Rusty" by those who know him at all, hoisted it in the seventh inning, just outside the realm of the infield fly rule. The San Diego second baseman, Alan Wiggins, roamed far off his assigned beat to field it because the right fielder, Tony Gwynn, lost it in the clouds—that's what he said—and once caught, Kirk Gibson, the authentic hero, tagged up and broke for home and scored.

It was the run that broke a 3-3 tie, and in the infinite wisdom of those who establish the intricate statistical system of the major leagues, that came out to be the "Game-Winning RBI." Just as unceremoniously as he had arrived—as a pinch-hitter for John Grubb, who had pinch hit for Barbaro Garbey—Kuntz disappeared from view, to be pinch hit for by Howard Johnson.

Having a somewhat more forceful hand in the outcome, an 8-4 score for the Tigers, was the former split end from nearby Michigan State, Gibson, he of the 6 o'clock shadow. Gibson, who never completed his course in shaving as a Spartan, hit two home runs, drove in five runs, and scored three, enough all by himself to handle the case. The second of his blasts endeared him to his countrymen.

Rich Gossage, exalted in San Diego as the incredible reliever, had come into the game. The Padres were back within a run again. The spontaneous chanters were attempting to vex the Padres pitcher with their needling. "Goose-busters!" "Goose-busters!" they cried.

What vexed him more was his second serve to Gibson, which the crusty Tiger returned to the right-field stands. Two associates being aboard, Detroit now led by four runs, and the issue could best be described as no longer in doubt.

It perhaps went unnoticed by thousands keeping watch on Gibson high-stepping it around the bases, but Gossage sagged with dejection on the mound—even his pork-chop mustache seemed to droop—and stared straight ahead, realizing that he had delivered the pitch that put the Tigers out of reach. Better things are expected of a piecemeal pitcher said to be earning $2 million a season.

This was the game, Sparky Anderson had said, that he was looking for from his unsurpassed team. Neither the Tigers nor the Padres had scored more than five runs a game. The Tigers always got away to the good start, but had scored only two runs after the third inning in the first four games.

Their pitcher of the day, Dan Petry, an eighteen-game winner, had been set off with a three-run lead in the second game, and had blown it. The Tigers gave him another three-run lead in this one, and darned if he didn't blow it. Kirk Gibson to the rescue.

The Padres appeared to be ill at ease under such close national scrutiny. Their starters started poorly. Their combined ERA was an atrocious 13.94. Their finishers finished well, until the $2 million man made the scene. Their pitching coach, Norm Sherry, spent almost as much time on the mound as those in his charge.

No less than symbolic of the Padre performance was that their main offense was a journeyman who plays many positions, but in this series served one unfamiliar to the National League. Designated hitter Kurt Bevacqua won San Diego's only game with a three-run homer, his first since June, only his sixth in the last six years.

Darned if he didn't hit another Sunday night. Just when all celebrants were preparing to exuberate, Bevacqua quieted them with his long ball in the eighth inning. That was why the Padres were back within a run of the Tigers when Gibson met Gossage.

By this time, Anderson had left nothing to chance. He went to his bull pen for *Los Compadres Latinos*, Aurelio Lopez, commonly called "Señor Smoke," to be followed by Guillermo Hernandez (Villanueva), who has endeared himself to all from Grosse Pointe to Hamtramck. Except the Tigers exchequer, for during the week Willie spit out his demand to be paid much more than his current $400,000 salary, suggesting $2 million for openers. He lost his opening argument, as he gave up the eighth-inning home run to Bevacqua.

This evening then, belonged to Señor Smoke, who humbly and nobly accepted his fate as winning pitcher. "This is the most beautiful moment in my life," he said, mellifluously laced with his accent, imported direct from Tecamachalco, Puebla, Mexico.

THE YEAR EVERYBODY HIT .300

JUNE 4, 1987

You can't travel far enough to get away from the frightful stories. Ed Hinton goes all the way to Japan and runs into it, the home-run deluge. But Ed was looking for it, and with 290-foot fences, you're going to find it. They've gone so home-run bananas in Japan they think that Bob Horner is Babe Ruth. Born-again Fatso.

(I saw a picture the other day of Horner and Japanese comrades gathered on the mound around a distressed pitcher. Now that's a conversation I'd like to have eavesdropped on. How does Amelican who can't speak it encourage Japanese pitcher in native tongue? The usual routine is that they always slap the pitcher on the rump and go back to their position, and a slap on the rump is part of the universal language of baseball.)

Well, I get to Dallas the other day and the first headline that leaps out of the *Morning News* sports section is, "A Reduction in Quality Arms Has Rocketed Home Run Totals."

Editorialists across this country are engaged in much hand-wringing about the avalanche of home runs being struck in the major leagues. Ozzie Guillen of the White Sox hit one the other day, matching his career total. Luis Aguayo, small Phillies infielder, has already three rockets more than he ever hit in a season. Jerry Royster is hitting home runs, and so is a kid named Karkovice, whose batting average is .098 for the White Sox.

The White Sox are heavy on the minds of the Metroplex because they hit ten out of the park against the Rangers in two nights. They roughed up old Charlie Hough so the other night the locals considered it brazen effrontery. Charlie throws the knuckleball, and like Phil Niekro in Cleveland, they consider him a state resource. They didn't blame Charlie. They blamed the pitching coach, Tom House, whom you may remember as the bull-pen pitcher who shagged Henry Aaron's 715th home run.

Maybe the pitching *is* lousy. There are a lot of strangers suiting up in the big leagues. Clubs are desperately shuffling through their farm-system cards and picking any kid who can throw hard, never mind if he can pitch. There is a difference. Some are barely out of phys-ed class, some are barely weaned.

The prime suspect, though, is the ball. One umpire says there's so much rabbit in it you don't have to call the ball-boy for replacements. You drop it in the bag and it multiplies.

Let me tell you of a season long ago, one very much like this one in which offense reached the state of obscenity. Don't laugh when I bring up 1930, and throw it out as ancient history brought up by an old goat. They used the same kind of bats, and the balls had 117 stitches, or whatever it is, and home plate and the pitcher's mound were sixty feet apart.

It wasn't so much home run. The home-run record for eight-team seasons wasn't set until years later. It was the rainstorm of base hits that gave that season something to be remembered by. National League players went to bat 43,747 times in 1930 and made 13,260 hits. The league as a whole batted .303—*.303!* Never has it happened before or since.

The Phillies, then playing in an old trap called Baker Bowl, batted .315, lost 102 games, and finished last. Seven Phillies hit above .300. Their problem wasn't easy to hide. The pitching staff had a mass ERA of 6.71.

The Giants batted .319, which led the league, but that didn't win the pennant. St. Louis won it with pitching—Bill Hallahan, Jess Haines, Flint Rhem, and Burleigh Grimes—but the Cardinal earned-run average was above 4.00.

The slugging percentage of the National League that season—that's total bases divided by at-bats—was .448, of the American League .421. The National scored 7,025 runs, the record for an eight-club season. Only 892 were home runs, only 673 in the American.

This would testify to the unnatural liveliness of the ball, for such reasons as the fences were longer than today, and long pop flies that clear fences don't necessarily distinguish good hitters. The year of 1930 was a year of line drives, the trademark of the true hitter.

It was a season that stood apart from all others of the time. It was the season when Bill Terry was the last of the National League's .400 hitters. The season before, the National League batting average was .294. The following season it was back to a sane .277.

I don't recall that there was any great commotion about it at the time. Americans like offense, base hits by the score. Suspicion was that the ball was juiced up, but not necessarily on purpose. Your grampa might recall that just three seasons before Ruth had his sixty-home-run season, and once the stock of lively pills ran out, which might have been 1930, the leagues went into a conspiracy favoring the shell-shocked pitchers.

BASEBALL GOES TO COLLEGE

FEBRUARY 2, 1961

It had been too long since I had seen Tubby Walton—with his clothes on, at least. He had been on the last occasion, if memory is accurate, running around the Health Club at the YMCA wrapped only in a Turkish towel, which is a new achievement for the towel industry.

Once upon the days of Herbert Hoover's poverty-stricken regime, there wasn't a towel made that would have spanned the breadth of William Hewlett Walton. In contrast to the economy of the times, he was as big as a side of beef, and it was then that he earned his degree as Tubby.

"Nobody ever ast my name befo'," Tubby said in his native tongue, "except the revenue man and a traffic cop. Ain't ten people in Atlanta know I'm William Hewlett Walton."

Tubby got so fat because he ran a restaurant called "Tubby's Home-Cooked Meals."

When his weight blew up to 350 pounds, and when he found he was giving away more meals at the back door than he was selling up front, he closed up his kitchen and quit.

Those were the days when the baseball scout was a rare breed, and Tubby was one of them, and indeed a rare breed. Tubby's scouting practices went beyond the general limit of his contemporaries. He was a progressive. He organized what he insists was the first baseball school in the history of mankind and attracted young geniuses to come unto him.

"This was 1928," he said. "You show me a baseball school befo' that and I'll eat Branch Rickey's fedora.

"One day at my modest little restaurant, Bird Hope come in for lunch. He was the coach at Fulton High School. Tubby's Home-Cooked Meals was just down the street.

43

" 'I got a little boy that can hit a curve ball,' Bird said. He talked with a little whine.

" 'Ain't no boy can hit a curve ball, Bird,' I said.

" 'This boy kin,' Bird said. 'Look a little like a Indian and kin hit a curve ball.'

" 'Bring him out,' I said. I ast him to bring him out to Tubby Walton's Baseball University, of which I was the president. President of a university and couldn't read or write. It was located at Almand Park, and our campus was a skin diamond and a chicken-wire backstop.

"I got this pitcher who was sorta mean. Later got in jail. I tole him to knock this Indian down and then curve him. This mean boy low-bridged him, then that Indian-looking boy hit the next curve ten miles.

"I tole Bird I'd take him without any further examination. The boy tole me his name was Luke Appling. He went on out to Oglethorpe University and I kept watching him and I finally signed him for the Crackers. Rell Spiller give him $1,000 and me $500.

"Luke later sent me $500 after he got to the major leagues. He shouldn't of done it. I lost it in the restaurant.

"I had this boy in my university named Leroy Waldrop. He tole me, 'Mistuh Walton, a boy out in Clayton County I know can hit anybody.'

" 'Ain't nobody kin hit anybody, Leroy,' I said.

" 'This boy kin,' Waldrop said, 'but he can't get away. His daddy's got him plowing.'

"I told Waldrop to get that boy up to the university at 9 o'clock the next morning and I'd let him be our guest for a spell. He showed up the next morning wearing tennis shoes, white duck pants, and old cap. I told him to get a bat and have a swing.

"He reached back and picked up a bat and never even looked at it. All my athletes always looked at the label. If it wasn't Babe Ruth or Al Simmons or Jimmy Foxx, they wouldn't hit with it.

"Hugh Casey was pitching. I told ol' Hughie to bear down, and this tall, lean ol' plowboy hit a line drive off him, and kept hitting 'em.

"Kid Elberfield was the dean of men, and I told him we better drive this boy out to his house personally and talk to his daddy ourselves.

"I remember just as we drove up the last hill before we got

to the farm, the boy said, 'Mistuh Walton, get Pa to let me plow and play baseball, too.'

"His daddy turned out to be a school teacher. He sat on that porch and rocked and read every word in that contract.

" 'It sounds like he's joining the chain gang,' his daddy said.

" 'It does sound like that,' I said, 'but they'll pay him for his work. They don't pay on the chain gangs.'

"I signed the boy and his name was Cecil Travis. I took him to Chattanooga and Joe Engel paid me $300. Cecil never got a dime."

BOCCABELLA
FROM
POCATELLO

JULY 1978

No game has more fun with nicknames than baseball, and none wastes as little time on tact. A baseball player sees a "Moose," or a "Horse," or a "Whale," and he calls 'em like he sees 'em.

The Baseball Register, published each year by *The Sporting News*, and *The Baseball Encyclopedia* are indispensable archives of nicknames. But they make it plain that today's appellations are less colorful. Maybe it's because the fine art of lobby sitting—practiced during the long hours when players sat around their hotels shooting he breeze—has vanished. Maybe it's because teams no longer have to suffer through long, hot train rides. For whatever reason, today it is left to the press to do the fancy naming. Tom Seaver may be "Tom Terrific" to the sportswriter who needs a catchy lead, but he's Tom to his teammates. Steve Garvey is Steve, Rod Carew is Rod, and even Reggie Jackson is just Reggie. Of course there's Catfish Hunter, but that was owner Charlie Finley's doing: Finley also tried to persuade Vida Blue to adopt the cognomen "True," but the pitcher resisted.

So the real classics of baseball naming remain enshrined in baseball's century-long memory. *The Baseball Register* has always tried to be very polite about these names. It would insist that "Moose" Solters was called "Moose" because he had a deep voice; or that "Harry the Horse" Danning was called that because he played the nags. Pshaw, "Moose" was called that because he looked like one and "Harry the Horse" was so-called because his face was shaped like Whirlaway's. And Fred Walters was called "Whale" because he was as big as one.

Baseball players waste no time monkeying around, which reminds me that there was an outfielder known as "Monkey"

Epps, and you're on your own there. Players can be as cruel as playground kids, and often just as innocent. The nicknames they bestow are sometimes just natural reactions to a face, shape, or personality. They're graphic and to the point, which is to say, Bob Fothergill wasn't known as "Fatty" for nothing. And when the big leagues took their first look at tall, lean, drawling Cliff Melton, they knew he was "Mountain Music."

When Bob Seeds first planted his big feet in the Cleveland clubhouse, he became "Suitcase." The Athletics took one look at a new outfielder who became "Mule" Haas because it looked as if he ought to hee-haw. Clyde Milan ran with such speed and grace they called him "Deerfoot" in Washington. New York, being more sophisticated, interpreted the same traits in George Selkirk as "Twinkle-toes." Monte Stratton's neck was so long they called him "Gander."

All of this tomfoolery is more acute in baseball because of the leisure of the game, and because the athletes are less stereotyped. Football tackles can all be described in one word— *big*. Guards are short and dumpy. Centers are always stooped. Basketball players are always tall. Hockey players can all buy their clothes off the same rack—medium. And jockeys are miniature men.

But in baseball, a pitcher can weigh 155 to 250 pounds; thus Hal Brown became "Skinny," and Walter Brown became "Jumbo."

The old Philadelphia A's had a crafty little second baseman who always led the American League in walks and was known as "Camera Eye" Bishop. Bobby Veach, who played beside Ty Cobb, was called "Peek-a-boo" because of the funny way he peered through a crook in his arm at the pitcher. Jim Galvin was known as "The Little Steam Engine" because he huffed and puffed while he pitched. "Dirty Al" Gallagher always looked as if he needed laundering, and "Shanty" Hogan was another Irishman who flunked hygiene.

When the Boston Red Sox gave a sawed-off outfielder named Gene Rye a chance, he naturally became "Half-pint." They'd have been stumped if they'd ever learned his real name was Mercantelli.

But get this one: With all the Smiths in the big leagues, what do you suppose Salvatore Giuseppe Persico changed his name to? Joe Smith. Didn't change his luck at all. In thirteen games in 1913, he batted .156.

Meantime, all the Smiths were using every colorful instrument to bring their names alive. There were "Klondike," "Riverboat," "Skyrocket," "Broadway Aleck," "Oil," and those two paragons of modesty, "Phenomenal" and "Wonderful Willie," all Smiths. And, lest we forget, "Bull" Smith. The broadcasters had to be careful with that one.

Naturally, all Rhodeses are "Dusty," all Indians are "Chief," all Latins are "Chico," but Lew Whistler wasn't "Mother." Nor was Ernest Jeanes called "Blue," but "Tex" instead. How Ulysses Simpson Grant Stoner ever became "Lil" remains a nagging mystery.

Some were not left to survive one nickname alone, but became endowed with full titles, as in Jim "The Human Mosquito" Slagle, Moe "The Rabbi of Swat" Solomon, Frank "The Naugatuck Nugget" Shea, Amos "The Hoosier Cannonball" Rusie, and that classic fellow who should make the Hall of Fame for pitchers with names that rhyme, Heine "The Count of Luxembourg" Meine.

There were some, though, whose names stood alone—they needed no tampering—names with funny sounds like Blong and Binks and Zuverink, and names that described careers, as D'Arcy Fast, whose delivery wasn't but whose career was. And one of my all-time favorites, Elmer Klumpp, whose thirteen-game career between Washington and Brooklyn was just that—a "klumpp." He batted .115.

Wherever will you find more distinction than in such names as Decatur Poindexter Jones, Ambrose Puttman, Camille O. Van Brabant, Clayton Emery Van Alstyne, and Jonathan Trumpbour Matlack, who is still alive and well in Texas. I reserve for my personal favorite Carden Gillenwater, an outfielder who should have been an inventor.

Some relied on their destinations or identification, as Boccabella who played for Pocatello, and Duffalo who pitched for Buffalo before they made the majors. It was Dave Philley who paid off on the daily double, having played for both teams in Philadelphia before the A's moved. Unfortunately, Nathan Detroit was never a Tiger.

Before approaching the best-in-show name of them all, let me assure you I've never known how virtuous was Jacob Virtue, nor how happy was Aloysius Joy; but I have realized how laborious it is to introduce the now-retired pitcher Calvin Coolidge Julius

Caesar Tuskahoma McLish, one of the rare Indians never known as "Chief." With a name spread that covers everything from B.C. to H.E.W., it's obvious that baseball popped up with the bases filled when it finally settled on "Buster" (ugh!), declining a glorious opportunity to improvise. A nice man as he has lived, but sure to be cursed the day he dies—by his stonecutter. And with that, Adios Aloha, who was part Hawaiian, part Mexican, part outfielder, and parting shot.

The Wide World
of Football

ROY THOUGHT HE WAS RIGHT

OCTOBER 1966

. . . The score was 0-0 and we had the ball on our 23 near the sideline. We had a play which faked toward the sideline and came back. Stumpy (Thomason) was carrying the ball and fumbled, California's Riegels grabbed it while it was still in the air. It was my business to block halfback Benny Lom, but when Riegels got the ball it became Lom's job to block me.

Riegels took two steps in the right direction, but as I was bearing down on him, he headed for his own goal. Lom was caught short and we both set out after the ball-carrier.

We ran like a team, with one stride behind Lom, who finally caught Riegels at the one. Lom grabbed Riegels by the right shoulder with his left hand and spun him around. Then I hit him high and spilled him into the end zone, where he lost the ball and we recovered. I've never been able to understand why we didn't get a touchdown, but they gave the ball to California on the one.—Frank Waddey in Bob Wallace's *Dress Her in White and Gold.*

Roy Riegels is, indeed, a remarkable figure of a man. Weaker mortals have been known to crash-dive under the load he has carried. Harrowing, nightmarish, pride-searing stuff that shreds one's emotions like the fringe of a hippie's leather jerkin.

Most legends achieve that status by the normal course or routine. Winning the big game with a dropkick. Making the spectacular catch hanging over a fence with the bases loaded. Upsetting Harvard. Beating Don Budge. Breaking Nurmi's record. Using the first rear-view at Indianapolis.

But some make it like Roy Riegels. Like Mickey Owen—the

52

passed ball that lost the World Series game. Like Aaron Robinson—who forgot to tag the runner and lost the pennant. Like the marathon runner—who ran part of his race in the back seat of a car.

Or Snodgrass, or Merkle and a bundle of others whose acts were committed under circumstances of merciful obscurity.

Roy Riegels became confused, reversed his field and carried the football in the wrong direction for California in the Rose Bowl game of 1929. Frank Waddey, later a major-league baseball player, was an end for Georgia Tech, beneficiary of Riegels's run, and he tells you his part in the addling event.

But have a look at it from where Roy Riegels stood. First place, he was a center, and centers spend half the game looking at the world upside down. They aren't supposed to know how to carry a football.

The first quarter had just ended and the two teams had changed fields.

Then, as he says himself, "If I had it to do again, I'd still run in the same direction, for I surely thought I was running the right way." Riegels is now sixty-three years old. He lives in Woodland, California, a small town twenty miles north of Sacramento, and operates Roy Riegels Chemicals Company, an agricultural fertilizer firm with four outlets in that fertile valley.

He is splendidly preserved, blessed with the kind of patience that heaven reserves for such individuals as need it, and looks at life through pastel-blue eyes that twinkle. Amused, no doubt, at the curious Homo sapiens who gather about him in inquisitive awe, and verbally paw at him like a timid feline.

The fame of Roy Riegels bounds. "It is with me, I suppose, as long as I live," he said. "You run the wrong way with a football in front of 60,000 people and it's pretty hard to lie out of it."

Not only in the Rose Bowl, but in earshot of the first national football broadcast audience. Also, in a game shot full of enough crank incidents to mark itself forever, anyway. And the crazy score, 8-7.

"I was embarrassed," he said, "when I realized what I had done. But that soon passed, and then I reached a stage when mention of it would cause me to bristle. Soon that passed and it has never really bothered me since, except in cases of people trying to exploit it.

"Some fellow circulated a story that my mother had finally

seen fit to forgive me. It was pure fabrication. My mother had been dead five years."

Ministers have used Riegels as a sermon topic. Coaches have used the old story to soothe the souls of plagued players. Lecturers have prattle on it from civic club rostrums. Any kid runs the wrong way, Riegels is begged to write him of the chances of his pride healing.

There is one severe oversight. Lost in all this sideshow atmosphere is the fact that Roy Riegels was a fine football player. His teammates had already elected him captain for the next season. Associated Press made him the center on its second All-America team. California invited him to remain and coach the freshman team for a year.

Georgia Tech has invited him and Benny Lom, whose tackle saved at least four points, back to mingle with the members of the team in whose direction he ran. They are all here for the Georgia Tech–Army game, but the center ring is Riegels's. The first thought that strikes you the moment you meet him is he has obviously been running the right way ever since January 1, 1929.

WOODY HAYES
—AT PEACE

MAY 28, 1982

COLUMBUS, Ohio—From his office on the second floor of the Military Science Building, Woody Hayes can look across Woody Hayes Drive—a Woody Hayes drive used to be three yards and a cloud of dust, this one is a boulevard—upon the north end of Ohio Stadium. It cannot be called the house that Woody built. It was thirty years old when he arrived. But it was the house that Woody filled for nearly thirty years.

"Since that stadium was built in 1922, there have been more changes on this earth than in all the years, back to the birth of Christ," the man himself said.

He had been talking to one of his old centers, Danny Fronk, now an investment broker, when I walked in. They were to meet for lunch.

"By God, those kids call me all the time," he said, cheerfully and proud. "Two of my old players arranged for me to have this office."

It couldn't have been a more likely location for such a student of the military and kibitzer of generals. If Napoleon had had Woody Hayes on his staff, we'd probably all be speaking French today.

He sat at a crescent-shaped desk. He was surrounded by books—on his desk and in a tall wall-case back of his desk. *The Second World War*, by Winston Churchill; *Leaders* by Richard Nixon, *History of the U.S. Marine Corps; Guns of August; Einstein; Adolph Hitler*; William Buckley; Henry Kissinger; Gerald Ford—their works and others, but not a football title among them.

On the wall above his head was a *Sporting News* cover portrait of Pete Rose. "I admire that young fellow," he said. "I think he sent me that."

One title not likely to be seen among the Hayes collection

55

is *Football/History and Woody Hayes*," mainly because it probably never will be finished. "I have 85 percent of it written," he said. "I have to put it together, but I'll probably never do it."

He spreads himself about the country making speeches. His desk calendar was dark with engagements. He uses a plain lead pencil. He was due to address a convention of dentists in Phoenix, then on to San Francisco for a Boys Club of America appearance, to Chicago to an NCAA meeting, then back to Columbus for a banquet. That very evening he was the main speaker at a commencement exercise.

"I do about twenty-five of these a month, luncheons, dinners, conventions." He has his price, and it varies. When he was offered a fee of $5,000 after speaking before a Boy Scouts of America congregation, he said no. All he wanted was a pair of $125 hunting boots. On another occasion, before a service organization, he accepted a necktie instead of a $1,000 check.

His fascination with life and people runs as deep as he is a fascinator. He grew up the son of the high-school principal in Newcomerstown, a rural community of about 5,000 east of Columbus. "It isn't easy being the principal's son," he said. Being a football star helped ease the stress. On his way to fame at Ohio State, he apprenticed at Mingo Junction, New Philadelphia, Denison College, and Miami of Ohio. His first bowl game wasn't the Rose, it was the Salad, which soon wilted.

The phone rang. It was Bud Wilkinson. His son, Jay, now a businessman, was coming to Columbus. He wanted Woody to make some time for him.

"Oh, yes, I see every Ohio State game at home, some on the road, not all. I just can't. Occasionally I get all worked up, but only twice or so. I was at the spring practice game and they left that quarterback [Mike Tomczak] in too long, and he broke his leg in two places."

His secretary, a brunette named Sandra, appeared at the door. A Dr. Zimmerman was calling about the speech in Phoenix.

"When I was coaching, I pointed for only three games a year," he said, Dr. Zimmerman having been attended to. "I started pointing for Michigan in spring practice. You know who I saw the other day in Minneapolis? Murray Warmath. He coached for two of the greatest, Bob Neyland and Earl Blaik. And Bobby Dodd, he was such a helluva coach I had him here for spring practice one year.

"I'm sorry Bear Bryant didn't quit sooner. I think he coached himself to death."

His unceremonious departure, his exit on the toe of a boot as warlord of the Scarlet and Gray, has tarnished none of his romance with Ohio State. Not ten men on the street can tell you who's the president of Ohio State. They can tell you who the football coach was the last thirty years. In the minds of most, and probably him as well, he is the true spirit of the Buckeye.

It ran in the family. His son Stephen, now a judge in municipal court, was a football player. "I tried to get him to go to a smaller school where he could play," Woody said. "He said, 'Dad, I'd still be back in Columbus every Saturday.' "

The Gator Bowl, Charles Baumann, the Clemson linebacker, that wretched night in Jacksonville, weren't introduced as subjects. What is there to be said now by a man born seventy-one Valentine's Days ago.

Instead, I said, "When the fall comes, and the leaves turn, and the stadium fills, do you miss it?"

"I'd coached long enough," he said. "I'd coached long enough." And he looked out across Woody Hayes Drive toward the stadium.

DAMNING INDICTMENT OF GARBAGEMEN

JANUARY 9, 1986

We may not make a university student out of him but if we can teach him to read and write, maybe he can work at the post office rather than as a garbageman when he gets through with his athletic career.

It has the quality of a line out of a stand-up comedian's mouth in a dingy nightclub. Read it again to make sure your eyes are working.

It was spoken in a courtroom. A lawyer said it, representing two staff members standing trial as the accused. The fact that they are from the University of Georgia is almost coincidental. It is the most damning indictment of college athletics and its relationship to education that I may ever have read. It reads like the defense scored one in the wrong basket.

The year Georgia played Texas in the Cotton Bowl, two members of the team who had already flunked out at the end of the fall quarter were allowed to play in the game. The defense was, you couldn't blame the coaching staff. The two players were in school because of federal decree, so why shouldn't they play?

Georgia fought, bled, and died to keep Cedric Henderson on the basketball team while he was making no pretense of trying to get educated. He finished the season, then took flight. If you had to make book on his destiny, postal worker wouldn't get a call.

It doesn't take much to get me lathered up over such as this. Persons who can't read or write have no earthly reason for taking up space in college. How do you educate those who don't recognize words and can't make letters and sign their report card with an X?

We are coming to the point where we must decide what college is for—education or a refuge for illiterates hired to put on shows for television, for which the school is paid a handsome fee. We have known that what came out of the opening remarks to the jury of this attorney, Hale Almand, is going on, but it is the first blunt admission seen in type, and it shocks.

At least if he can't make the grade, he can learn to read and write and become a postal worker instead of a garbageman—gad, what a savage appraisal of what the college athletic world has come to! The hope is that the athlete will become another Herschel Walker. The prospect is that he might. The reality develops that he won't, that he misses by a few light years, and in the end, all the academically deficient misfit has to show for college is a monogram sweater, programs with his picture in them, a few clippings, some hotel towels, and a lot of memories.

Some, who really came to college for an education and won't get away without one, tough it out until they master it all. It took Ronnie Stewart six years, but he stuck it out and got his degree. Willie McClendon came back from pro football and hit the classroom. He wants his degree.

Heaven knows how many others walked away and hadn't read a book and never looked back. The University of North Carolina System was surveyed a while back, and the chancellor was appalled at the scores that came in. Actual graduation statistics were much below what they'd been advertised. With pride, Dean Smith at Chapel Hill underscored the fact that this wasn't the case with his basketball players.

A discharged instructor named Dr. Jan Kemp is charging that she was fired at Georgia because she objected to treating athletes preferentially at Georgia and spoke out against it. The court will decide on the merits of her case, but the public will look at lawyer Almand's crass admission that indeed athletes are treated preferentially and decide what to make of that. Surely you don't kick a star out of school, one who attracts the television networks, draws national attention, and puts money in the university's pockets. Is that what he is saying? Surely Boston College wouldn't have flunked out Doug Flutie, Auburn wouldn't have flunked out Bo Jackson, Georgetown wouldn't have flunked out Patrick Ewing, who brought in a bonanza of $12 million—and you get the point.

Is that what we've come to? Have college athletics become

the academic garbage heap? Is lawyer Almand making a confession for all of America's athletics departments? You can bet your Phi Beta Kappa key he isn't speaking for Georgia alone.

The college people (NCAA) meet in New Orleans next week and one of the major items to come up is Proposition 48, or whatever it has become since some whittling and wheedling. That would have restricted college athletes to those who came out of high school with a 2.00 grade average and a 700/15 test score. There's a big push among athletics people to soften it, weaken it.

That pretty much tells you all you need to know.

ORAL ROBERTS GOES MOSLEM, SO TO SPEAK

JANUARY 7, 1987

Let me get this straight, now.

Bill Curry is going to coach the football team at Alabama. The same Bill C-U-R-R-Y who gave his heart to Georgia Tech as a player. Who palmed footballs to John Unitas, Bart Starr, and all those famous quarterbacks. Who played for Lombardi and Shula, was one of George Plimpton's books and one of Ed Garvey's union presidents. And who was 1-9 and 1-10 the first two seasons he came out head-coaching at Alma Mater.

My first reaction as I come out of my daze is that I'm glad to see Alabama has decided to go straight.

(The same Bill Curry who has two kids and a lovely wife named Carolyn, and wears the dark glasses on the sidelines even if it's cloudy. Right?)

I guess that means Alabama has given up on Bear Bryant's resurrection. It has been a lot longer than three days.

Twenty years ago it wouldn't have happened. Alabama and Georgia Tech weren't even speaking. One reason Georgia Tech isn't in the Southeastern Conference is Alabama. Alabama wouldn't touch anything from Georgia Tech without first scrubbing up. They hated.

Some of them still hate. Else Dr. Joab Thomas, the courageous president, wouldn't have to take his telephone off the hook, or check his life insurance.

That's the kind of Roll Tide mentality Curry is walking into. They can't understand a coach who looks upon the college president as his equal. They're used to the coach telling the president where to park his car, where to sit and how he wants his eggs, not some coach standing up talking about purity and sounding interested in education and looking humble.

They're not used to this. It's culture shock. You could sense their pain when President Thomas started talking about "a high level of integrity." Dern it, there goes our annual bowl trip, even if this one was to El Paso.

They're used to the coach talking about kicking butts, winning championships, and mamas and papas and bowl games. If education happens to rub off on a misfit here or there, good for him.

It is lovely for Curry to bring enlightenment to Alabama, but only if it improves his own career. Take Steve Sloan. What an admirable team they make, Curry and Sloan. Mr. Clean as twins.

The difference is Sloan doesn't have to worry about winning. He gets the job with the safety belt. He's the athletics director, and he has an Alabama diploma—a real, actual Alabama diploma.

It's not as if you never expected Curry to leave Georgia Tech— of his own accord. It's just that if you had to guess the last place he'd ever have gone, the absolute last, the University of Mongolia might have come first, but Alabama wouldn't have been more than a neck back. Picture Oral Roberts joining the Moslems and you've ot it.

Georgia Tech once spoke proudly of having only three paid head coaches in all its football years. Now it has had seven. Bobby Ross makes eight. Of all those coaches, only one has taken leave for another school. Curry.

John Heisman left because of an unusual divorce arrangement. "I have agreed that wherever Mrs. Heisman lives, I shall live in another place to avoid embarrassment," he said. She chose Atlanta. He went to Penn.

Another burr under the saddle of the real hard-core Crimson may be that Alabama has hired the only losing coach Tech ever had. Bud Carson was close. He finished 27-27. Curry leaves behind a record of 31-43-4, and a constituency patient enough to brook such an adjustment. Throw a couple of 7-4, 8-3 seasons at the guy in the van with the "Roll Tide" horn, the red hat, and a wife named Myrtice—and you ain't Alabama, anyway—he'll allow you to pick out your own noose. Curry may have mad his first misstep in staff selection. If ever a fellow needed Alabama Red on his side, guys who know the territory, speak the native tongue and have some roots, it would seem to be him. Instead, he's cleaning out the old gang and walking in with all these nice new guys who dress good and smell metropolitan. Lord, it's a gamble.

So was going to Tokyo. The plane might have crashed. Nevertheless, today we find Bill Curry in Tuscaloosa not Tokyo. At Bryant-Denny Stadium, not the Japan Bowl.

I'm not sure I'm ready, or that anybody is, for him to take his stance at The Capstone and cry out, "Roll Tide!" Not with feeling. Bill Curry "Rolling Tide?" C'mon. I'll wake up tomorrow.

"COMMENT VONT LES CHIENS!"

NOVEMBER 27, 1985

If you were among the gallery at the Scottish Rite Game, you will recall that on the first play a manicured hand reached outside uniform #92 and slapped down a Georgia Tech pass.

The Georgia Bulldog is developing an international taste, plumb suave and debonair. You will recall that the captain of the national champions in 1980 was an import from Spain, Francisco Ros, born in Barcelona and shipped to the U.S. as a boy.

This young fellow wearing "92" is fresh from the south of France. The named is pronounced "Tar-DEETS," as the French say it. The address is 6 Carrefour, Biarritz, a resorty beach town resting between Bayonne and St. Jean de Luz, on the Gulf of Gascogne, twenty miles from the Spanish border.

There is a distinct difference in the background of Frank Ros and Richard Tardits. Ros got his training for football in the high schools of Greenville, South Carolina. Tardits got his on the rugby fields of France.

Richard Tardits didn't come to the United States to study the peculiar customs of these crazed Americans and report back to *le professeur*. Richard came to play, which is what a coach likes to say only about the best of them. Which isn't to say that that describes Tardits in his present apprenticeship.

Georgia, as a rule, doesn't recruit France. Didn't this time. Young Tardits recruited Georgia, and Georgia's gain is the University of Toulouse's loss. "That is where I would have gone if I had stayed in France," he said. "I was recruited by Toulouse for rugby."

As it turned out, Tardits lucked out, and it looks as though Vince Dooley may have as well. Tardits is not a military brat foaled in France while his poppa was stationed there. He is as French as truffles, Balzac, and fromage de Camembert. He had never seen a ball with points on it before. He had never seen a game played with one until he watched on the sidelines as Georgia played Alabama. As hellish a scene as that was, he was swept up in it and since has played in the rest of Georgia's nine games.

He made his first tackle against Clemson. He sacked his first quarterback in the Tulane game. He batted down two passes and had another sack among his four tackles playing for the junior varsity against Georgia Tech.

Dooley, though, said he had played his best game the day before. "He was outstanding scrimmaging the varsity Friday. He had four sacks, then came back and played the game on Saturday, bruised as he was."

Put it this way, Tardits has been on the campus less than a year, was introduced to football only last spring, and Saturday will find himself in the midst of the very personal war between Georgia and Georgia Tech for the championship of a state that's as mysterious as Mongolia on Rue de Carrefour. He will be the only player on the field with an accent like Louis Jourdan.

Tardits finds himself absorbed by a world of balmy passion, inhabited by wacky people dressed in red, driving red machines and shrieking, "How 'bout them Dawgs!" The nearest thing he has seen to the Georgia-Florida scene is bullfighting in Spain.

He wasn't sure what to make of it at first, but after a season in the trenches, he has a fresh understanding.

"I think it is really great," he said, "all those people in red shirts and black pants and those houses on wheels, going about saying, 'How 'bout them Dawgs!'"

He laughed in English. "I love it. They are crazy just for a game. It is the only way to make a sport."

To his neighbors in Basque France, it may seem that Richard is serving in a Foreign Legion. Actually, it is the manifestation of a strange urge. It was not an American education that lured him. After all, Americans send their kids to France for continental polish. Richard was attracted by this American football. His father, a contractor in Biarritz, encouraged him.

The family had friends in Augusta, and the friends had a friend named Dr. Mixon Robinson, a former Georgia end, now the team orthopedist. Tardits was invited to Augusta, and the summer and fall of 1984 was spent in the Americanization of Richard. In January, he was accepted at Georgia, and when the call for football went out, he showed up.

"One of the coaches told me one of the walk-ons was from France," Dooley said. "I said, 'That's interesting.' "

"Some walk-ons stay a few days, some just disappear, some stick it out. He began to catch our eye."

Tardits was tried out on offense at first and told to block the lineman facing him. "I just jumped at him, and I grabbed him by the legs," he said with a laugh. "I didn't know what 'block' was."

Dooley said, "I expect you'd better try defense," and a defensive end he has been ever since, now 225 pounds of French fury.

Rugby is played without bodily protection. All the pads, the helmet, and the cage were new to Tardits. "For three weeks my neck hurt from the helmet. I know now why we need it. Football is much more violent than rugby."

He will not go home to Biarritz until it is all over. Travel is expensive. So is education. To stay beyond a couple of years, he must be impressive enough to earn a scholarship. Upon which the student section will learn how to chant, "How 'bout them Dawgs!" in French.

"Comment vont les Chiens!" Give the man a C for his high-school French.

"WHIMPER, LION, WHIMPER"

It was the day of the sixth game of the World Series. Autumn in New York was at its loveliest, but only one with the resonant tones of Ted Husing still sounding in his eardrums would have taken the train to the 215th Street station to see Columbia and Colgate, two winless teams, play a football game. Columbia hadn't beaten Colgate since 1964, when Archie Robert was quarterback, and hadn't beaten anybody since 1983. The old fight song, "Roar, Lion, Roar," has been reduced to a whimper.

Columbia is breaking in a new coach, Larry McElreavy, third of the decade. The last one took his leave after railing out in his despondency at a slipshod punter. Nothing remains of the glorious days when Husing, first and most glamorous of a new breed of broadcasters, painted the scene at Baker Field on our old radio.

Baker Field sits on the northern tip of Manhattan, where the Harlem River takes its leave of the Hudson, where the Henry Hudson Bridge, the Bronx, and New Jersey all come together. Once there were 32,000 seats, but the old stands have been replaced by about half that number cast in cement, a cozy little theater of convenience, an old Ivy League priority.

In ten minutes, Colgate had a 10-0 lead. One thing Colgate can do is put the ball in the end zone. Twice the offense has scored thirty-nine points but lost to Lehigh and Bucknell.

A crowd that half-filled the seats soon became restless. Enticing as the scenery was, there was little to keep those of Columbia persuasion engrossed.

"Why don't we buy tickets to a game that a lot of people come to?" asked the lady in an adjoining pew. "I don't feel like I'm at a football game when I see the stands half-filled."

"It's more private this way," her husband said, soothingly.

"I like popular events, with a lot of people cheering and interested."

"Give them time, dear. This is a new coach."

Ted was of Columbia loyalty. The son was of Colgate, and was carrying on with such glee that a couple of elderly men of the Blue, who looked like research scientists, were taken to suggest that he move. He did when a group of late-arrivals told him he and his bride were in their seats.

"Why don't we get tickets to the Yale game?" the wife said again. "That would be nice."

"Yale beat us, 47 to nothing," Ted said.

Last year a Colgate fullback named Chubb had run the opening kickoff back for a touchdown. Now he broke loose on a draw play for a long gain.

As Colgate neared the goal line, a voice from above cried out, "Look out for the draw!"

Sure enough, Phelan, the quarterback, called the draw and Chubb carried for another long gain.

"Come on, you wimps!" cried the voice from above. Ted's wife looked around disapprovingly.

Columbia finally got on the board when Policastro punted out on the one-yard line and Phelan was tackled in the end zone for a safety. The score was 24-2.

"Why don't we keep doing that and catch up?" asked the wife.

Ted smiled and patted her hand.

Not to be discouraged, she said, "Let's do a wave."

Just before the half, Columbia intercepted a pass and Putelo threw to Brown for a touchdown. Joy spread around the home rooters, but the placekicker, who had been warming up vigorously on the sideline, missed the extra point. Oh, well, it was something to build on, anyway. Columbia never scored again and Colgate won, 54-8. The Lions led Villanova, 28-14, at halftime the next week, and the rare fragrance of victory was upon the wind. But alas, they never scored in the second half and Villanova won. Now the nonwinning streak is up to thirty games, but those of Columbia carry on with a stout spirit, and those who visit grieve at such despair in such elegant people in such an inspiring setting.

"Won't you join us at halftime?" they asked. Tailgating is a halftime sport there, and after a glass of wine and a sandwich, I headed back to the train to be delivered to the dungeon of the city.

This is where college football breathed its first in America, before catching the wagons west and south to become the foundries of Oklahoma, Alabama, Texas, and the rest. Eight teams became the "Ivy League" in the 1930s, and they cling to standards long since lost in migration. Columbia once played and won in the Rose Bowl, and Husing once rattled chandeliers speaking of its might, but sad to say, it isn't that winning has vanished, but even the hope of winning.

ARTLESS, BUT FOR ART'S SAKE

JANUARY 13, 1975

Super Bowl IX will be remembered as the one when the game plan seemed to have been lost on the way to the stadium. Played by two teams that looked as though they might have chosen up sides after they got there. On television it must have looked like a rerun of an old Falcons-Saints game, or Laurel versus Hardy.

I knew we were in a recession. Well, the Super Bowl beat us to the depression. If the national economy follows suit, we're in trouble up to here.

It was so depressing the Minnesota Vikings started leaving the field before the clock ran out. Trying to beat the crowd, I guess. It was their most impressive run of the day. Honestly, being as cold as it was, noses had a better day running than they had.

They carried the ball twenty-one times and gained seventeen yards. Based on that average, our pioneering forefathers would be about as far west as Knoxville by now.

The best the Minnesota offense could do was score two points—and they counted for Pittsburgh. You do this by moving the ball backward. The play was good for ten yards—into the Minnesota end zone. Something happened when Fran Tarkenton tried to pitch out to Dave Osborn and Tarkenton wound up covering the ball for the ultimate in football humiliation—the safety.

The Vikings were still holding the score down, though. When the first half ended 2-0, you were beginning to envision a 3-2 final. The Vikings would hold. Somehow they'd get in position. Fred Cox would kick a field goal and that would be some kind of relic to put in our 1975 time capsule.

But this was one day the gods in charge of such things weren't having any of that stuff. They were playing to the gallery. They went the sentimental route. Pure, cornball American plot right down to the tears. They went for the rumpled old gent wearing the thick eyeglasses and cigar and talking like your high-school principal.

All these years Art Rooney has been trying to get here. Just hoping to rub shoulders with a championship. Nursed the Pittsburgh Steelers through 0-10 and 1-9 seasons, kept answering the bell for the next round. Never made an enemy. Never stirred up a fuss. Never missed Mass. If he ever disapproved of anybody, he only thought it. Never said it out loud. Finally, the team overcomes insurmountable odds and makes it to the title fight.

But this is not to be, say wise men who know these things. "Minnesota has been here before, knows the pressure, the tilt of the field, how the week gnaws and nags," they say.

To show you how the Great Director Up Yonder wasn't letting anybody else roll his dice, check this for the bouncing of balls, switching of momentum, swinging of pendulums, as they say in the broadcast pulpit.

Roy Gerela almost misses the ball kicking off the second half, the ball does crazy things and winds up in the hands of an old fullback up front who's in there for blocking purposes. Bill Brown is so surprised he fumbles on Minnesota's thirty-yard line. A rookie named Marv Kellum, who is unknown to anybody but Mr. and Mrs. Kellum of Lecompton, Kansas, covers the ball.

Terry Bradshaw, the strong but dumb quarterback, also bearded, turns Franco Harris loose twice and the second time he's in the end zone after running nine yards, and nobody realizes it, but at 9-0 the game is over.

Marv Kellum, mind you. A walk-on, who didn't even cost a draft choice. Got to Wichita State too late to catch the plane that crashed but to the Super Bowl in time to catch the loose ball at the right time.

"I knew we were going to score," Harris said later. He's a powerful man of 230 pounds. His face is all angles and a Nazarene beard and his hair a mass of black ringlets. "We were moving the ball. It was bound to happen." See what I mean?

There was nothing else about the game, though, to recommend it to Canton, Ohio. It was about as classic as intramurals. There were so many fumbles it began to look like soccer. You know, hands off. Even a big-busted stripper got fumbled three times by two security men before they could break up her dash across the field at halftime.

Blocked punts, skied kickoffs, missed field goals, a conversion kick that struck an upright, a pass reception that became a fumble, and an interception—because Pittsburgh's safetyman Glenn Edwards hit John Gilliam so hard the ball took light again and came down in Mel Blount's arms around the goal line—and then the craziest play of all, Tarkenton throwing two forward passes on one down.

L.C. Greenwood batted the ball back in his face on the first and Francis wound up and pegged it again about forty yards downfield for a completion that didn't count. Greenwood did this so many times Tarkenton could have become the leading rebounder in Super Bowl history. Five times it happened.

"I figured I might as well throw it," he said of his unique second effort. "Mean Joe Greene was standing right there waiting to swallow me whole if I kept it."

I don't know when these guys are ever going to get hold of themselves. They've been playing Super Bowls now since 1967— and these big, strong, well-paid professionals get stage fright. They go on like a kid playing his first piano recital. The defense plays it like hell-drivers. Greene, Greenwood, and their gang, even with Dwight "Mad Dog" White still bug-infested, literally strangled the Vikings.

"We don't choke up," Tarkenton said. "I don't feel like it's my blackest day. It's been a good year. We're better than twenty-four other teams in the league." Who's to say?

They announced before the game that it was being telecast around the hemisphere to such places as Venezuela, and the rest of the Caribbean and the Virgin Islands. I just hope it didn't get into Cuba. Castro may have seen it and decide that it's time to invade.

Fore!

FATHER AND SON DAY AT AUGUSTA

APRIL 14, 1986

This is a story I'm not sure I can write. Athletes choke, writers choke. Jack Nicklaus has brought me to the brink of my choking point.

What comes muscling into my mind is all the negatives: The broadcaster who, after interviewing several players, came to the rash conclusion, "His fellow pros no longer fear him"; the awful tee shot on the third hole, a duffer's slice through the pines and the azaleas, almost into the second fairway; and the overstroked putt five feet past the pin on the ninth hole, both part of the seventy-four strokes of his first round in the Masters. The fiftieth, four more than he is old.

But in a time of need, when American golf is losing face, foreign players are about to take over even our beloved Masters, who should ride to the rescue? Who should answer the call when the bearded old gentleman in the top hat cries out from the billboard, "Uncle Sam Needs You!"

Not one of the newly monied youth, comfy and cozy in their fresh prosperity, safely placed in the *PGA Guide* for the year, from Azinger to Zokol. And who live from tour pot to tour pot.

But out of the backroads of our memory comes this codger, this battle-hardened old trouper who had been brushed aside, this man who said, "I sort of felt everybody had written me off." What does Jack Nicklaus need with one more green jacket? One more major to hang on his wall? One more fat check to share with the IRS?

Seriously, don't confuse the return of Jack Nicklaus with anything patriotic. He was a man with bloodshot pride, who hadn't won a tournament since the Memorial (his own) two years

74

ago, who had $4,000 to show for 1986 on the American tour (at an expense of $100,000). This was one he won for Jack Nicklaus and all the Nicklauses. His son caddied for him and his mother was here for the first time since he was an amateur, and every member of the gallery became a Nicklaus as he turned for home and they began to sense he had a chance to win again.

He birdied the tenth hole, he birdied the eleventh, and just when there was a rustling among the throng, he bogeyed the twelfth, and they sagged. Then he birdied the thirteenth, and when he reached the fifteenth, 500 yards with the green treacherously situated above a pond, he gave them a signal that all was not lost. When he sank the eagle putt, the cry that arose startled all the wildlife in the forest. He was now two strokes back of the leaders, seven under par with three holes to play.

This was the Masters that the son of Santander had pronounced his. "The Masters is mine," Severiano Ballesteros had said. "It belongs to me."

When he followed Nicklaus to the fifteenth hole, he began to lose his grip on ownership. It went down with a gurgle when his approach hit the pond, and he dispatched himself with three putts on the seventeenth. It was on the same hole that Nicklaus put his brand on it.

His approach lay fifteen feet from the cup, and a chance at taking the lead. He crouched and peered at the line through his squinty old eyes, then he stepped over the ball. And stood, and stood, and stood until it seemed he was transfixed. Finally he made the stroke, the ball found the route, and it dropped into the hole. He threw up both arms in exultation, and we didn't know it yet, but Jack Nicklaus had won his sixth Masters.

Some runs had been made on the leaders, but none serious and none lasting. I'd thought earlier what a shame if Jay Haas should win a Masters on the day he wore that dreadful shirt, and that all the other Haases I'd known in sport had nicknames like "Mule," "Bruno," and "Moose." Then his charge ended on the back nine.

Corey Pavin had a hot flash, but an eagle on the fifteenth was followed by a water shot on the sixteenth. Tom Watson fired and fell back, fired and fell short. Tom Kite had his chance down to a ten-foot putt on the eighteenth green and missed again.

All the foreign brigade but Greg Norman went peacefully—

Bernhard Langer, Nick Price, and Tommy Nakajima—until finally it was Norman, the Australian, who threw the U.S. Open into a playoff at Winged Foot two years ago. The putt was twelve feet long on the eighteenth green, and the ball drifted left. There would be no Norman conquest. The green jacket could be returned to familiar shoulders, where it would feel at home and had that old familiar look.

Eleven years have passed, and that's a long time between championships. For an economic measure, check this: Nicklaus won more for this one ($144,000) than for winning all the other five. He was thirty-five, now he's forty-six. His plane had propellors, now it's a jet.

They'll never believe you when you tell them Jack Nicklaus won the Masters again. He's supposed to be a golf-course designer and land developer who plays in his spare time, only he doesn't know that. "I hope there's some more golf left in the old body," he said as a benediction.

And for all those bloody intruders who would wade ashore and take command of our treasures of golf, there's a message here from old General Golden Bear: "In a pig's eye."

THE MIDDLE NAME IS HOGAN

APRIL 13, 1987

Let's see what we have had here this harrowing week:

• Two seniors made the cut, Tommy Aaron and Bill Casper. A third named Palmer shot himself out of it on a course his game forgot.

• If Nick Price had shot another sixty-three on Sunday this year, he would have won by five strokes—and been given a saliva test.

• The first left-hander since the Japanese Hagawa made the field. Ernie Gonzales began double-bogey, double-bogey Friday, and sayonara.

• Two sons caddied for their fathers, Ozaki and Nicklaus.

• Scott Verplank hit his second shot into the cup for an eagle, he wiped out taking ten shots on the fifteenth hole, which was a record until Jumbo Ozaki came along a little later and took eleven.

• Hal Sutton three-putted from five feet.

• Curtis Strange eagled #5, the toughest par-four on the front nine, but this year he blew on Saturday instead of Sunday.

• A guy with a beer cap and a beer bag and a beer belly had his chance to win the Masters until the last hole. For the last three rounds, Roger Maltbie, who comes and goes, was close. So was his last putt on the seventy-second hole.

• Greg Norman wonders where it'll come from next. Last year it was Nicklaus with a sixty-five on Sunday, this year it was. . . .

A player with the middle name of Hogan won the Masters. (The name came from his grandmother, not Ben.)

A Georgian won the Masters. Not just a Georgian, a Georgian whose hometown address is Augusta, who grew up just down the road from Augusta National Golf Club.

They were wearing out the old tried-and-true "local boy makes good" angle in the press building last night. It has never played here before. Only two other natives of the state have won the Masters, Claude Harmon, a club pro who grew up in Savannah—and was here this week—in 1948, and Tommy Aaron, one of the seniors who made the cut, from Gainesville, in 1973. No player from Augusta ever came close before, except Ed Dudley, the club pro, who finished third two times. I'm not sure he counts. He came from Philadelphia.

Larry Hogan Mize won it the hard way, like making your four at the craps table. The first blow he struck landed in the ninth fairway. The seventy-first landed in the heart of the cup on the eighteenth green, the end of a four-foot putt for birdie.

Then he had to stand around and wait for Severiano Ballesteros, Greg Norman, Ben Crenshaw, who'd led most of the way, until he missed another green and two-putted on the seventeenth, flunked again.

So they set out down the tenth fairway, native son defending home and honor against these foreign intruders, the whooping and the hollering of hometown supporters ringing in his eardrums.

"C'mon, Larry! Attaboy, Larry! Go get 'em, Larry!" they cried.

Larry Hogan Mize has not been known as one of the best of finishers. He let the TPC championship get away from him last year, the Kemper Open twice, the second time in a six-hole playoff with the same G. Norman. He's a nice, clean-cut, mild-mannered youth of twenty-eight who speaks softly and smiles gently.

"Never got a chance to get a word in at home," an exuberant sister said.

Out went Ballesteros on the tenth, a short putt astray. Mize put his approach to the right of the eleventh green, the way the real Hogan used to play it. Norman's second shot was on, but a long way from the pin. Mize took aim with his sand wedge from about forty yards out, and the ball hopped, then rolled and rolled and struck the stick, which was a good thing considering the speed.

Birdie! The nonexuberant Mize became suddenly exuberant, hopped and danced and skipped to the hole, removed the ball while bedlam broke out around him and Rae's Creek flowed behind him. Poor Norman had thirty feet left and a putter in hand, and when he missed, they cheered. You had to forgive them.

This was for the kid from down Washington Road in Evans, the kid from Augusta Prep. The Mize boy who used to drive by Augusta National on the way into town. These are dreams that come true.

That's the way he put it. "Dream of a lifetime," he said. If he didn't shed a tear at the jacketing ceremony, he should have. Nicklaus held the coat for him, Jack Nicklaus himself, one he used to come to watch in the Masters.

"He finally brought it home," John, the gray-haired lower locker-room attendant, said. His eyes were misty.

"You-all kept me pumped up," Mize told the people. "You-all sounded like you were behind me."

That was a dialect they could recognize, and they knew what "you-all" means. He lives in Columbus now, but he belongs to Augusta, and if there was ever any doubt about it before, put it away.

You know, a funny thought just passed through my mind. Nobody from Georgia Tech ever won the Masters before. That includes the man in whose name the Masters was created. Bobby Jones. Think upon that.

NICKLAUS AND WATSON, HEAD TO HEAD

JULY 10, 1977

TURNBERRY, Scotland—What was intended to have been the 106th British Open turned into the Tom Watson–Jack Nicklaus match play series.

What have we here? said the Scots, as they turned toward their homes in Ayr and Girvan and Kilmarnock. This little game of the shepherd they sent to America comes back to them almost recognizable. They had scuffled and scrambled around the dunes and the humps and the hollows of Turnberry Friday and Saturday, and sat down to wonder if this was what Tom Morris, Willie Park, his brother Mungo, and the Auchterlonies had played.

What they had seen was the last day of Augusta 1975, with a cast of two. They're reasonably certain the Loch Ness monster turned up as twins. What had been a nice little seaside course that aspired to greater things had been desecrated. It's called Ailsa, one of three at Turnberry, and it had been given a new finishing touch, dressed out in new finery, and sent out on the runway like a new girl in the burlee. After four days, it was put to shame.

It wasn't all Watson and Nicklaus, as elegantly as they executed. Ailsa was double-crossed by the weather. She was built with wind in mind. All these seaside courses in the British Isles are. This week there wasn't enough wind to move a toy boat in a tub. The weather Friday was straight out of the book of the Atlanta Classic, complete with the traditional thunderstorm, and Saturday would have done Augusta proud in April. There wasn't a cloud in the sky nor a puff or a blow.

It was in these ideal conditions that the pairing that had brought Watson and Nicklaus together for matching sixty-fives on Friday was resumed. It had come off Friday like a movie staging, first Nicklaus and then Watson stealing a stroke and taking the lead until they arrived at the clubhouse in a dead heat at 203 strokes for fifty-four holes. The final-round pairing was automatic.

So at 1:30 P.M Saturday, they went at it again. When they were done, it had to be reserved for posterity among match events of all time: Dempsey and Tunney, Swaps and Nashua, Ahab and Moby Dick, Hillary and Everest, The Old Man and The Sea.

Jack Nicklaus has emerged in the role of "old-timer;" Tom Watson, the new kid on the block. When Nicklaus sank a five-foot putt for birdie and Watson missed the green on the second hole, the Old-Timer was suddenly up by two. When he rolled in a thirty-foot putt on #4, a par-three overlooking the island of rock called Ailsa Craig, he had them all saying, "Aye, Loddie, experience always tells."

See, not only has Nicklaus won more major tournaments than any golfing man who ever lived, he also has more seconds and thirds on his wall. On points, he is the British Open champion of all time with three seconds, two thirds, two fourths, a fifth, and a sixth. He hadn't won since 1970 at St. Andrews. Rightfully, it was his turn.

After four holes, it would seem that God and the Queen agreed. It was historically prescribed that Watson now would bend. The metal would give. This was Nicklaus he was trying to match in, not some kid with shaggy hair, thin enough to clean chimneys and a degree from Wake Forest.

Well, Watson kept chipping away. He seemed to be saying to himself, "Tom Watson doesn't choke. Tom Watson doesn't choke. Tom Watson doesn't choke," and sportswriters of the United States should turn in a paper with it written fifty times for Monday's lesson.

Watson birdied the fifth hole. Nicklaus missed the green and settled for par, which is five. Nicklaus drove to the rough on the seventh, and it cost him a stroke. Watson birdied again. Nicklaus parred. Now the margin was one.

Nicklaus left himself a forty-foot putt on the eighth, 427 yards, par four, called Goat Fell. Watson put his approach close for a birdie. Nicklaus parred. It was a whole new day again.

The Scots were surging and clawing around the course now, ignoring ropes and the stilted commands of the Royal and Ancient committeemen. Finally, in the middle of the ninth fairway, Nicklaus and Watson agreed to ask that the gallery ropes be restored and the stampeding spectators be herded behind them.

Somehow or another, I never thought of Scots behaving in such a raucous Bronxian manner. I've seen better manners on subways at rush hour.

Watson suffered the indignity of another bogey here, but the second of only two the whole match. Nicklaus went one up again with his par.

Next, they came to the tenth and eleventh holes, a dramatic meeting of earth and sea. Hardly more exciting than the tee at #9, which sits on a crag close by the Turnberry lighthouse. Neither drew any blood here, but on the twelfth, Nicklaus rolled in another putt for a birdie, and the margin was two. Watson got back into it when he put his approach about twelve feet from the hole and sank it to Nicklaus's par on the thirteenth.

Now, the key shot of the round. The fifteenth hole is 209 yards long, par three, called Ca Canny. Nicklaus's drive was on target and left him about a twenty-five-foot putt. Watson pulled his to a shelf above the green, sixty feet from the hole. Out came his "Texas Wedge," and with the blade, he rolled in the putt that put the dagger to Old-Timer. Instead of looking the birdie-prone fifteenth and seventeenth holes in the eye with comfort, Nicklaus was again in chains. It had to be reminiscent of 1972 at Muirfield, when Lee Trevino chipped in and brought the curse down upon Nicklaus's grand-slam gesture.

Once again, the seventeenth hole leaped up and bit Nicklaus, as it had Friday. On both days, he missed wee putts of three or four feet, and Watson's birdie put him in the lead again, and to stay. Nicklaus drew out his big gun on the eighteenth—he'd been driving so erratically he'd relied too much on his one-iron—almost drove it into the gorse, but reaching the green, discovered Watson there two feet from the pin. It was over. The Open may have seen better, but there is evidence that this could surely be entered as a candidate for Most Superb. Watson had birdied four of the last six holes, seven of the last fourteen, and he had taken the finest player in the world and decisioned eye to eye, cheek to cheek.

In the end, it was the American Open abroad. One had to reach to the bottom of the Top Ten to find one not of us. Tommy Horton of England finished tied for ninth with several at 284. Just eight years ago, that would have won it by eight strokes. I suppose that's progress.

A NORMAN CONQUEST AT TURNBERRY

JULY 16, 1986

TURNBERRY, Scotland—The impertinent wind whipped sassily across the narrow road between Patna and Kirkmichael and had the tall grass in the fields taking bows. The crooked little road led to the village of Maybole, then down to the Firth of Clyde, which popped into breathtaking view as the rented Sierra crested a ridge.

There in the distance, like a huge knob deposited when the earth belched a few million years ago, arose Ailsa Craig. Its notoriety is guaranteed in sport as long as golf is played, for Ailsa appears to stand guardian of the Turnberry course, where The 115th (British) Open—even royalty is not allowed to address The Open on a first-name basis—was in session at that very moment.

Through the morning, radio's prophets of doom had warned that the day at Turnberry would be fraught with hazards. "The northwest will be showery in the morning with winds of force 6, sometimes gusting up to force 8," said a broadcast gentleman with a burr developed by overexposure to haggis.

Horror stories were already being told in the press tent. Players coming in from morning rounds had that wild-eyed look of witnesses to a massacre. Raymond Floyd, our national champion, had played both sides in thirty-nine strokes, including an eight on a par four. His mood was best described as truculent.

"Nothing I have done anywhere, any time would help me here," he said, when asked if his triumphant experience over seaside Shinnecock Hills might be a reminder to his game.

Greg Norman had made the dangerous pronouncement that

"the tougher the course the better, and I would like to see the wind blow." Now the Australian was in at seventy-four and crying, "Uncle!"

"I don't want it any tougher than this," he said. "You're talking about some of the greatest players in the world being humiliated out there."

A clue to the kind of British Open #115 had been was that Tom Watson and Jack Nicklaus had both finished their Sunday rounds before Ian Woosnam, Gordon Brand, and Jose-Maria Canizares teed off.

Ian Woosnam, Gordon Brand and Jose-Maria Canizares, I said—defending champions of the Ivory Coast, the Zambian Open, and a Spaniard who last won in Kenya.

The last time Watson and Nicklaus were at Turnberry, they might as well have booked the Ailsa course for themselves and sent the rest of the field home. They made history the Scots will never forget. They helped destroy it this time— Watson, especially, but we'll get to him later. The witness who took the stand to testify for the aggrieved and deflated Yanks against this scenic ground.

This time the championship was a Norman conquest. Some curmudgeon said Sam Parks could have won this one. The truth is, over four days of shipwrecking weather, Gregory John Norman held up through gale and wind, thick and thin, sloshed through the last five holes Saturday like G.I. Joe on the front, played the course and the elements even par, and never complained. His disposition never varied, from sunny, matching the sun-bleached tone of his hair, to pleasant.

He's the guy who arrived last week saying, "The tougher the course, the better I like it." His scores, 74-63-74-69, prove he wasn't playing the Bijou. Depend on the Aussie for candor, for spinning no webs.

Norman broke into golf caddying for his mum, then read two books Nicklaus wrote, *Golf My Way* and *55 Ways To Play Golf*. He could now write his own title, *From 27-Handicapper to Scratch In Two Years*, which has been the true story of his golf life. He was sixteen before he touched a club, and he took off like a rocket.

This was the major that didn't get away. Three had—the U.S. Open of 1984, the Masters last April, and the U.S. Open again just a month ago.

"I finally crashed the barrier," he said. He finally beat the "choker" rap as well. He had heard they were beginning to whisper behind his back.

The United States would like to claim that Norman saved the day for the Red, White, and Blue. He has settled there, bought a place and established residence at Orlando, and plans to live there. But the truth is, he no more saved the face for the U.S. Open than Martina Navratilova at Wimbledon or Ivan Lendl at the French Open, or any more than Gordon Brand, who went off at 125-1, saved face for his backers. He still finished second, they still lost a pound.

The victory is Australia's, for the roots of his game are there and the Australians were celebrating, and no Florida cracker ever had an accent like his.

He didn't slip in the back door, either, as did Sandy Lyle a year ago at Sandwich. He went out the leader Sunday by three strokes and finished leading by five. It is true, there was no one in the chase to put fear in his heart. Severiano Ballesteros moved up with a sixty-four, Bernhard Langer with a sixty-eight, but the sun was out, the wind took a holiday, and there was nothing in Brand, Woosnam, Faldo, Koch, or Tommy Nakajima to cause the tremors, not like hearing the footsteps of Nicklaus or Watson behind you.

Gary Koch was low American at eight over par. From 1970 to 1983, Americans owned this open, until the rise of Ballesteros. Raymond Floyd, the U.S. Open champion, made no run at it after the second day. Saturday he had announced his own retreat: "I am out of the championship." So much for the Transatlantic challenge.

THE "ARMY" MUSTERS ONE MORE TIME

APRIL 14, 1985

It seemed a cruel sentence that at such an early hour Arnold Palmer should be called upon to do something he had never done before in the Masters. He would tee off before the grass was free of the morning dew and play the second round by himself. Of such scheduling was the "rabbit" born, the now-extinct player who lived by aspiration and Monday qualification.

Of course he had done something the day before he had never done before in the Masters as well. He had played a round in eighty-three strokes, and this was his penalty.

The chips fall where they may in golf. Score determines starting time, and since there was an uneven number of players in the field, the lowest scorer was condemned to play alone, accompanied by what is known in golf as a "noncompeting marker." This is a club member who plays along to attest the score, and in this case it was Charlie Coe, a member of Augusta National and former U.S. amateur champion.

By the turn, Coe was gone. He limped off, complaining of an ailing knee. Dan Yates, of the Atlanta family Yates, replaced him, but as a marker only, not as a player.

Following a player making an early-morning start with a marker, one would naturally expect much privacy and solitude, a stroll through the forest. It was at the twelfth hole that I came upon Palmer and his scorer. There has been no hole more significant in Palmer's relationship with the Masters than the twelfth, the Golden Bell that angles 155 yards across Rae's Creek to a horizontal green guarded by a bunker. It was on the twelfth that a favorable ruling, belatedly made as he played the fourteenth hole, provided the margin by which he won his first of four green jackets.

Now Palmer's tee shot found creek water. His second attempt hung on the fringe of the green, but he stubbornly stroked the putt into the cup and saved bogey, at which point a startling roar arose that caused the pines to quiver.

There would be no solitude, there would be no privacy. As Palmer made the turn around Amen Corner, astonishingly, about a thousand followers made the turn with him. His "army" had not deserted him in his most poignant moment.

They were there, trailing him, urging him, cheering him, appealing to him to call upon the last vestige of tigerish spirit within him and rise once more. The old tiger was trying to give it back. You could see him, almost hear him answer back, as best a fifty-five-year-old player can with a swing that never was a classic.

"Arnie's Army" would have shrunk to a platoon, you would have suspected, yet here they were again out whooping and tramping after him as if it were 1960 again. "Go, Arnie, Go" on their breath again, the monoplane overhead towing its banner again. The clock turned back again for two delicious hours.

Ring out the new, ring in the old. Bring back the good old time of twenty-five years ago. Damn the kids, the Hallbergs, the Stewarts, the Stranges. Give them the old established firm of Palmer & Co.

It had the air of a reunion, the old gang getting together one more time in honor of their man. When he approached each new green he was greeted by a fresh gallery, and it followed all the way to the eighteenth, where the number was inestimable. The walking group seemed to have doubled. The number of newsmen had jumped from a dozen or so to twice that. It reminded me of that year Ben Hogan made his one last flourish in the Masters, when he played a round of sixty-six in 1967, greeted as he walked onto each green on the last nine holes by a standing ovation. It was moving, as was this.

It all had come about so surprisingly that it seemed to have been organized. It was a spontaneous outflowing of affection by those with a sense of the historical for a man whose style Augusta galleries have come to admire, and who in turn long ago learned how to respond, and who had meant so much to this tournament.

He was doing his best to give them a reward for their loyalty. He came around in even par, but there was no chance he would make the cut. He was on the board in Las Vegas as a 10,000-to-1 shot. The next best sentimental moment his "army" could count on will be that time when he succeeds Gene Sarazen or Sam Snead as one of the honorary starters.

He talks, though, as a man for whom that day is not yet imminent. He doesn't expect to be young forever, but "I haven't given up on winning yet, Seniors or anywhere." The $1,791 he has earned on the big tour this year came from making the cut in the Tournament Players Championship.

"They continue to make me want to play," he said of his loyal followers, "but if I shoot many more eighty-threes, I'm going to have to reconsider that."

This had been a phenomenon in sports. It was something for the museum of your mind, the old crowd coming out to see Astaire dance again, the original Sugar Ray shadow-box one more time, Aaron swing for one more fence. Who was it—John Updike?— who wrote of Ted Williams, who had no time for applause, "Gods don't answer mail."

Here's one who does. The reply is swift, the reward immediate and satisfying to those who have become members of America's most recognizable gallery in sports. Here is one idol who has realized the full value of being idolized, and has repaid in kind.

EXIT OF THE LAST GREAT AUTOCRAT

APRIL 8, 1976

It was inevitable that some day we would have to accept that there would no longer be a #77 with Red Grange inside it. Now fat tackles wear it.

That the "Four Horsemen" would eventually become three, then two, then one. That there would be a center field in Yankee Stadium without DiMaggio in it. And that Judge Landis would leave baseball a vacant chair.

Nobody really expects Sam Snead to play forever, or A.J. Foyt to race until infinity. Or that Gibraltar will even make it to Doomsday. Even Kelso had to hang it up.

However, the odds were in favor of Clifford Roberts. His wasn't the kind of name you'd find on banners spread across stadium facings. No crowd ever raised a chant in his name, "We want Roberts, we want Roberts!" His face never made bubble-gum cards. People never lined up waiting for his autograph—except at the bottom of a check—but somehow or other, our world of the beat and the deadline, and the men of high places, fast decision and the thousands who cheer hadn't made proper preparations for the Masters without him.

No more of those news bulletins of propriety and careful rhetoric signed at the bottom, "Clifford Roberts, chairman, Augusta National Golf Club." Nor those Wednesday-morning press conferences before the Masters, during which he sat owlishly stern before the flowers of the American press, whose attitude was sometimes as civil as a judge with gout.

This Wednesday he held his last. The man who created America's fifty-first state used his last one to pronounce himself retired. His years approach eighty-two, and they have worn on him. Monarchs, emperors, czars usually live it out to the end, but Clifford Roberts had been looking for a stopping place.

Don't think for one minute that Augusta National Golf Club wasn't—isn't—one of the last of the autocracies. The major reason it survived, grew into the national institution it is through the image of the Masters is that it was an autocracy. If you get to heaven and find it's run by committee, ask for a transfer.

The power was not self-endowed. In his book *The Story of Augusta National Golf Club*, so fresh off Doubleday's presses even the stores don't have copies yet, Roberts tells of the meeting in January 1933 when Grantland Rice, the sportswriter who was a charter member, stood and made the motion that operation of the club be left entirely in the hands of Bobby Jones and Roberts, and that all meetings be dispensed with.

All members present rose and gave the motion a "rousing aye," he reports, and thus it has been all these forty-three years. The only commandments this place has ever known have been the two who founded it, and, since Jones's death in 1971, Roberts alone.

It's not as if Roberts is turning in his key to the washroom, or catching the next boat to St. Helena. His hand, while not as firm as it once was, will still be close to the helm. It was the discussion of this unwavering status of his until cutoff date that colored the meeting with a tint of comic gravity.

The man who'll succeed him as chairman of the Masters, Bill Lane of Houston, Texas, a fellow of modest physique and a ten handicap, sat at Roberts's right during the press conference in the main hall of the press building. A head table had been set up on the platform in front of the scoreboard, a little touch of Augusta National transferred to the urgency and the tin-roof clatter of the newsroom down to the spread of a white tablecloth.

"I'm not going to call on him to talk today," Roberts said of Lane, "because I am chairman of this tournament until its conclusion, and I don't want any interference."

It's the kind of moment in which you're not certain if you should laugh or clear your throat. Roberts's humor is sometimes drier than an eleven-to-one martini. He meant it, but you also were supposed to laugh.

William H. Lane will be taken care of in other places and other times. He came from Maryville, Tennessee, where everybody works for Alcoa, as did his father; went first to Georgia Tech, then to Tennessee after interruption by World War II; and today operates a large food-processing conglomerate in Texas. It appears that he has charm, poise, an affable manner, and a lot of other savoir faire a fellow acquires after he leaves Maryville, Tennessee.

It was the conclusion of a long period of speculation, and of search during which no applications were solicited, and during which nearly every kind of name from a football coach to a movie star was introduced.

"At long last I've been fortunate enough to find a successor," Roberts said. "It's no secret that I've been looking for one for a long time. He has arranged his affairs to be able to take on this duty.

"He is the right age, fifty-three. We can expect him to be able to last another twenty-five years."

And so the transfer of command was as simple as that. Word of it had already leaked out around the grounds. With a committee action, it would have broken in several newspapers and over radio stations days ago. In typical style, when asked whose decision it was, the Last Great Autocrat answered, "Largely mine."

THE U.S. OPEN CLOSES ON PALMER

JUNE 14, 1984

MAMARONECK, New York—Arnold Palmer won't be playing the United States Open. Roy Vucinich will. Jerry Pate won't be playing the U.S. Open. Rocco Mediate will. Neither Sam or J.C. Snead will be playing the U.S. Open. Rafael Alarcon will. Bill Casper, Gene Littler, Jim Simons, Orville Moody, and one of the USGA's all-time favorite rednecks, Dave Hill, won't be playing the Open, but Roy Biancalana, Jack Skilling, Robert C. Friend, and Chien-Soon Lu will.

This is the golf tournament of the people, by the people, and for the people. This is the tournament you might say the Constitution guarantees. I forget which amendment, but you'll find it in there somewhere.

This is the tournament that comes with democracy. Every man who can swing a two-iron has his chance. He doesn't have to belong to a club. This is a tournament even for the player from Unattached.

Sometimes it seems half the field is made up of "unknowns," as the headline writer sees them. How many times have you picked up the sports section and seen the banner line, "Unknown Leads Open."

"Unknown" has led the Open more times than Jack Nicklaus. Once in a while, he'll sneak up on the field and win it. He'll use the name of Jack Fleck or Orville Moody, then fade back into the scenery, rarely ever to be heard from again.

"Unknown" won it at Rochester in 1968, a lively Texan with a Mexican name and the need of a clothing coordinator. Lee Trevino didn't fade away into the scenery. He became part of it, and still is. Thursday afternoon at 12:28, you can catch him teeing off at Winged Foot Golf Club in the company of Severiano Ballesteros of Spain and Hal Sutton of Louisiana.

You don't have to be royal or ancient, wealthy or handsome to play the Open. You don't have to know the right people or have the right stuff. You don't have to have a college degree, or name your politics.

You can't buy your way into it. No way you can politick an invitation; for that matter, there are no invitations. You either play your way into it, or you're out of it. You can't get there with some Oriental order of merit, or Occidental either, or by winning Somebody's Classic on the PGA Tour.

Even winning the U.S. Open brings with it no permanent invitation. The warmhearted USGA welcomes you as long as you can play your way in. This is for the national championship, and there are no passes.

That's the reason Arnold Palmer won't be here. "For all he has done for golf," as it came across on morning television, he wasn't awarded a place in the field, which might have cut out Roy Vucinich, Rafael Alarcon, Robert C. Friend, and friends. When they told Ben Hogan, who won it four times, that he had to start qualifying again, "The Hawk's" jaw tightened, he turned and walked the other way, and he hasn't looked back.

Palmer never took it personally. There has been nothing stuffy in his behavior. He never stopped trying to qualify. It was only this year, after thirty-one years, that he couldn't make the field, and he took it like a trouper. After all, look what Red Grange did for football, and Jack Kramer did for tennis. They don't invite them back to play in the big championship.

"If you don't play well enough, you shouldn't be in the Open," Palmer said. "I didn't play well enough and I shouldn't be there."

Give the old boy a standing ovation. If the Swede Nelson Award for sportsmanship is out of circulation, bring it back and plant it on his brow. Arnie won't be here in the flesh, but he'll be here in spirit, the old commercial spirit, he and his tractor. Give the old machine a whirl and see how she runs.

Last year, Palmer finished in a tie for sixtieth place at Oakmont, a course he knows so well. The year before, he never made the cut at Pebble Beach. He hasn't been closer since the year at Medinah, when he tied Tom Watson in ninth place. But he loves the stage. They come to see him play, exult with him, and die with him.

This really wasn't the place for him, anyway. When the Open made its last run at Winged Foot, he was twelve over par. Nobody came closer than seven strokes of par. Hale Irwin had to score no better than three over par the last day to win it when it seemed Tom Watson had only to survive the last eighteen to win.

Winged Foot surrenders pars grudgingly. It's a grouchy old crock of a course laid out to demand your best and penalize you for anything less. There are going to be a lot of Bradys and Kirbys and Puskariches and Tuckers and Roy Vuciniches who will be wondering what they're doing here before it's done. They may want to put in a call to Latrobe, Pennsylvania, and say, "Arnie, come back. They may not need you, but we do."

THE GREAT INTIMIDATOR

MARCH 1978

Hardly any mortal man intimidates me more than a caddie at one of the classic golf courses of the world. Muirfield, Cypress Point, Seminole, Augusta National—I mean, one of those dramatic pieces of acreage that seems to have been rendered to golf by celestial appointment.

Whose members sneer at any other form of physical exertion as common. Whose single-minded purpose is *gawf*, no swimming pool with squealing kids or tennis courts, and if you showed up with a female partner, the course would suddenly be declared unplayable.

Once at Muirfield, I dumped a tee shot into a pothole bunker adjacent to the green. There was barely room enough for me and the ball in the burrow, much less room for a swing. The caddie was an old Scot named Alex Morrison, who handed me the proper weapon and gently suggested that I bump the ball out the way I'd come in and make a fresh approach.

Stubbornly, I struck away, aiming at the flag. The ball did indeed reach the lip of the bunker, there quivered, and fell back at my feet. The worst thing that could possibly happen, happened. Old Alex said nothing. His silence almost smothered me. Meekly, I bumped the ball out the backside, rolled it onto the green, and got down in double bogey. It may have been two holes before old Alex even belittled himself to speak to me again.

I want you to understand, first and foremost, that Leon McClatty doesn't deal with his clients with the offended air of an adviser ignored. He's patient, willing, always at hand with counsel when consulted, will read greens as palmists read hands, but Leon has a face that can't be controlled. If a picture is worth a thousand words, Leon's face is worth 10,000. I've read novels, by classic literarians, that didn't have the expression of Leon's face.

Leon is a caddie at Augusta National Golf Club, where he caddies for the Masters, and other exceptional players. His regular client for the Masters is Tom Watson, a person who needs no further elaboration. Leon caddied so well and Tom played so brilliantly last year that together they won the Masters.

Leon has borne the bag, held the pin, stood riveted at the side of his player before the piercing eyes of thousands. He has known the glory of sharing victory on the eighteenth green, and of bearing the winning bag back to the bagroom.

Not just that, but Leon plays to a five handicap himself, and taught Jim Dent how to play the game when big Jim was growing up in his neighborhood in Augusta.

Alex Morrison may know Muirfield, but Leon McClatty knows Augusta National. He pulls on his white uniform designated for any day of the week just as it is for the Masters, and goes out to his "office" nearly every day the club is open for play.

I've just returned from a play-out with a group of gentlemen— some my age, most younger, some who were players, some who found it a struggle. One of the worst drawbacks of playing Augusta National is this awed feeling that you're playing a shrine. When you spit, you want to blot it.

There was nothing stuffy about this group of ours. Carl Reith, our host and friendly neighborhood exemplar of the left-handed putting stroke, had organized more cagily than that. My main handicap was Leon.

It was nothing in Leon's manner. He couldn't have been more civil or sympathetic. He coaxed jauntily. He advised with sincerity, especially when he saw more than a mere bearer of clubs— "big-toter" is the lowest level of caddying—here was a golf-scientist accustomed to finesse and manipulation.

"Here is a fellow used to Tom Watson's shots," I kept trying not to remind myself, "and here is he out with a fourteen-handicapper, and every time I hit the ball I'll bet he wants to throw down the bag and walk back to the caddie room."

I hated to face him the second day. When I parred the first hole, a great peace came over him. "Seventeen more like that," he said. He grinned widely. It was thirteen more before the next one came.

Pull a shot, his face writhed with agony. Hit it fat, his face set like cement. Occasionally, after he'd counseled me on a putt and I'd made my stroke, I could hear him say softly, "Hit it, hit it!" Or, on other occasions, "That's too much." Softly and with regret, not venomous.

"I'd like to make you happier, Leon," I said once, "but I'm not Tom Watson, you've noticed."

"No," said Leon, "he's right-handed." A scoutmaster couldn't have been more tolerant.

But the face he couldn't control. It spoke of a thousand agonies. When I hooked a tee shot into the creek on #12, his face said, "Swing through the ball!" I said, "Well, Tom Weiskopf took thirteen here."

Leon's face said, "You ain't through yet." He said, "Weiskopf took twenty for two days," and handed me another ball.

What Leon does is make you dreadfully sorry you can't shoot him a little seventy-five, or even a seventy-eight. All this does is make you choke and wish that Leon could be a cart. A cart just sits there and never says a word, can't grimace, and never caddied for Tom Watson.

THE RESURRECTION OF PHIL McGLENO

MAY 19, 1983

I've been around in this game. I've seen 'em play from Marrakech to Jakarta. I've seen big ones win and little guys with a lead blow it and never make it back.

I saw Arnold Palmer play for Wake Forest, and King Hassan play for Morocco. I saw Lee Trevino rise from the bilge water of life at Baltusrol and become a name in the Hall of Fame. I even saw a left-handed golfer win a tournament once. He's back again where it happened—Bob Charles at Atlanta Country Club.

I've seen holes-in-one in the heat of it, Billy Joe Patton in the Masters, Gary Player in the U.S. Open. I've seen Jack Nicklaus win one he should have lost, and lose one he should have won. And I've seen husbands and wives sob on each other's shoulders because he'd won, and if he hadn't, they'd have been on their way to a dingy little pro shop in Steubenville.

But yesterday I met Mac O'Grady. If I had met him a few years ago, I'd have met Phil McGleno, and that's a sad story. A year ago, Mac O'Grady/Phil McGleno couldn't have gotten into the Atlanta Classic unless he bought a ticket. This year they sent a car for him—and his wife, Fumiko, an appealing lady who has a delicate hand in this story. An O'Grady married to an Adyagi of Japan, if you please. You begin to get the feel of Mac O'Grady, on tour.

This should be a book, but I have neither the time nor the space. I bring before you a thirty-two-year-old man who has worked as a dishwasher, cook, busboy, waiter, and grinder, and has picked up stiffs for a mortuary. Who has been humiliated in the best and worst of circumstances, and who has ridden a bus across the country back to California from some of them.

The first time I heard of Mac O'Grady, he was in shock from humiliation for which he shall never forgive the British Empire. He had gone over to play the European Tour, and made a decent living. He had the British Open made in a qualifying round at Glasgow last year when he became imprisoned in a pothole bunker and took fifteen strokes to break out while two British pros stood by in hysterics.

"His name really isn't O'Grady. It's his mother's name, and he took it because he thought it would be to his advantage over here," an Irish reporter said, being Irish down to his imagination.

His name is O'Grady in anger. It was his mother's name, but his now mainly because he is ashamed of the McGlenos. His mother, whom he adored, died when he was fifteen. Within two weeks, his father was remarried. "I was crushed. I couldn't believe it. The change was so devastating I had to leave home," he said. Brothers were on drugs, home life gone to pot, the neighborhood so tough each day was another fight to survive. He split.

In 1972 he began working on a record that no other golf pro will ever choose to challenge. He missed the first of sixteen straight attempts to qualify for the tour. He was in the lead, then shot 80-80 and missed by two strokes.

"I rode a Greyhound bus from Florida back to California, and I rode a bus from Texas, and I don't know how many times I was catching buses back to California after missing out. Have you ever ridden a bus across the desert?"

On the seventeenth try, last fall at Ponte Vedra, he cashed in. He started out 79-76 and had one foot on a bus back to California again, when all of a sudden he tied the course record at the TPC Club, finished fourth, but even then wasn't ready to leap head first into the fun.

He had grown up in Los Angeles. He had known more heartaches there than you ever saw in an old-time tearjerker, and a few good turns. One old pro who let him down, another who picked him up, the courses where he'd caddied and where he'd played. He passed up the first stop at Tucson so he could make his start on the American Tour in Los Angeles, at Rancho Park, the municipal course he knew so well. The old pro who had let him down showed up and O'Grady smothered him with kindness. The old pro who had picked him up was with him the day he followed a sixty-seven with a round of seventy, then on the way back to his car dropped dead in the parking lot.

There was another man named Raphael, who has a restaurant in Palm Springs. Raphael was O'Grady's port in a storm, and his life was one storm after another. "I must have spent $50,000 trying to get qualified for the tour," he said, "and a lot of it came from Raphael. The tortures of adversity have played against me for so many years."

He is a sentimental man who may burst out in a philosophical rash without notice. He keeps a diary at the end of each playing day, and some days the diary will say such a thing as, "I hope for my sake the cool collective aura of patience will guide me into successful harbors."

He has an advantage known by few, if any. He can play as well from one side as the other, once shot a sixty-five left-hander, and putts left-handed. He has, tongue in cheek, written the USGA requesting amateur status as a left-hander since he plays professionally as a right-hander. He hasn't had an answer yet.

He came into that harbor he was looking for three weeks ago. At Harbourtown he led the Heritage after two rounds, finished third for the biggest haul of his life, $20,300, and time on television. After nibbles and chips of $600 to $742, it was like catching a hot pair of dice in Vegas.

His time on television brought out the real Mac O'Grady, who said to his interviewer, Steve Melnyk, "Ask me any question on any subject and the more intellectual the question the more intelligent the answer."

This guy's gotta be in my next movie.

SHEDDING
LIGHT ON
DONALD ROSS

JULY 14, 1987

DORNOCH, Scotland—There is hardly any daybreak at Dornoch, for there is hardly any nightfall. In truth, golf could be played, by those so fanatically inclined, around the clock this time of year. But dawn in its regional form had arrived, and en route to an early tee time, Willie Skinner, the professional at Royal Dornoch, was engaged in a discussion of the man in whose name this expedition into the heartland of the Highlands was made.

Donald Ross left his distinctive brand on American golf as the most revered designer of courses of his time, if not of all ages. Dornoch, about 220 miles north of Edinburgh, was his birthplace. He grew up in a home on St. Gilbert Street, a few doors from a thirteenth-century cathedral, and sang and played in a brass band as a boy.

Enriching the broth of his background was time spent as apprentice to Old Tom Morris at St. Andrews. Thus schooled, Royal Dornoch brought him back as professional and greens-keeper, which was the custom then, until he took leave for the United States around the turn of the century at the age of twenty-five.

The conclusion jumped at by many Americans is that Royal Dornoch was the first course designed by Donald Ross. In the first place, golf courses were not designed in the old country, they were laid out across the bosom of the land, taking what pitch and roll and hillock and vale that nature gave. The most esteemed courses of the British Isles never felt the dent of any kind of machine.

So nobody designed Royal Dornoch; it just happened. As the

101

professional, Ross was more a clubmaker, an art he picked up from Old Tom Morris, and a right accomplished player. Willie Skinner seemed a trifle offended at all the glory attended upon Ross, his long-ago predecessor.

"He has no fame in this country. If you asked club members a few years ago, they wouldn't have known about him," Willie said. "If he had anything to do with the design of Royal Dornoch, it was only in the shaping of a few greens and bunkers. Golf has been played here since 1715. His real fame was made in America."

Eventually, that fame filtered back through Americans coming to Dornoch. Pinehurst became Ross's American base through association with the Tufts family, and there, like an outdoor museum, rests his masterpiece, bearing the laboratorical name of Pinehurst #2. He designed or redesigned more than 600 courses in the United States, all distinguished by their greens, elevated and contoured in a way you never forget once you've putted one, a seeming effort to re-create those left behind in the homeland.

Royal Dornoch plays along and above the Dornoch Firth, which widens into the North Sea, putting to glorious use wasteland known in these isles as links. The first six holes are a lovely stroll down to a wee valley, then comes the seventh, reached by a strenuous climb up Struie Hill along a pathway marked by rest benches installed in memory of departed members. The seventh is called the Pier hole, followed by Dunrobin, because that castle is in distant view, playing back down to the sea, and #9, Craiglaith, the first par five. The course plays 6,577 yards to a par of seventy, and no par comes cheap.

To remind you of where you are and where you have been, and command your departing respect, Royal Dornoch gives you three finishing holes to bring you to your knees. The sixteenth climbs 405 yards to a green atop a cliff, the seventeenth plays 406 yards back to the valley to a green wearing a necklace of bunkers, and the eighteenth hole, called Home, runs back up the hill, 457 yards toward the clubhouse clock, and blessed relief.

Here on this golf course, now in its third century, there is one incongruous annoyance. Bombers from a nearby air base continually split the air with their sizzling sound, doing maneuvers overhead.

Everywhere is the infernal rabbit, the greenskeeper's

nightmare. They dig holes in fairways, set up housekeeping in warrens along hillsides, and have no fear of golfers. I counted twenty-seven along the seventh fairway, happily chomping away.

"We poison them and we shoot them, but they keep multiplying," one of the course crew said.

Dornoch is a quiet village, about 2,000 in residence. Donald Ross returned a few times, but once in America, that became his home. There is no trace of his family here, though the county is named Easter Ross—as against Wester—and Rosses abound. He died in Pinehurst in 1948, and 600 monuments commemorate his name in America. The news has been a trifle late reaching his hometown.

Two Men and Some Horses

FROM BARBER COLLEGE TO KENTUCKY DERBY

FEBRUARY, 1972

The only alumnus of Molar Barber College who ever owned a horse that won the Kentucky Derby revisited the old campus town the other day. Business has been pretty good since he got his diploma, so he felt safe leaving his comb and shears in the attic.

Don't laugh. There was a time when Fred W. Hooper was never without the tools of his trade, for he never knew when his steady right hand was going to have to start feeding the rest of his body again.

I would like to make this the real tonsorial heart-warmer of the month, with pictures—Fred back on the senior line at Molar, walking up and down among the chairs, shaking hands and talking to the graduating class like a president mixing and mingling among the midshipmen at Annapolis. That never came off, I'm sorry to report. Molar Barber College used to be over a drugstore on Marietta Street, but it isn't anywhere anymore.

While a haircut academy provided Fred with a means of survival for a few years, it was also at Molar that he realized he didn't care for a permanent career of mowing men's skulls.

"When those broken-down bums walked in off the street and I had to smell their breath while I tried to trim their hair, I knew I didn't want to be a barber," he said.

The Hooper audience and the scene of his appearance were about as far removed from the unshaved, unwashed scene of the sodden inhabitants of packing boxes as pickles from perfume.

He had the membership of the Georgia Thoroughbred Breeders Association before him at Piedmont Driving Club Friday evening.

It's a quarterly sort of thing in which those Georgians who believe in the future of racing in the state gather to hear from a personality who can encourage them. None, however, has appeared before with the dramatic qualifications of Fred W. Hooper, a seventy-four-year-old of Baptist faith.

In the first place, he himself is the first Georgia-bred who came back to the home state bearing such enviable Thoroughbred stature, for Fred is a man of international impact in horse breeding and racing.

You see, he was introduced to the equine society at an early age. "When I was eight years old, my daddy used to say, 'Son, go feed the horses.'"

In those days, Fred was one of a family of eleven children scratching out a living on a farm in White County, of which Cleveland is the place people go when they "go to town." The barn was built of logs. The Hoopers were built of hardier stuff than logs, and Fred's emergence from the abject obscurity of Appalachian zero to the winner's circle at Churchill Downs reads like one of the great lies.

Back to horses for a minute. "My daddy used to tell me to hitch up the team and haul a load of apples into town. One day a neighbor asked me if I'd take something in for him, and he loaded it on under the apples and I never knew what it was. On the way, a revenue officer stopped me and wanted to know what I was hauling.

"Well, to make a long story short, if that officer had reached down one layer of apples farther, I'd have spent the next few years in the pokey, for the 'secret' load was moonshine."

Hooper's course from the soil of White County to Churchill Downs ran through the world of shaves and haircuts (he entered Molar at seventeen), prizefighting (he was heavyweight champion of Muscle Shoals, Alabama), ditch-digging, and finally construction. This was the key he used to unlock the rest of the world—construction.

Hooper arrived in Bunnell, Florida, when U.S. Route 1 was being built, got a job, saved enough money to pick up two old trucks another fellow hadn't been able to pay for, and that was the groundwork for Hooper Construction Company.

What Hooper Construction has built, I can't tell you, but his contracts ranged from drydocks to highways, and today the company is cradled in the nest of General Development Corporation, Fred Hooper, member of the board.

Not everything he touched was converted into money, but near-about. He won the Kentucky Derby in 1945 with the first thoroughbred he ever owned, Hoop Jr., bay son of Sir Galahad III, bought at Keeneland Sales for $10,500. Hoop Jr. didn't just win. With Eddie Arcaro up, he won by six lengths "with something left," it said on the chart.

Four years later, Hooper was back with the overwhelming favorite, but a mile and a quarter wasn't Olympia's kind of race. A mile was, and he led at this point but faded to sixth, then eventually became a star of stud and breeding in the Hooper stable.

It was 1961 before he was back again with a colt named for a construction foreman, Crozier, and Crozier came down the stretch on top but lost it at the wire to Carry Back, one of those thoroughbreds that thought no race was over until he won. Hooper stopped over in Atlanta on his way to see Susan's Girl meet Numbered Account in the three-year-old filly match of the year in the Acorn Stakes at Belmont. Susan's Girl is another home-bred from the farm in Ocala and just off victory in the Kentucky Oaks. Overall, in the past twenty years, thoroughbreds out of Hooper Farms have won over $10 million, twenty have been $100,000 stakes winners, and this from a man who confesses that he has really never been one to pay a lot of attention to exotic bloodlines.

"I don't know the answer," he said. "You never know where a runner is coming from. They have a saying in racing that you breed for the best and hope for the best, and I guess that explains me as well as anything."

LITTLE OLD BOYS IN COLORFUL SILKS

MARCH 4, 1987

When Fred Hooper was young and reaching for the stars, he shipped a colt named Hoop Jr. to his farm near Montgomery for training. Hoop Jr. was the first thoroughbred he owned and in time won the Kentucky Derby for him, but more than that, Hoop Jr. became the rock on which one of America's horse empires was founded.

Hooper is eighty-nine years old now, still breeding classic stock and still winning classic races. His latest star, Precisionist, was bred in his own barn, and, when he was retired this year, had earned more money than any horse ever foaled in Florida.

So it was that Fred Hooper came home to Alabama Tuesday night to a sight that he never expected to live long enough to see. Horses with little old boys in colorful silks were being raced around in circles and sums were being bet on their noses, all legal and above board, at an adult preserve called Birmingham Turf Club. Fred Hooper had come to see with his own eyes, still full of twinkle, and sat in the opulent lounge of the Turf Club, seven floors above the rocks and rills and rolling hills of somewhere in Alabama, and marveled at it.

Across the room, Bill Shoemaker looked out across the spread and tried to remember if he'd ever seen a track opening before. He has worked under contract with the Turf Club, offering himself for interviews, starring in seminars, and on this first-nighter, practicing his art aboard a three-year-old named Burt's Dream.

"I'm trying to think," he said, "and I can't remember seeing a track open before. I sure can't remember riding in one."

He won't take back to California any sweet memories of this one, the historic Inaugural Stakes, dripping with tradition, except that he and Burt's Dream were first out of the gate. At the end of their mile journey, Burt's Dream had become the first horse to finish fifth in the history of Birmingham Turf Club.

The Inaugural was a race until the field turned for home, and there it belonged to a five-year-old mare named Queen Alexandra, who outclassed the ten trailers and returned the favor of those who had sent her to the post even money. The Queen has had an uncommon career, travels well, and adjusts like a good trouper. Her owners, the Rosenthals of Ocala, Florida, have chased stakes at her level from Nebraska to Florida. She has won seven of her last eight races, fifteen of thirty-four in her ubiquitous career, and now has won $585,570, with $19,890 on opening night at Birmingham.

Afternoon around the backside was at once hectic and drowsy, hectic in the racing secretary's headquarters, drowsy around the barns.

To a hard-boiled horseman, a horse race is a horse race, first night or closing night. Cot Campbell had dropped in to visit Natania, five years old and striving to please. Wade Rini rated her smartly, saving her for the stretch. Then Natania tore out of the pack and caught everything but Queen Alexandra and her small package, bearing the name of Omar Londono.

Naturally, such a glorious occasion was attended by much speechmaking. Birmingham had done itself so proud that Atlanta should be jealous. A young lady named Judy Thompson had drawn her kind of people together, and it wasn't until the moment that this lady chairperson stepped forward for a few modest words, and the lyrics of "The Impossible Dream" blared forth over the public-address system, that those who produced this miracle near Irondale—Merritt Pizitz for one, and Todd Robins, the builder, for another—had a right to get teary-eyed.

Cars blew in from Georgia, high rollers among them. You could tell by the smoke screen laid down by their exhausts. High rollers never bother to get their valves ground. By 3 o'clock, three and a half hours before post time, cars were lined up two abreast at the grandstand gate.

There was frustration. A floral delivery man couldn't locate a lady trainer he had a gift plant for. A squat, bearded old groom in Sal Campo's barn growled, "Are you anybody with authority?"

Somebody from the racing commission had kept his veterinarian waiting an hour.

Flow at the mutuels windows was more a crawl. Bettors and clerks were new. The machines were new. The terminology was new.

"I'd like a $2 combination ticket on #5," one daring plunger told a lady clerk. By the time she was through, she had punched out $18 worth of tickets.

A bettor standing nearby said, "Now, if I bet a horse to finish third, he has to finish third, doesn't he?"

That was all right, he was assured, but it would be just as well if he finished second or even first.

It was, considering all the perils of first nights, something to remember, like a marriage, for better or worse, for richer or poorer, and at the end of the first nine races in Birmingham, the Turf Club clerks had handled $750,572 bet by 13,140 patrons concerned with improving earnings, as well as the breed.

Only 174 more days to go.

ASSAULT IN THE STRETCH

MAY 3, 1987

While the favorite was being loaded in a van on the turn for home, down on the other end of the track at Churchill Downs, Alysheba, his brown coat glistening in the late sun, finally concluded a broken-field run through the stretch to the wire three-quarters of a length in front of Bet Twice, and thus the bizarre 113th Kentucky Derby finally had a winner. For a time, it had looked as if the mile-and-a-quarter course might be littered like a battlefield.

First, there was Demons Begone, darling of the bettors at 2-to-1, odds surprisingly short in this field of seventeen. Pat Day, his rider, pulled him up in the backstretch after he had lagged along near the rear, far off his usual pace. He had developed a bleeding problem, and if you're looking for history, he is the first favorite that never finished a Kentucky Derby.

Meantime, the rest of the field sprawled on through the slowest Derby since Cannonade's 2:04 in 1974, and, once entering the stretch, began to sort out the doers from the die-ers. Chris McCarron and Alysheba had saved themselves along the rail, and now they could see daylight and ran to it like a fullback. Only trouble was, every which way they tried to run, Bet Twice was there. Like a horse setting a pick.

"He come in, and he hit me," Craig Perret, the jockey aboard Bet Twice, insisted.

Three times they seemed to bump, and at least once, at the eighth pole, it seemed that Alysheba surely would go down. McCarron would later exclaim that he didn't "because he is such a great athlete. He overcame so much. The colt went down to his knees," he said, a little carried away with his plight.

This is the same colt that bumped another named Leo Castelli, a horse not a person, winning the Bluegrass Stake last week, bringing his number down. Now here he was in another stretch imbroglio, but that's not the half of it.

The other half is that this amazing athlete, whose daddy, Alydar, three times watched Affirmed cross the wire in front of him in the Triple Crown of 1978, had every excuse to cough up the bit. Instead, he ran down Bet Twice and beat him to the wire. While all this was taking place, there was no challenge behind them. Avies Copy, out of the field, sloughed home third, Cryptoclearance, Templar Hill, another field horse, and Gulch right behind, and then it was five lengths back to a gasping Leo Castelli, the same.

The trip had taken two minutes, three and two-fifths seconds, but considering the traffic he was in and all the bodily contact, Alysheba was lucky to finish it by sundown. This was a race in which the prize should have been a Purple Heart.

Alysheba still wanted to fight some more in the winner's circle. He stalked stormily about under the blanket of roses, and Jack Van Berg, his trainer, his arms full of roses, his bald head standing out among the hats and haircuts of owners and relatives and stable hands, finally calmed the colt before he stomped somebody.

Here is a man who has won more than 5,000 races, but now he had found his choking point. "I couldn't say a word on television," Van Berg said.

The pater of the Texas family of owners, though, made up for Van Berg's shortage of verbosity. Clarence Scharbauer—Van Berg calls it "Scarbor"—is as Texas as his postmark, Midland. He talks with a cactus drawl and points with pride to his status in the world of quarter horses. "I'm vice-president of the American Quarter Horse Association."

His father-in-law, the late Fred M. Turner, won the Derby in 1959 with Willie Shoemaker aboard Tomy Lee. Dorothy Turner Scharbauer was in the same state as Van Berg, tearful and choked up. Clarence, though, said, "We were here in 1959, and that was quite a thrill, but ah tell yew, this is a helluva thrill today."

Of course, the doubting begins. What if Demons Begone hadn't come down ill and run his race? What if he had been on lasix, the prescription for bleeders? Just about every horse in the race was on something. Alysheba and Masterful Advocate were both on bleeding medication.

"He bled pretty severely," Pat Day said of Demons Begone. "I could tell going under the wire the first time he wasn't the same horse he had been in Arkansas. He gave no indication before he had any problem like this."

It's not that Alysheba hasn't had an ailment he could talk about. In California last winter, the colt came up short of breath, something to do with his epiglottis, and went into surgery. He was out the better part of three months before running fourth in an allowance race at Santa Anita in early March.

There is nothing like the mounting anticipation before a Kentucky Derby, the wailing tones of "My Old Kentucky Home," the arrival from the barns of the horses, accompanied by stable hands and trainers in suits and knotted ties, fit for posing in the winner's circle. Then there's no letdown quite as bottomless as the failure that follows.

Four hundred colts were nominated for the Derby this year. The odds against any reaching the starting gate are 20-to-1. The price of entering totals $22,000. The ecstasy of victory brought $618,000 to the Scharbauers and connections this year, but that's only money. The name on the billboard at Churchill Downs will always be there—"Alysheba 1987."

But always there will be the nagging. Could they have beaten the best? What kind of race would it have been if Demons Begone had been there at the end? If Bet Twice had been able to get his run out? If, if, if. . . .

STEVE CAUTHEN, WITH ACCENT

JULY 18, 1984

LAMBOURN, England—By the time he was sixteen years old, Steve Cauthen was already a national celebrity. Network shows chased him. Book publishers tried to muscle in on rights to his life story, whatever life a kid can pack into sixteen years. And he hadn't yet been aboard Affirmed on the way to the Triple Crown.

Check back to what most of us were doing when we were sixteen years old: trying to get the right date for the prom, learning how to drive—horsepower instead of horses—and still on dad's allowance. Cauthen was on his way to being a teenage tycoon.

He had grown up with horses. His dad shod them, his mother trained them. They lived from track to track. Usually, they could be found in the tack room on the backside. The Cauthens had some runners of their own, none very good.

Seven years have passed. Steve Cauthen is now a man of twenty-three. His voice has deepened, even developed a trace of a Kentucky/English accent. You find him in this little town, which isn't too far from Walton, Kentucky, as a refuge from metropolia.

I'd seen him ride at Newmarket a few days before, just after he'd been suspended for rough stuff. He tried to force his mount through an opening that wasn't there, and his impatience had cost him twelve days off the saddle. Not only that, but also the choice ride aboard Diamond Shoal in the Queen's Cup at Ascot. (He began serving his time July 14.)

Cauthen had come out smoking that day at Newmarket, driving a longshot named Elegant Air home first, followed by another winner aboard Desirable at 30-to-1 and two places in six races, which comprise a day's card at English tracks.

The old man on the bench in the Lambourn square cheerily gave me directions to Cauthen's cottage, then with a twinkle in his eye, said, "You'll think you're in no-man's-land when you get there."

He was right. Up the hill by the school, the lane got more narrow and soon ran out of topping onto a gravel squeeze with a pasture on one side and a white fence with a "Montana" plaque on the other. At the foot of Greenways, the name of the lane, sat a little brick cottage without a mark of identification, but for the BMW sedan in the parking space. Stillness was everywhere, the kind broken only by an occasional whinny or moo. This was solitude in the complete form, in Berkshire, twenty-eight miles south of Oxford in rolling, tumbled hills not unlike Fayette County in Kentucky.

Lambourn leans more to the jumping horse, but here is where one of England's leading trainers, Barry Hills, keeps his stock, and since Cauthen addresses Hills as "my boss," here is where Cauthen has come to station himself.

Cauthen made the run to England after a long losing streak in California. In some judgments, he was pictured as a onetime big winner who hadn't been able to cope with defeat, with the attention that followed him, and with the suspicion that he had been a flash in the pan.

"I came over here," he said, "because Mr. Sangster made me an offer, and it seemed the thing to do then. Besides, I'm keen on traveling and seeing other parts of the world." He has come to like the international life, and on most Sundays, when British tracks are closed, he can be found riding in France or Italy. It's a short drive to Heathrow Airport and a quick hop to Paris or Rome.

Robert H. Sangster, his sponsor, traces his fortune to the football (soccer) betting pools. More lately he has become known in the United States as one of the bidders who forced the price of a Northern Dancer yearling up to $10 million at the Keeneland Sales. At the same sale, Cauthen sold one of two yearlings he had an interest in for $265,000 while home during suspension.

He is a curiosity over here, simply listed on race programs as "S. Cauthen." Few Americans come to ride in England, where the courses are all grass, and in most cases one long straightaway. At Newmarket, some races are into the third furlong before the horses appear in the distance over the rise a mile away.

Cauthen, to the British punter, is known as "The American." He has gained respect as a grass rider, but still functions here in the shadow of Lester Piggott, a wee man with a face like a dried apricot. Cauthen stands fourth in the jockey ratings, behind Willie Carson, Pat Eddery, and Piggott.

"Some people think it's strange that I stay over here when there's so much money to be made in America," Cauthen said. "There's not that much to be made over there, and that's not everything in life, anyway. There's an atmosphere about racing over here. What they do here, they've been doing a long time. I like the tradition."

There was little talk of the "old" days. He doesn't look into the past. The child Cauthen is no more. The shy waif has been replaced by a world-wise entrepreneur. He could find no place to hide in America. He has here. He goes out for the week, riding from Ayr to Ascot, covering a great number of the fifty-nine racecourses in this country, then flees to Lambourn for a break.

He cut a lot of ties when he came here. "I miss my friends and my family, but when you talk of being homesick for racing back there, no, I don't get homesick. Besides, being around here is about like being around Lexington, anyway."

There's a sign of permanence about the little brick cottage, but the little man of twenty-three appears to have no priorities set. When he feels it's time to pick up stakes and go back to America to ride, he'll do it, and he has no fix on that.

"I'm playing it by ear," he said, which might have a double meaning. The sounds of Lambourn—the peace, the quiet, the whinnying and the mooing—do fall lightly on the hearing system.

Tennis, With Love

ESPECIALLY THOSE WHO PAY TAXES

JULY 6, 1986

WIMBLEDON—A gal from Texas with a Czechoslovakian drawl had just brought new distinction to Fort Worth, but the event represented no news in world tennis. Martina Navratilova had won her seventh singles championship under the mauve-and-green flag of Wimbledon, meaning nothing had changed again at the top of the women's game on this old ball.

Now, a gray-haired lady in a dress of sheer blue, which fluttered in the breeze, walked out upon Centre Court at a pace brisk for one of ninety years. She smiled broadly, displaying a brilliant set of dentures, when she was introduced.

"On this one hundredth anniversary of The Championships," a voice said, "His Royal Highness, the Duke of Kent, has invited the oldest living champion to present the trophy, Mrs. Kitty Godfree, winner of the women's singles championship in 1924 and 1926."

Unblushing, Mrs. Godfree wrestled a tray, large enough to hold a suckling pig with an apple in its mouth, into the strong hands of Fort Worth's most international resident. They embraced, exchanged courtesy kisses, and the deal was officially stamped and sealed in the presence of the beaming Duke and Duchess of Kent, official royal custodians of the game.

Since 1978, Wimbledon has been returning this same result on the feminine side, off and on. The off years belonged to Mrs. Goolagong Cawley of Australia and Mrs. Evert-Lloyd of the U.S.A., but the last five years have been Navratilova's. During those years, she has lost only two sets. Since 1983, there has been only one #1 in women's tennis.

Chris was her victim five times as Evert or Lloyd, Andrea Jaeger, wherever that child may be now, the other. This time the final embodied a conflict of some international nature, involving two players who grew up within two miles of each other in Prague and now pay taxes in Texas and Florida. Navratilova lives in Fort Worth; Hana Mandlikova's residence is at Boca West, up the road from Miami.

As far as the European press is concerned, this championship was all Czech. To Prague, so the story goes, it was Czech vs. Unknown. Since Navratilova accepted Americanism in 1975, she has been declared a nonperson in her old country. As far as Wimbledon is concerned, she is American. Ladies' singles champions have come from six countries, the official book reads, and Czechoslovakia is not among them. On Church Road, Texas rules the waves.

Mandlikova has kept the lines to the old country open. She travels on a Czech passport, drops in on the folks now and then, and, in some cases, registers out of Prague. But her economic base is capitalistic U.S.A., for that's where the gold is.

When she was eleven or twelve, Hana was a ball girl for Martina at a Prague tennis center. They have traveled the world, on varying yet similar courses, until they finally came together again at the top of the heap.

Not exactly a sort of "fancy meeting you here" kind of thing. They had met last September in the final of the U.S. Open, and young Ms. Mandlikova had prevailed a day after she dispatched Evert-Lloyd.

She had that much of her program working for her here. Thursday she put the wood to Evert-Lloyd again. Saturday, on a blue-gray overcast day, laced with rain before and after, she gave off menacing notices to Navratilova at first, with right much effrontery for a former ball servant.

Mandlikova bounded about the tired grass with that fawnlike figure of hers, broke serve in the second game, and had run up a 5-2 lead, and the gallery was moved. Still, there is something ominous about the air of Navratilova, who moved about with her businesslike stride, not like one who had come to Centre Court to be somebody's tragedy.

Navratilova made it 5-3, with the loss of only one point; then came the critical point. Hana's serve now, and there was a decidedly detectable sag in her gait. Some of the steam had gone from her strokes. It was pressure time. This was a game that must be won, otherwise Hana lost control of game and match and became the little ball girl again.

Navratilova broke her. The tigress took charge. It wasn't over, but it was over. It came to a tie-break that was a 7-1 wipeout for Navratilova, who then, between lecturing and cheering herself, snarling and squealing between shots, turned Hana into a girlchild again. She won it, 7-6, 6-3.

The grass must endure one more day of fierce warfare. Two more advertised as middle-European play for the men's title. It's another Martina-and-Hana story, two who have picked up their beds and taken leave to become floating corporations. Boris Becker, the West German, lives in Monte Carlo. Ivan Lendl, the Czech, lives in Connecticut. Bring us your tired, huddled masses, especially those who pay taxes.

100th YEAR
OF WIMBLEDON

JULY 7, 1986

WIMBLEDON—The 100th Lawn Tennis Championship of the All-England Club had just been committed to history when the winner committed his first error of the day. Boris Becker dropped the trophy at the feet of the Duchess of Kent, recovered, blushed admirably, and began the second year of his reign at a pay scale of $196,000.

The logical men's final had come out to be not so logical after all. All signs during the fortnight pointed toward an eventual collision between Becker and Ivan Lendl, #1 on grass against #1 in the world. It was over in three sets—two hours and four minutes. It wasn't a rout, but if there was ever any serious doubt about the incumbent champion defending gloriously, it was of short duration.

Tennis is a game of asterisks. It seems not to be whom you play or how you play, but where you play. Lendl, the Czech from Greenwich (Connecticut), has won more money than any player in history, is #1 on the computer that rates the professionals, and had plucked Becker's feathers four of the last five times they played.

Since Becker won Wimbledon last year, he had won only two of nineteen tournaments. Lendl has won the U.S. Open, the French Open, the Masters, the AT&T Challenge in Atlanta, and the heart of his accountant. Yet he was never the favorite here, either in Ladbrokes wagering parlors or in the hearts of the gallery. He wears his own tailor-made suit of sackcloth and ashes, thoroughly convinced he is the object of public hatred.

"Unfortunately, McEnroe is not here," he said the other day. "Next year I'm going to pay his air ticket and hotel and maybe he'll come."

He would also scorch the grass off Centre Court, for that is where the asterisk comes in. On any other surface, Lendl is supreme. On grass, he might as well wear hobbles. On grass, even a Matt Anger gives him problems.

But on grass, Boris Becker is, at the baby-faced age of eighteen, twice the champion at Wimbledon. Lendl is the best in the world. Becker is the best on grass, but not much tennis is played on grass. It is for cricket, for football, baseball, and golf, for lawns and for grazing. To contradict what I said recently, only one other major tournament in the world is played on the slippery surface, and even the Australians are experimenting with artificial grass.

Before a royal box spilling over with royal highnesses, dukes and duchesses, princes and princesses, earls and counts, generals and marshals, ministers and ambassadors, the Right Honorable Maggie Thatcher herself, and a four-star lineup of old champions, Becker set forth with what would be the policy of the day on his first serve. He aced the Czech.

Lendl first broke Becker, but Becker broke him right back and took the first set. It was about the time a baby began crying in the second set that Lendl launched a pair of double faults. The mother thoughtfully removed herself and squalling child, whereupon the umpire, a dentist named G.H. Grime, said, "Thank you," speaking for all packed into the old theater.

Becker completed Lendl's double-fault despair, broke his service, and in the fifth game of the second set, Lendl, visibly crestfallen, sent up the white flag. Even after he took a 3-0 lead in the third set, he lost his grip when Becker snarled back from love-40. Becker won five straight points, two with rushing volleys at the net, and the set was tied 5-5. The finish was academic, and the 6-4, 6-3, 7-5 verdict was rendered.

Winning this one was of some pressing importance to the West German. "Last year I was nobody," he said. "This year I proved I can be a Wimbledon champion."

Last year they looked upon this yellow-haired nobody with question. Was he merely a flash? Did he luck into a friendly draw and benefit from the unscheduled defeat of John McEnroe?

This was convincing. Only elegant champions repeat at Wimbledon. However, Becker's status will be more firmly established the day he finally meets McEnroe in the final, which will surely happen once The Brat takes leave of his new and temporary duty of diapering and pramming.

210th YEAR OF U.S.A.— ABROAD

JULY 5, 1986

WIMBLEDON—Gad, what an emotional hour. Lying there in the early morning, hearing the sounds of New York, Lee Iacocca introducing Ronald Reagan, and the moving chorus of "God Bless America" crackling over the little radio.

The Brits were acknowledging our 210th birthday with grace. It was the Fourth of July, and here I was in the lap of the Mother Country—such good losers are they—but I wasn't feeling myself. I was homesick.

I missed the good old U.S.A. I missed Atlanta. I missed Rilman Road and the solitude of my writing place in the trees.

I missed the Braves. I missed cheery Chuck Tanner. I missed my office and the accursed telephone. I even missed traffic on the freeway and Grizzard—not much, but I missed them as an entry. Ah, first news of Ted Turner's Goodwill Games appeared in *The Times*. It was negative. Eleven American boxers wouldn't be making the trip. They were military personnel and our generals had ordered them to stay out of Moscow.

The British will be distinguished by their absence. The Commonwealth Games, quite serious in the minds of the United Kingdom, take place in Edinburgh in mid-month, and Grand Prix meets pop up over here almost with every breath, bearing coveted points convertible into money.

Television indulges a considerable amount of its time in the Cornhill Test Matches with India. They move about from Old Trafford to Lords to Edgbaston, and I might say that watching cricket on television can be an emotional balm. It's like watching a fishing line, or broadcast of a funeral procession.

Mike Gatting, a fellow with an Oberkfellian chin and pirate's

125

swagger, will have produced another boundary, meaning a clout over the wall, which counts six runs. England have—note the clash of tenses, but such is the style of the British press, "Oxford are," "Cambridge have," etc.—been at bat since breakfast on Thursday. I'll keep you posted.

On one of the outer courts at Wimbledon, old, gregarious Tony Roche was having a go at Bob Lutz in the over-35s, a class that has no identity beyond these confines. Lutz spent most of his life as Stan Smith's doubles partner. Roche once was Australia's finest. Now his craggy face is lined with valleys, but good humor is still within him. He needed a fast decision, for he is Ivan Lendl's coach and his client soon would be on Centre Court jousting Zivojinovic. It was no contest. Roche won two fast sets and was gone.

It was an event of such sportsmanship that only five officials were necessary—Centre Court has twelve—excluding the "let" caller, the guy who Lutz even bantered with a bit, and questioned nary a call, causing myself to be reminded, as I am each day, to give thanks that this Wimbledon is being played with the well-received absences of John McEnroe and Jimmy Connors, and the tempests they created.

Ian Woolridge, a columnist of wide range and great humor, spoke of this in the *Daily Mail* this very morning.

"Are we missing John McEnroe? Like a toothache."

"The very proximity of that screeching, whining mini-megalomaniac wound up the whole of Wimbledon to a steel-springed tension . . . It was like sitting on an unexploded bomb."

On the other hand, hear this from Ion Tiriac, the Romanian with the handy appearance of a terrorist. "Dis game of tennis, she drop dead if McEnroe don't come back soon," he say.

A reminder, though, that he manages both Boris Becker and Slobo Zivojinovic, and without a McEnroe to engage, he is like a bullfighter without a bull. Business is not as good, even for a noncapitalist, ho, ho, ho.

BATTLE OF BRATS— PAST AND PRESENT

JULY 4, 1982

WIMBLEDON—After three and a half hours of acute concern with aces and deuces, forehands and backhands, and a duel by racquet on the sacred lawn of Centre Court Wimbledon, to the delight of a stadium choked with swivel-headed viewers, John P. McEnroe, Jr., of Douglaston, New York, the defending champion, and James S. Connors of Belleville, Illinois, champion eight years ago, found themselves exactly where they were when they started. Even.

This process of establishing the world champion of tennis, an event of such social significance that it attracts nobility and celebrity in swarms, was becoming no less a labor of sweat and grime than plumbing. The world's #1 player, as well as a computer can determine, was playing the world's #3 player. To this point, each had won a set by 6-3 and each a set by 7-6, such a score being possible through the invocation of the tiebreaker some years back.

McEnroe had won the first set, Connors the second, McEnroe the third, Connors the fourth. By no measure, official or otherwise, was McEnroe expected to be under such heat. He had been the dominating figure in men's singles these two weeks, and the chalk had said he would win.

McEnroe is "The Kid," twenty-three years old, in his prime. Connors is "The Old Man," approaching thirty and mellowing to the point that cast iron would melt in his mouth. That creates an interesting contrast between Connors and the John McEnroe that is.

McEnroe left Wimbledon with the prize last year, but in such disrepute with the parliamentarians of the All-England Club that he was even denied the honorary membership that traditionally goes with the championship. He had snarled his way through the tournament and in the end had left his reputation a total wreck.

He is an unfortunate youth who appears to be quite disappointed with this planet. He never smiles publicly. If there is any happiness inside him, his features are lying. The poor fellow could start a war just saying, "Good morning."

The majority of the 20,000 holding the precious seats had come to see him lose, and rejoiced in making known their preference. This was due not altogether to the Boy Scout that Connors has become, but what McEnroe is and to the memory of what Connors used to be. He need only take a glance across the net to see himself as he was in his early years as a pursuer of the treasure of Wimbledon.

"It was life or death with me when I first broke in," he said. "The money meant a lot to me because I had none. Now that the money is made, I play for the tennis."

The once-naughty kid from the toll-taker's family in Belleville now gets laughs. McEnroe gets scowls.

Now at the deadlocked point of the match, by which time England was past teatime and America was into lunch, this match began to take shape, to assume a monumental gilding of the hue of the match between Jack Crawford and Ellsworth Vines fifty years ago, sometimes called the greatest final ever played at Wimbledon.

It was in the forty-seventh game of the five-set marathon that Connors played his trump card. He broke McEnroe's serve and took the lead, as in each of the previous sets. He finished him off in a love game that saw McEnroe chase with futility an unreturnable serve to his backhand side.

Eight years, four hours, and fourteen minutes later, Connors had what he wanted again. "It means more, of course," he said. "I was twenty the first time. I'm almost thirty now. I don't know if anybody has ever won Wimbledon, then won again eight years later."

Bill Tilden won nine years apart, 1921 and again in 1930. Tilden's was no record Connors coveted.

On the matter of manners, both deported themselves as royalty would have it. They took their turns questioning the calls, but Robert Jenkins, the Welsh umpire, maintains an orderly house. McEnroe got through the week with only a fine of $500 for an offense defined as "verbal abuse." Leading finee of the week was the Australian Mark Edmondson, victim of Connors in the semifinal. Poor chap, they socked him to the tune of $3,800, mainly for waterfront language.

The Duke of Kent came forth once more. Presented the large trophy to Connors and a small medallion to McEnroe, who in this moment of depression heard one small call from the recesses of the gallery in his behalf. "We love you, John!" some wee voice cried out.

It had been a day spent under grim and brooding skies for a war between two men. "Kill or be killed," as Connors put it. Between one American who plays tennis like Pete Rose plays baseball, and another adrift in a strange world and with serve to match. It comes off like a one-bladed windmill.

The victory comes up somewhat shallow for Connors. He beat the best that was here. But absentees were Ivan Lendl, Bjorn Borg, and the pride of the Argentines, Guillermo Vilas, and José-Luis Clerc. These were caused by distaste for grass, by choice, and by war.

In the end, something nice did come to McEnroe at the end of a long day. The committee of All-England announced that, though one year late and deposed as champion, he had nevertheless been elected an honorary member.

Louis, Ali, Frazier, and the Warriors

A NATURAL RESOURCE GOES TO REST

APRIL 21, 1981

Louis became Barrow again Tuesday. In death they returned the name by which he began life and returned the body to the soil. The beginning and the end were of contrasts as broad as a chasm, and reflect the American legend. Joe Louis Barrow came out of a sharecropper's cabin in East Alabama and was buried in Arlington National Cemetery, a ground sacred to Americans who come here to honor their military dead. Just a few days ago, General Omar Bradley was put to rest here. Just up the hill from the old heavyweight champ's grassy plot is the Tomb of the Unknown Soldier. In death, he'd be keeping good company.

When he came into the world, the odds were about as long as they can get. He left with millions watching. The services were nationally televised by Cable News Network from the Memorial Chapel, an oddly shaped creation that looks as if it may not be finished yet.

This was the second service. The first was in Las Vegas and was akin to a carnival. The casket was placed in a boxing ring in the sporting annex of a gambling casino, performers featured Frank Sinatra and Sammy Davis, and at the end they gave the corpse a standing ovation.

The service here was left to the clergy, representing a broad spread of faiths. Catholic, Protestant, Jewish, and Muslim participants were advertised, and all performed except the Muslim, who was a no-show. The interior was lighted up by the frequent flashes of photographic bulbs, most of them belonging to freelance fans responding to the appearance of anyone of fame.

In that sense, it was like a Hollywood premiere set to the score of "Amazing Grace" and "Rock of Ages." Several hundred gathered along the street, in parking lots and across the way in front of the Fort Myers Base Exchange, straining the gallery ropes for a glimpse of anyone of notoriety.

Muhammad Ali arrived about noon, usually stoic, but wherever he went, the center of attention. He never became quite convinced that this wasn't his show. Jersey Joe Walcott entered quietly. Joe Frazier came later, and equally as noiselessly. Billy Conn came in the company of Edward Bennett Williams, lawyer, franchise owner, and butterfly of Washington society.

They would have been late, but this was one time the corpse was late for its own funeral. Services were scheduled to begin at 1 o'clock. It was 1:15 before the honor guard wheeled the casket in from McGuire's funeral parlor, where it had been on display during the morning.

A few old cornermen and fight handlers were here. You can always pick them out, bent and gnarled, looking out of place without a towel on one shoulder, a water pail in one hand, and a mouthful of cotton swabs. They were like sponges for a kind word or recognition.

Before any of them, a fellow in a jacket that said "World Champions 1958" on the bosom stood around the church door as any onlooker would. He turned out to be Lenny Moore, the old Baltimore Colt, who had driven over.

"I never met him, but I wanted to be here," he said. "He was the black man we could all look up to, before Jackie Robinson, before Campanella, before any of them."

Joe Louis didn't have to go around calling himself "The Greatest." "Brown Bomber" said all that needed to be said of him. He never had to pound himself on the chest or his ego on the back. He held the world heavyweight title longer than any other man, and that said enough for him.

He was solid American gold. It may read like solid American corn, but here was a man who loved his country and put it where his heart was. Out of the purses of two championship fights, he peeled off $100,000 for the Army and Navy Relief Fund. He had ninety-six exhibitions for fighting troops around the world during World War II, and that can't be translated into a cash figure.

The money he earned in the prime of his time was frittered

away by people he trusted. Leeches were onto him. It was never accounted for. The disgrace of it all is that he wound up living on the house in Las Vegas. "Greeter," they called him at Caesar's Palace. It had a nice ring to it.

It was there that I was able to sit on the periphery of one of Louis's richer moments in later life. They threw open the hall and put on "A Testimonial to Joe Louis" at Caesar's one night. From all up and down The Strip, they came in for a gig, the big and the loud and the small and the grasping. Of all the guests of the evening, one in particular stood out. He had come all the way from Hamburg, West Germany, to pay tribute to Joe Louis.

Americans have made much of the triumph of Louis over Schmeling in 1938, gaining much, much more of a political nature in time than was relevant. It was a blow for democracy over nazism, or so it became. Above the fact that it was the launching of Louis.

On this night in Las Vegas, Max Schmeling, now a gentleman of distinction and affluence, had come to speak his testimony to the Brown Bomber who had knocked him into humiliation. They stood on the stage and embraced and they spoke like brothers, and that was a moment to remember. Really, more so than this day they put Joe Louis to rest on a hillside at Arlington National Cemetery with a twenty-one-gun salute. Then they lowered him into the ground, and that is all that remains of the great fighting man, except a memory that shall become a national resource.

ALI GOES
TO COLLEGE

JUNE 1972

"It's tough to be the greatest in the world," Muhammad Ali, born Cassius Marcellus Clay in Louisville, Kentucky, was saying as we drifted along through one of Auburn's tree-shaded streets. "You can't get careless. You have to be on guard all the time for somebody is goan to try to knock yew down."

He lapsed into accentuated dialect at the end of the sentence, and rolled his big brown eyes, to emphasize his point.

The former heavyweight champion of the world of boxing was engaged in the process of explaining why, though there was no question about "The Greatest" in his mind, he was no longer champion of the world, or even of Ken Norton.

"A nobody," he said, not sneeringly. "Nobody ever heard of him. He couldn't fight. Just another bum of the month. I didn't take him seriously. I didn't train like I should. It showed in the way I fought. I didn't believe I could be beat.

"I believe God was punishing me for the way I live. My problem now is making myself work, and they need me."

Boxing needs him, he meant. The Big Game.

"They need me. They got nobody that's got charisma, they got no poems, they got nobody picking rounds, they got nobody can shuffle, and they ugly."

He was on a treadmill on a large college campus in a small Alabama town, and the incongruity of it all made an incuse impression. It came back and back again, especially after we had arrived at the Lambda Chi fraternity house for dinner. Here was this black man, not back in the kitchen sweating over a hot stove and dirty dishes, but the guest of honor at dinner, and young, bright-faced, white college men gathering in close to hear and touch him as apostles gathering at some philosopher's feet.

There had been a press conference in a little theater room

135

at Haley Center, then dinner at Lambda Chi, then off to Auburn Coliseum, where 5,000 to 6,000 gathered in to hear the most unlikely lecturer who ever stalked a stage in East Alabama.

("Who-all has spoke here before?" he had asked Jimmy Tisdale, director of Horizons III, a subscribed student activities group. Barry Goldwater, Rod Serling, Ted Kennedy, and a sterling lineup of letters, brains, and politics, he was told. "I'm not just a fighter," he said. "I'm brilliant. I match wits with the brains of America, and I win.")

There came a break in the swift pace, when he returned to his room at the All-American Motel ("Welcome, Muhammad Ali") to refresh his weary body and dress for dinner and lecture. A kind of sobering mood came over him in the privacy of his room.

"You're seeing a side of me not many sportswriters ever see," he said. "They see me, the fighter. You're seeing me on the college side."

"How far did you go in high school?" I asked.

"I don't know. About the tenth grade, I guess. They gave me my diploma, though, not because I passed all my work, but because I won the Olympic heavyweight championship," Ali said.

"Your name, Cassius Marcellus Clay, it is melodious. Beautiful. Classic in its own right. Why did you have to change it to become a Muslim?"

"I didn't change it. Muhammad Ali was bestowed upon me. It's an honor, like the pope makes a guy a cardinal. I am an officer and that is my title. Muhammad Ali was a warrior 1,400 years ago. He rode at the head of his troops and never lost a battle," he said.

"I don't know too much about him, but that's what they tell me."

"What now for you? What goals? What ambitions? What is important to you now?"

"Money," Ali said. "I own a $250,000 home and two Rolls-Royces and have four children to support. I want to make $2 million to go in the bank and make interest for me. Once I lived on principle. Now money is my principle."

Twilight had settled over Auburn, poetically named for "The Loveliest Village of the Plain," Goldsmith's Auburn. Cars wove their way along the streets lined on both sides with other cars already parked. Students scurried about, furtive figures in the gloaming, moving in and out among the traffic, mostly couples aimed in the direction of the Coliseum, which rises with startling abruptness above the flat land.

Cliff Hare Stadium stood dark and out of it on the left. Jimmy Tisdale had attempted to interest Ali in the slur that Howard Cosell had directed at Auburn's most cherished alumnus, Pat Sullivan, at the time of the Heisman Award. He may as well have dropped the name of Boozer Pitts. It never took. Football is a foreign matter to Ali.

"Look at 'em," he said, speaking of the thickening crowd as we drove along. "See, at your fraternity I made a hundred friends, like you say. These people, they're all coming to hear me. All these cars, they're coming to see me. In Alabama, a little ol' black boy like me, and all these people coming out to hear me."

It was not an offensive monologue. It was spoken in the manner of one marveling at a phenomenon, as much as anything else. For indeed, it was.

There was a quiet wait in the reception room of the athletic offices, heavily draped in reminders of the glories of football—a stuffed Tiger, a portrait of Pat Sullivan, an award to Coach Ralph Jordan. Peace once again seemed to settle over Ali temporarily.

"After being on top all the time," he said, in a solemn key, "I'm not getting used to being the underdog. But it's embarrassing to the guys that beat me, when people start talking about rematches they say Ken Norton, you get a $200,000 guarantee and Ali, you get $275,000. It's still me they need, not them."

The lecture was not Zola. Not Emerson. Not Thoreau. It came out blurtedly, "The Intoxications of Life," as if its proponent was not quite sure of it himself. Ali raced to its end, mercifully closed it out with one quick summation that missed the 5,000 or 6,000, then opened the floor for audience participation.

He became Cassius Marcellus Clay, or Muhammad Ali, as you will, again.

JOE FRAZIER WILL NOT FALL

MARCH 9, 1971

Joe Frazier kept his title Monday night at Madison Square Garden, but Cassius Clay won the consolation prize for finishing second. A free trip—to the hospital.

The "dumb, ugly, flat-footed man" from Philadelphia is still king of the heavyweight beasts today, much to the surprise, consternation, and physical discomfort of Clay, who not only flunked boxing during the course of a fifteen-round exercise in blood and mayhem, but also clairvoyance.

The fist, in other words, proved mightier than the mouth.

Before the first blow was struck, Clay went before a closed-circuit television audience that stretched around the world and precociously confided that he had very special plans for Frazier for the evening.

"They will be shocked at how easy I will beat Joe Frazier, who will look like an amateur boxer compared to me. They will admit that I was the real champ all the time."

"Frazier will fall in six," he said, reading from a prepared statement.

Clay had been sent into a tirade at the weigh-in ceremony when John Condon, who directs Garden boxing publicity, introduced him as "former heavyweight champion of the world."

"I'm sick and tired of all this mess," Clay raged. "All this 'former' talk has got to stop. I'm going to get all this mess straightened out tonight. That dumb, ugly, flat-footed Joe Frazier can't fight. He can't even talk."

No prizefighter ever set himself up more perfectly for the kill. Not only did Clay lose for the first time, he came to the end of the perfect career in such a humiliating manner that he had to be drayed to a hospital to be X-rayed for what by this time has probably been diagnosed as the equivalent of a broken jaw.

He went the distance. Fifteen rounds. He gave an abundance

of punishment, but he absorbed a bunch. When this self-ordained "greatest" disciple of the sweet science delivers by proxy the message that he is "just satisfied not being knocked out," the world is ready for a return to humility.

Frazier gave him the kind of beating that may get Muhammad Ali demoted to Cassius Clay and require him to turn in his turban and his camels. The Arabic name has not been made official, but resulted from his mixture of religion and boxing.

As a spectacle, it was the kind of event that would have made W.C. Fields die laughing—if he weren't already dead. It may have been the first time two men from Philadelphia drove to New York in their Cadillacs to beat the tarnation out of each other, and Fields was the man who made Philadelphia immortal with a touch of uncivic humor that has withstood the ravages of several ages.

On the other hand, it was the first time that New York—or any place—has paid $1,352,961 to see two guys from Philadelphia—or any other place—fight. It was the world's richest indoor sports event, and the complete fiscal success won't be determined until results are in from the outlying television precincts, such as Thailand, London, and Japan.

The atmosphere became so conversational during the fight that referee Arthur Mercante motioned both Frazier and Clay to cut out the lip service and get to fighting.

There was a man who earned his fee. Mercante became so involved on one occasion that he struck Frazier in the face with such force that Joe wanted to stop and count heads.

Also, both gladiators took turns at demonstrating overconfidence. In the fifth round, Frazier, mimicking Clay, dropped his hands and invited Clay to hit him. And if I read lips properly, taunted Clay with "Now who's better?"

After the seventh round, Clay leaned across the ropes and yelled, "No contest."

By the ninth round, Clay had Frazier bleeding at the nose a second time. Frazier's right cheek was puffed and his eye was peering through a slit.

Clay idolizers leaped to their feet and shrieked his adopted name. It was mass hysteria. On occasion, Clay responded. But soon he ran out of response.

At times he dawdled on the ropes and allowed Frazier to have at him, but Frazier, apparently sensing the strategy, played pattycake with him. The fight reached such a state of inactivity that the booers took offense.

Thirty seconds of the fifteenth round were gone when Clay suffered the humiliation of his life. With the whole world watching, he took a left hook to the jaw and went down. Flat on his pants, his tasseled feet flying abruptly into the air. Posterior over teakettle, I think is the expression.

If there had been any doubt—and three officials' cards later proved there wasn't—that dissolved it. Clay was hurt and happy to end it on his feet. His jaw puffed like a grapefruit. Frazier could have stuffed him and mounted him in the family den.

Frazier had not fallen in six. Clay, who had promised to crawl across the ring and concede, "You are the greatest," if he lost, barely crawled to the dressing room. It was only a stop on the trip to the hospital. That was the last seen of him, except by his private court.

He had been wounded where it hurt the most—where he talks.

THE ANGEL, THE DEVIL, AND THE CHAMP

MARCH 12, 1961

Floyd Patterson and Ingemar Johansson would fight for the heavyweight boxing championship of the world Monday at 10:30 P.M. in Miami Beach Convention Hall, and this was the man who had brought it off. His name is Bill MacDonald. He is round-faced, portly, and with a matching disposition. You know, all the world loves a fat man.

He stood on the deck of his yacht at Bal Harbour on a bright Sunday morning. The breeze was gentle. The harbor water lapped lazily at the hull of *Snoozie.*

Men of the fight game and newspapering were gathered on the fantail. MacDonald stood among them wearing his navy blue commodore's coat and cap.

He is rich and a sportsman. He made $7,000,000 manufacturing mobile homes. He said so himself. He once was the doorman at the Dempsey-Vanderbilt.

"I bought 'the door' for $750 and made $8,800 in one season," he said.

He finances golf tournaments for the PGA, owns racehorses, owns 45 percent of Tropical Park racecourse and three minor-league baseball clubs. Then a man named Dave Feld came to him and told him he thought he could get Patterson-Johansson for Miami Beach. MacDonald would have to help.

"I met Cus D'Amato at the World Series and we talked," MacDonald said. "They were talking about a $600,000 guarantee at the gate. I said $400,000. D'Amato said the fight was going where he said, because he was Patterson's manager.

"When he came down to $400,000, it was a deal. In other words, I underwrote the fight for Miami Beach. D'Amato later told me that after he talked to me, he knew the fight was going to go only one place—Miami Beach.

"I looked into it good first. I didn't want to get in a racket with hoodlums and crooks, and you know how boxing is known. I liked D'Amato. He's an odd guy, but I think he's honest. That sold me, his honesty.

"A fellow's trying to get me to buy Sonny Liston's contract now. I don't know. He's a good boy, but I just want to make sure if I buy him I don't buy a lot of guys in the back room, too."

In Convention Hall Sunday afternoon, Billy Graham was preaching. Where 14,000 fight fans would sit and shriek for blood and slaughter eighteen hours later, 14,000 people had come in out of the tropical sun to listen to this magnetic man.

You could hear the voices singing even as you parked your car. It was on old-time hymn we used to sing in the little white clapboard church on a Sunday morning in North Carolina.

In the lobby of Convention Hall, members of the fight mob, going to and from the press room, would stop and talk in hurried tones, then rush on.

"Christ-a-mighty," Mumbling Sam Sobel said, waving a burning cigar dangerously near the nose of a listener, "this so-and-so thinks he can push me around, and I . . . ."

George Beverly Shea sang "All Hail the Power of Jesus' Name" in the background.

"Damn, what a helluva mob that guy's drawed in there," said an intellectual. "You see de money dey just carried out?"

Billy Graham's powerful voice poured through the public address system now. The worshipers had opened their Bibles and were reading the text for the day's sermon. Behind and above Graham's head, a huge blue-and-white banner read: "Jesus says, 'I am the way, the truth and the life.' "

The 14,000 sat now and listened intently, and you stood and thought of the incongruousness of it all. Here, one man battled the devil man-to-man, fought, strove, beseeched souls to save themselves. More than 900 persons had marched down the aisles the night before and joined him.

On the next evening, the place would be turned over to the slaughterers, the morbid whose idea of entertainment is the sight of a left jab stinging the cheek, a hard right to the skull, or a referee in white vigorously counting out the benediction over the fallen body of some poor pug. They would pay up to $100 for seating space.

In the kitchen of the white stucco house at 2815 Pine Tree Drive, Floyd Patterson was getting a haircut. He stuck his hand out from under the barber's apron. He said he felt fine. He said this was no ritual. He said he was just getting his every-two-weeks haircut.

"I understand that some people won't get their hair cut before a match or a game because it is supposed to be weakening," the heavyweight champion of the world said. "Do you think there's anything to that?"

"It comes from the story of Samson, I guess," somebody said. "A lot of baseball pitchers don't shave before a game."

"Oh, I don't shave either," Patterson said. "There's something about the beard that toughens your skin, I think."

A photographer crept in from the living room and began snapping pictures of him from all angles with a camera shaped like a stick of bologna. Patterson paid no attention.

In the dining room just outside, Cus D'Amato shifted restively in his seat. "Too many people coming in this place," he muttered. "It ought to be quiet around here today."

This is a residential home in a quiet, middle-bracket residential section. Patterson and his party rented it for a month for $2,300, without downstairs furniture. Everything but a few chairs and a dining table was moved out.

"I'll have a steak tonight and I'll go to bed at 10 o'clock and get up at 10 o'clock tomorrow morning," Patterson was saying in the kitchen.

He said he'd sleep most of that time. "I haven't dreamed much this time. Last time I kept dreaming that Johansson's right was on the way to my chin, but I always woke up before it hit."

When someone mentioned Sonny Liston to him, Patterson said carefully, "If I beat Johansson, I think that Sonny Liston is the next man to fight."

Friday evening he had gone to Convention Hall. "Billy Graham wanted to meet me," he said. Patterson is a Catholic convert.

"We are giving up the hall Monday night only," Graham told the audience. "Every other night I will preach here. Monday night, Floyd Patterson will preach."

Patterson enjoyed telling the story. He grinned pleasantly and said good-bye. Outside, Sunday was bright and sparkling. Outside, 2815 looked just like any other house on Pine Tree Drive.

INJUSTICE IN
A WASTELAND

SEPTEMBER 27, 1976

The United States in all its Jeffersonian smugness needs something like the Ali-Norton decision to remind us that we haven't perfected justice yet.

Ken Norton has a lesser chance than most. Even a mass murderer can carry his appeal to the Supreme Court. The best Norton can do is to carry his to the New York Athletic Commission, which is very good at weighing in fighters and insisting that bearded ones shave, but has all the clout of Lassie.

I had seen Jersey Joe Walcott earlier in the course of events. I couldn't resist turning during the late going at Yankee Stadium Tuesday night and looking over my shoulder at Joe Louis, who sat directly behind me wearing a big, brown Texas Ranger's hat with upturned brim.

The Brown ex-Bomber was attentive, but emotionless. I should have known so. He has gone through more than fifty years without using his face as a message board.

The interest there was in their fight nearly thirty years ago, when Walcott floored Louis twice and discovered that he had come to the Garden alone. Louis was so certain he had lost his title that he took a walk in disgust. He had to be brought back to the ring to have his hand held aloft in victory while the world booed.

Several years later, Red Smith, the noted columnist, told me, "I'm convinced now that Louis won. We're always inclined to overreact at the time on the monumental nature of what we're seeing, and then simply because Walcott was of sympathetic circumstances, off the welfare rolls and father of a large family."

I doubt that I shall ever be so generous. I have a much clearer version of what I saw now than I'll have twenty years from now.

Muhammad Ali, as a talent, is like a fire burned down to smoldering ashes. His act at Yankee Stadium was a hodgepodge

144

of old Ali-isms. He couldn't quite get a handle on just how he planned to mesmerize Norton, and what he gave the crowd was a series of disorganized flashbacks to what he used to be.

Norton does not wilt. He gazes upon Ali's sophomorisms as if he sniffed a rank odor. George Foreman is the kind of psyche that gets to Norton. He carries it in his fists. Norton fears that awesome fellow as he would an ogre.

Norton is a college man. He went to Northeast Missouri College intending to become a teacher, and, after two and a half years, gave in to a venturesome spirit that drove him to the Marine Corps.

There he learned how to fight, both with fists and weapons. He's better than poolroom smart. He can even read and write and act, though Ali sneers at the fact that Norton has done most of the latter with his clothes off.

The air had cleared somewhat Wednesday morning. Ali and Norton no longer shouted insults at each other. Ali had even thrown a punch at Norton after the eleventh round, a little something extra after the bell had rung. It was convincing evidence of frustration.

The morning after, while Bob Biron, a distinguished gentleman who manages Norton, spoke of an appeal, and Norton spoke of a rematch, Ali spoke of retirement. "It is not far away," he had said Tuesday night.

"How Ali can pretend to be the greatest fighter in the world without giving Ken a rematch is beyond me," Biron said.

"Let him beat George Foreman and he can have a rematch with me," Ali said. "He got to beat Foreman, then I fight him. I'm not going to fight 'em both. I fight the winner and that'll be my last fight."

There must have been something strategic in Ali's fifteenth round. He fought it backing up, as if he were saying to the judges, "See, I got it won and I'm taking no chances."

It sold. The judges bought. They went his way. It decided the championship of the world. It went to the elder adversary who fought the last few rounds defensively.

There is no sports event quite as chaotic as a heavyweight title fight. It's a disorderly, humorless orgy in mayhem even on its best behavior.

The route through Harlem—the burned-out buildings, the garbage heap, the skulking dopies gathered around dark alleys—

gave you a preview of the evening. Police contributed to the riotousness of the occasion. They're on strike. Those not on duty are striking, and even those on duty added little to the security of the spectators. One demonstration after another developed, and if not boisterous enough, the off-duty fuzz recruited from the herds of wild teens roaming the stadium inside and out, like rabid coyotes.

Forty thousand were expected. Ten thousand fewer showed up, scared off by the frightening scenes outside the gates. Patrons of the "sweet science" in the $200 seats were trampled. It's the worst buy in sports.

BEFORE ALI'S LAST STAND

JUNE 1980

LAS VEGAS—In any other American town with a mayor and a main street, you can always look at the fight mob and say, "That's the fight mob."

Except in Las Vegas. The whole town looks like the fight mob, at least those that show up along The Strip, which is all a traveler ever sees. So, around Caesar's Palace, the temple of chance, the mob had gathered, and was gathering, slapping bare flesh, clucking at one another in a junkyard jargon without subjects or predicates, and prepared to attend the worship services in Sports Pavilion. There His Reverence Muhammad Ali was going on shortly. Crowds had lined up in the searing sun of a 100-degree noon for the privilege of paying $3 a body to view the ritual of a man fighting his shadow.

The bimbos had turned out—the babes in tight pants, handkerchief halters, spiked heels, fluffed floozy hair, and the willing eye. Included among those of more legitimate connections were Mrs. Odessa Clay of Louisville, Kentucky, of some partiality to the son she had named Cassius, and Mr. R. Giachetti of Cleveland, whose interest is the party of the other part, Larry Holmes, born in the cotton and peanut province of Cuthbert, Georgia, but removed to Easton, Pennsylvania, at the age of five. There, soon to be abandoned by his father and reared by a mother who had her hands full with Larry and eleven others. However he may have looked then, in his hell-raising days, he was looking like the apple of a mother's eye now, heavyweight champion of one or the other of the alphabetically dissected worlds of boxing, and about to come into four millions for a few hours of exercise in a parking lot back of Caesar's Palace Thursday evening.

When Ali appeared in the ring for his workout, he appeared slimmer and trimmer than expected. With the mustache gone, he looked like a middle-aged loan shark. His hair had been dyed a darker shade. He looked almost as young as Angelo Dundee, his loyal trainer, had, through handy arithmetical reasoning, declared him to be.

"My guy laid off five years," said Angelo, "so in boxing, he's only thirty-three." He spoke of the period Ali spent in limbo fighting his draft board over a matter of joining the Vietnam war effort.

Ali is thirty-eight, and nobody his age has ever been heavyweight champion of the world. Holmes is thirty, and much is made of this, especially and significantly by a man who long attended Ali as his ever-present physician, Dr. Ferdie Pacheco, who will not be here. Pacheco says Ali has suffered brain damage, that his speech is slurred from it, that he is going to the well one time too many with the body that has given him fair warning to leave the game to the young.

There is some economic urgency in his scheme, I'm told. That of the $55 million he has earned in the ring, none of it remains. As if that isn't enough, it looks so easy. Holmes, that is, no more than a former sparring partner once pleasured to get a place on Ali's supporting cards. You'll find it more than fascinating that among the supporting events on this one is a twelve-round prelim returning the person of Leon Spinks, whom Ali lost and won the title to and from, to an old trade.

Once a bloated 252 pounds, full of rich milk and cherry pie, Ali is now down to a dancing 220. But had he ever fought at such a weight before? Oh, yes, Angelo Dundee assured a crowd he had attracted. "Against Wepner, I think it was, he was up to 230. He has gone in at 225 several times, I'm sure."

But he was younger and able to absorb much pummeling then, albeit inflicted by clumsy, oxen clods who weren't boxers but hammer-throwers. There was a slight bulge of suet over the beltline of his trunks, but the feet were agile, and he danced dandily as he shadowboxed, decisioning his shadow easily.

Now it was time to turn up the glow of the lights and go into his act. It had the sound of a tribal chief beating on the eardrums of his people. It was the old Ali, onstage.

"Hey, this is me," he began. "This is my last day. I'm really retiring. This will be the last day you'll ever get to see me work out. I got fat after the last fight because I had to trick Holmes into fighting me. I drank a quart of milk a day and ate half of a cherry pie, then I posed for that picture with my belly hanging out. Holmes see that, and he says, 'I'll take him.' "

"I shaved off that mustache. I lost all that fat. Hey, look at me now. Ain't I pretty?"

He transferred to the press gallery, but what was advertised as a conference turned into a continuation of raving monologue. "I got him so psyched out. . . .

"Hey, prediction: This might end in one round. . . . If I had trained like this for all my other fights, they wouldn't have lasted so long. . . . This will be a total mismatch. . . . I am super, super, super. . . . I wasn't born, I was hatched."

By this time, his father had fallen asleep. The crowd had dwindled, even the press drifted away. He had been going for forty-five minutes, and walking away from the pavilion, you could still hear the drone of his voice, driving on. The sound would follow you on into the night.

AN UN-FATHER'S DAY STORY

JUNE 1978

Let me tell you first that this is a story that will not warm the cockles of your heart.

Willi Besmanoff is the same fellow who once fought the best heavyweights the world had to offer and now is the star baker at Davison's, the department store on Peachtree. Willi once was the fourth-ranked contender in the world. Once he went seven rounds with Cassius Clay before he became a born-again Muslim—Cassius, that is. And in Clay's own hometown. Willi lost to the stars, but he made them earn it. A good "trial horse," they said of him, which means he could lose with grace, I suppose.

Willi grew up in Berlin, the son of an American-born father. He was seven years old when he began to notice that his dad, a medical doctor at the University of Berlin, no longer came home. Eventually his mother explained. Since the nazis had come into power, his father, fearing for his life, had made a run for it to the United States. Bailed out is what she didn't tell him.

Life went on. His mother became successful in the contracting business. Willi asked no more questions. Scarcely did his father's name come up. He never wrote. Never sent money. He'd vanished.

Willi went to baker's school and learned the trade under the gentle hand of a family friend. It was this friend, noting Willi's handiness with his mitts, who guided him into prizefighting, and, as always happens in fairy tales, the godfather Jim Norris should turn up one night as Willi was taking out the American, Don Ellis, in Dortmund.

When Norris invited him to come to America and fight under the auspices of the International Boxing Commission—how many times did you hear Jimmy Powers spit out that phrase on the "Friday Night Fights"?—Willi was elated. He would get to see his father again!

Not only that, he could pick up his American citizenship. Since

150

his father was American, it had been open to him until he was twenty-one, provided he came to the States. He'd never become a German. Not until he was ruled ineligible in the middle of the Helsinki Olympic Games did he realize that he was "stateless."

His first act on reaching New York was to start the search for his father. Lew Burston, Norris's matchmaker, suggested he forget it.

"I thought that was strange," Willi said, "but I was insistent. I had to do it my way. Lew told me, okay, he'd help."

There was a big-time gambler around New York in those times whose name was Mike Best. Actually, he was Mike Besmanoff, Willi's uncle, with an Americanized handle. He told Willi where his father could be located, but also with a suggestion that he should forget it.

A match was made for Willi in Milwaukee, and on his way to the fight, he stopped over to visit his father, who was living in Chicago.

"He fell all over me," he said. "He was so overjoyed to see me. He had all these plans, but usually there was the necessity of my money. He'd remarried, but he had never divorced my mother, so he was a bigamist.

"I was doing rather well in those days, and had a name. My wife began to see through it all and said, 'Willi, let's get out of here. All he wants is your money.' I couldn't see it that way."

When Willi and his wife said good-bye after a two-week visit, his father handed him a bill for $1,000.

"For what?" I asked.

"You owe me $1,000 for two weeks' room and board," his father said, this man who had abandoned his family. He told the old man he was crazy and left for Milwaukee.

After the fight, Willi discovered his purse had been attached *by his own father.* In the courtroom, the trial judge had Willi tell his story three times.

"He couldn't believe it. I'll never forget that judge's name— Krueger. A German name. My father had sent a lawyer up from Chicago to hold up the purse until he collected his $1,000," Willi said.

"You should forget you ever had a father," the judge said. "Give him $400 and forget him."

Willi paid him $400, "the best $400 I ever spent." He never saw or heard from the old man again, but since has learned of his death. "I never missed him as a father. How do you miss something you never had?"

Back in New York, Lew Burston could only shake his head and say, "I tried to tell you you'd be sorry."

The "Re-Americanization of Willi Besmanoff" took place later—ironically, also in Milwaukee. There his citizenship was restored. It can be said that he lives happily ever after, especially once he found Christ, and today he's the only member of his Baptist church in Forest Park with a German accent.

BEAUTIFUL RAY TAKES UGLY MARV

APRIL 7, 1987

LAS VEGAS—The retina is still attached. The eyes see more clearly than before because the view is better from the top.

The fox trapped the hunter. The calf killed the butcher. The fancy beat the bully. The bookmakers down the street are rolling in the loot. The gambling class played the wrong horse again.

Attention, all hands! Sugar Ray Leonard beat Marvin Hagler, who was not quite Marvelous enough. Sugar Ray Leonard is the new middleweight champion of the whole world, and it makes no difference what set of initials was or wasn't giving the party in the back yard of Caesars Palace Monday night.

A reformed welterweight, thirty years old—who had spent the better part of five years mowing the lawn, taking the kids to the pool, driving to the grocery store, sitting by the ringside talking about other tigers and feeling left out—got back on the other side of the ropes and turned "The Super Fight" into "The Fight of the Century" of this decade.

Dead men don't rise from the grave and fight again. Old boxers don't pack it in, then come back and win titles. Welterweights don't eat themselves twelve pounds heavier and suddenly show up as middleweights. Beautiful Sugar Ray Leonards don't beat ugly Marvin Haglers.

All the above matters came before a house of 15,303, including the talented and the famous, the more important of whom were three judges named Lou Filippo of Los Angeles, Dave Moretti of Las Vegas, and JoJo Guerra of Mexico. Guerra saw it Leonard's way 10 rounds to 2, Moretti 7-to-5, and, through some form of myopia of his own, Filippo saw it for Hagler 7-to-5.

As the end approached, there had been a vocal turn toward

Leonard. In the morning at the weigh-in, he had been booed. Weigh-in ceremonials once were events in the bedlam of Muhammad Ali's day. This one was as peaceful as a garden party, except for the light boos. Neither Leonard nor Hagler cracked a smile, spoke, or nodded, only stripped to their shorts and gold chains and stepped on the scales.

They were still seeing little with unjaundiced eye after the twelve rounds had been fought. Leonard stopped on the ropes after the decision was announced and told the crowd, "I don't want Marvin Hagler's belt. All I wanted was to beat him. I'll see you in six months and fifteen pounds heavier."

That apparently is the next mountain he will choose to climb— put on fifteen more pounds and challenge Tommy Hearns for the light-heavyweight championship. He fought Hearns once as a welterweight and defended his title on this same lot. The least Hearns could do is return the favor.

As long as two months ago, Leonard had said what his plan was and he never wavered. "I'm going to hit and run, but I'll leave him a few souvenirs," he'd said.

"I'm training to fight twelve rounds," he'd said. "I don't expect to knock him out. I don't hit hard enough."

No man could be truer to his word. He hit and he ran, and left a few souvenirs on Hagler's person. He went for points, not for blood. He hit and he ran and he taunted and intimidated, anything to cause frustration. It was a return to the old plan that had left Roberto Duran standing in the ring in New Orleans with his hands up in surrender.

What this tells you is prizefighters don't win fights with a scowl and a sneer. The guy you wouldn't like to meet in a dark alley isn't always the one who wins under bright lights. This was Little Lord Fauntleroy taking The Hulk. Popeye over Bluto again.

You don't want the guys with all the scars. You want the guy who hasn't been cut. You want the guy who's so bold, or foolish, that he doesn't mind risking another detached retina, he misses being a champion so. There was no risk in his eyes, no play on words intended.

If there was any doubt who would win this fight, Leonard covered that early. He won the first four rounds. He suffered mainly in the fifth and the ninth, when Hagler, the relentless stalker, became his most vicious self. Most of the time, though, Leonard kept him at such a distance, or at such close quarters, that he took Hagler's leverage away. The boxer gave the slugger a postgraduate course in the "sweet science."

As it came down to crying time, Hagler had only one chance left, a knockout, and by that time the steam was gone from his punch. Those who didn't have Hagler at the betting shop were on their feet chanting, "Sugar Ray, Sugar Ray!" and we have a new day.

As ebullient as was Leonard, the man with the mission accomplished, Hagler was dismayed, which is too mild a word to go with the anger in the eyes beneath that hairless head. He didn't say, "I wuz robbed" in so many words, but he did say, "A split decision should go to the champion."

In which case, Leonard would have been the robbee. Two tops one any time by my arithmetic, or my name is Einstein.

Politicians,
Politics, &
Other Games

A STRICTLY STOCK PRESIDENT

NOVEMBER 24, 1976

One of the presidents of the United States coached football before he made it to the White House. Another was outstanding at the rural recreation of splitting rails. Another was a noted hunter of wild game. At least one played tennis, but never to the point of making a nuisance of himself on the sports pages.

But never before have we had a president who started a stock-car race.

It should be brought to national attention that as Gerald Ford is succeeded by James Earl Carter, we are involved in more than a change of tenant, change of party, change of face, and change of hairstyle, but also a change in sport. Ford was basically a one-sport fellow. He skied, but he'd never have lettered at it. Jimmy Carter covers so much sporting ground he may need an athletic director.

Not only will Carter become the only president who ever started a stock-car race, he'll be the only one who ever knew Coo Coo Marlin, Soapy Castles, Elmo Langley, and Crawfish Crider personally, and had them out to his house for dinner.

To dig into the sporting background of our rising president, we must take you back to the farm life, where he broke in bird hunting and treeing possums with a man named Jack Clark, and shooting squirrels in the company of an old dog named Bozo. He fished anything that was wet enough to keep a minnow alive. He played on the high-school basketball team. He ran cross-country at the Naval Academy until he discovered that you can draw blood doing that. And he indulged first in hero worship at the shrine of a small-town welterweight boxer named Bud Walters. Softball came later.

Actually, Carter was brought up in a town with a sporty name. The family really didn't live in Plains, but out from Plains, in a spit of a village named Archery. Jimmy grew up going to the weekly baseball games of the Archery town teams, consisting of eight blacks and two whites.

"The extra man," he explained once, "was a backstop." The field had no foul screen.

He got to know Bud Walters on his peanut route. He'd boil peanuts and walk the railroad tracks into Plains peddling bags at ten cents apiece. Bud Walters was his best customer.

"Bud was everybody's hero in Plains," he said. "He had a bad accident when he was young and it left him with a limp the rest of his life. The fact that he was able to come back and be a fighter in spite of it caused everybody to admire him, and the people would drive into Americus to see him fight every time they had a card at the boxing club there."

Carter and teammates played high-school basketball under frontier circumstances. Plains High had no indoor court. The team had to practice outdoors, which brought wind and topography into play. Have you ever tried to fast-break—up hill? And shoot into a ten-mile-an-hour wind?

Cross-country campaigning is one thing. Cross-country running is another. After seven or eight meets at Annapolis, he gave up the running sport. "When you start spitting up blood," he said. "I think it's time to find another kind of fun."

His taste for stock-car racing would seem to have fallen rather naturally into his scheme, being southern and rural, except that it didn't happen that way at all. He got introduced to the game of the good ol' boys in Yankee territory. He'd never seen a stock-car race until he was already a naval officer, and then it came about out of humanitarian interest.

"There was this young seaman around the sub base at New London, Connecticut, who was always in trouble," he said. "Hit port and he'd be drunk, late reporting back, always on report, a real problem," he said.

"Then he developed some interest in mechanics working on an old jalopy, and when he started taking his car to tracks around Connecticut and Long Island, I started going along with him, mainly just to be in his corner and encourage him. From that point, my interest grew in stock-car racing."

The first time I ever saw Jimmy Carter, he was circulating

through the press box at Atlanta International Raceway, shaking hands, handing out cards, and soliciting votes for a race he wouldn't win to be governor of Georgia. His attire was properly "stock."

Once elected, when the stock-car tour hit Atlanta, he and Mrs. Carter entertained the drivers, crews, and wives at the governor's mansion. The guests got the dirt out from under their nails, sprayed themselves with aromatic water, and came dressed fitten for the occasion. It was an enormous social hoist for a ripsnorting sport developed in the illicit atmosphere of moonshining, and brought down out of the dusty unpaved tracks of mountain country.

"I found race drivers to be a different sort than I'd been reading about," he said. "People forget that A.J. Foyt is a millionaire, and that Richard Petty and Bobby Allison, for example, are very articulate fellows."

In the hunting field, he's better than an average shot. It came as natural to him as breathing, for as a boy on a farm, hunting was a way of life.

"Bird season was like planting season," he said. "When anybody had a good bird dog, everybody else knew about it and wanted to breed his dog to it. Then you'd watch the litter grow and you'd try to guess which one would be the good one."

From the time he was seven or eight, he hunted. By the time he was ten, he had his own gun, a .410 bolt action. But his first kill was a long time coming. He'd knocked down nothing but feathers until one day deep in the woods he fired and his first quail fell. Bird in hand, he dashed for the house, looked up his father, and told him of his great adventure.

His father took the bird, congratulated him, and said, "Where's your gun?" In his excitement, little Jimmy had dropped his new gun in the woods and abandoned it to make his dash for the house.

"I was three days finding it," he said, "which taught me a lesson."

Translated to presidential terms, I suppose it comes out: Keep your powder dry and don't leave any missiles lying around.

OUT OF HIDING IN HYDEN

JULY 6, 1978

After you've been in the fun-and-games division of journalism a few years, you begin to take other forms of life for granted. Everything out there looks like a cinch. Nobody else earns his daily bread chasing down press credentials, being held at bay outside some locker room like a vacuum-cleaner salesman at the service entrance, waiting for late planes, missing others that leave on schedule, and cursing games that start so late it's tomorrow before they'll end.

On taking leave from the sweatshop odors and the tobacco spray of the locker room to put the reverse move on Richard Nixon the past weekend—remember, he's the president who was always calling the coaches with his favorite play and telephoning to congratulate the winner of something big—I found myself in a whole new ball game, not to coin an expression.

A little mining town in southeastern Kentucky, Hyden (pop. 500), had invited the former president in to star at the dedication of a building in a sports complex named for him, and he had accepted. It was plumb peculiar that he had chosen such an obscure location for his coming out.

I'd selected the town of London as my base. It made a nice little mark on the road map and had a Ramada Inn. And, as it turned out, it was close to the airport where Nixon would arrive.

As I checked in, the lady at the desk said, "You're late. They've been checking in since last Sunday. They're all over the place."

When I walked into the little weekly paper office in Hyden, a woman sitting at the desk moaned, "Oh, no, not another one!"

I told her I was really there to cover the University of Kentucky swimming-team exhibition. Judge C. Allen Muncy, who runs Leslie

County, of which Hyden is the seat, had scheduled the mermen—
that's a word straight out of the old sports jargon—to follow
Nixon's speech.

The judge is a graduate of UK, not some hillbilly with a pot
belly, flinty eyes, and a swagger stick. He wears suits and ties
and a shine on his shoes. That's a part of Kentucky that has
a fierce pride, lives its own life, which is Republican in spirit,
and the rest of Kentucky—where the horses grow, the basketball
is dribbled, and bourbon is distilled—might as well be in Montana.

A sincere Wildcat would literally collapse at Muncy's attitude
toward basketball, a UK alum, mind you. "The only basketball
player I ever paid to watch was that fellow they called 'Pistol,'
from down about Mississippi someplace," he said. He meant Pete
Maravich of LSU.

I'd always assumed that credentials, the badges or tags of
admission to the press box, the field, or the locker room, were
mainly a harassment indigenous to sports. Something public, like
a president, or especially an ex-president, or the Senate or a
hearing, was just that, public. Sort of like a park. You walk in
because it's there, and you want to, and it's your tax money.

Credentials would be issued in the Laurel County courthouse
in London, I was told, between 5 and 10 P.M. Friday. The place
was crowded when I got there. I was nervous. This wasn't my
league. This was Helen Thomas' and James Reston's. I was a
strange face in a bunch of other faces that seemed at home
with each other.

You needed three accreditations: a press badge of identification
that would admit you to the airport for Nixon's arrival, another
that allowed you into Hyden—without that blue stub, you didn't
get into Muncy's town—and a white one that was most precious
and essential. It got you into the building where Nixon would
speak.

I was two-for-three. I wasn't issued a little white one. "There
are only 150, and if you're not on Judge Muncy's list, you don't
get one," said a woman named Johanna, a sloe-eyed, unflappable
wellspring of information as the press contact.

This was like going to the Super Bowl and being told you
had tickets to everything but the game.

Fortunately, the London Jaycees had set up an oasis at the
London Country Club to accommodate the thirst that so often
springs upon newspaper people, especially in dry counties. I

cooled my churning insides with a beer and did homage to the Jaycees. Fifteen minutes before Nixon arrived at the recreation center Sunday, I was still without a building pass. "Is this because I'm from Georgia, the state that gave you the Carter family?" I asked.

A local editor, one-armed and in a rage, had been shut out. He'd supported George Wooten against Judge Muncy in the last election, and since Muncy had won by only 129 votes, I considered his a dangerous form of spite.

I was loitering around the dignitaries' entrance, looking like a dog hoping for a bone, when another lady on the staff rushed up, Doris by name. "I've come to rescue you," she said, handing me one of the precious tickets.

"But what about Vernon Baker?" I asked. He was the local editor on the wrong horse.

"That's strictly local politics," Doris said. "I can't touch it."

I kissed Doris on one cheek, and then the other, and was working on a hand when she broke into my Adolphe Menjou display. "I'd like you to meet my husband," she said, introducing me to a man in a brown suit and metal-framed glasses.

"I hadn't planned to go any further," I said to Doris, but this shows you how far you have to go to get credentials when you're out of your ball game.

PAVLOV, WITHOUT HIS DOG

JUNE 25, 1974

MOSCOW—Now came the Big Pitch. Nine days we had been toured and feasted and wined and politicked. We had seen the Soviet Union from the inside of mayors' chambers to the moistly aromatic rooms where athletes train. From Moscow to Kiev to Tbilisi and back to Moscow, 5,000 tiring miles of Russia, the Ukraine and Georgia, by day and night—concluded by breakfast at the Tbilisi airport that opened with vodka and closed with champagne.

We toured the Kremlin on this day—even the former Mrs. Burton doesn't own that much jewelry—and were guided back to our bus for a trip into a narrow side street. These were government offices.

Our two visiting groups, now reunited and swapping tales of our adventures, were compressed into a conference room to get down to Hard Sell. The office was that of Sergei Pavlov, "chairman of the Committee on Physical Culture and Sport Under the USSR Council of Ministers"—the Soviet Union's athletic director, so to speak.

Pavlov, as had most of the other officials of sport, exemplified physical condition. He looked as though he could bend a crowbar in half. Stocky, thickset, but depicting agility, like a retired NFL running back. Nevertheless, personable, patient, and a smile that lighted up his handsome features.

A magnificently produced book called *Moscow-80*, welcoming the Olympics to the USSR, and another booklet in three languages detailing sports facilities, had been distributed. As we entered the conference room, a nine-page mimeographed paper was handed to us. It was Pavlov's presentation, explaining the USSR's plans for the Olympics of 1980, and the man himself stood before us, armed with a most articulate interpreter, to handle the questions of eighteen journalists ranging from Nigerian to Japanese to Israeli.

The home team had trotted out its big guns: K. Adrianov, chairman of the USSR Olympic Committee, who looks startlingly like the late Khrushchev; A. Zhernov, a member of the IOC committee; and a few athletic showpieces, such as Alex Medvid, heavyweight gold-medal winner in wrestling at Munich, and little Olga Korbut, who is virtually a household name in the United States, if not the USSR.

One commentary could not be overlooked in Pavlov's prepared statement. "We are unswervingly following the difficult road of détente," it said. "Implementing the Leninist principles of peaceful coexistence, the Soviet state has been coming out all the time in support of the social forces and movements whose activities help strengthen mutual understanding and peace among nations."

"If Chile got the Games in 1980, would the USSR compete?" This question was thrown at Pavlov by the editor from Tel Aviv, Moise Lehrer. Eight months ago, he was a tank commander in the Israeli army.

Pavlov fielded it neatly. "It is difficult to say. No one can determine what will happen in Chile by 1980."

What we wanted to know is what the spectator from outside the USSR border could expect in a country not encouraging tourism. What accommodations? What freedom of movement?

"That is our biggest problem," Pavlov said. "Moscow now handles 2.5 million visitors a year, but we plan the construction of new hotels and boardinghouses and holiday homes outside of Moscow. Olympic Moscow will provide visitors with all kinds of modern service.

"We shall also be prepared to handle 6,000 journalists and 1,200 commentators. The contours of the Olympic Village are quite clear today. The construction of a modern hotel complex with accommodations for 10,000 people has already started."

You see, projects in the USSR require no bond issues or public elections. You want it, you got the political clout, you go get it.

And about the countries not on the Soviet Union's friendly list? "There will be guaranteed acceptance of those nations with whom we have no diplomatic relations," Pavlov said, "such as Chile, Israel, and Taiwan.

"We are aware that men cannot play on fields where five minutes ago there were corpses. Politics are charged by those whose motives are politics," he said, rather sharply this time.

"We know that we have drawbacks, but we see our drawbacks better than you. We try to correct them."

"I can assure you," Adrianov said, "full observation of the rules of the Olympic charter."

There is no question about facilities. This was an application for candidature made in 1971—to be finalized in Vienna in October—and the USSR Sports Committee has not been asleep. Moscow's sports fixtures alone are overwhelming.

There are sixty-nine stadiums in the city; Lenin Stadium, the largest, seats 103,000. There are 1,500 indoor arenas, ranging from "palaces," one of the Russians' favorite terms, to "halls." There are twenty-six Olympic-sized swimming pools. The rowing channel, created in ten months at a cost of 13 million rubles, is considered the finest in the world.

Our group left the USSR Physical and Cultural Center aghast. Mike Hughes of UPI was convinced there's nothing like it in the United States, four gymnasiums and an indoor track for openers.

And if that isn't enough, Pavlov said "It has become quite evident that ten new facilities that meet all the demands of the morrow will have to be built in Moscow." Then he threw out such teasers as an indoor stadium seating 50,000, an equestrian base, and a cycling arena.

"Cost," he said, "is of no interest. We will be ready for four million people. The Soviet, I assure you, gentlemen, keeps its guarantees. Anything more that we might say would be called, as you say, 'Soviet propaganda.' "

There was still the question of what is an amateur in the Soviet Union, and what is an amateur in the United States, but it couldn't be answered there. Nor at the Hotel Metropole, where we repaired to another luncheon that might tie the record held by many. It was a six-glasser.

THE GAME OF INSURANCE

JULY 31, 1983

Lloyd's of London is located down a narrow, winding alley named Lime Street in the financial district. There is a Lloyd's Avenue nearby, but it has no connection. Neither does Lloyd's Bank, the chain you see all about England. Both the banker and the insurance broker came from Wales. Edward Lloyd's coffeehouse down on the waterfront became the center of marine underwriting, and from that it has grown into this, the most widely known name in the world of insurance.

This would not seem to be on the sports beat, but while in England, between Wimbledon and the British Open, I took a run down to Lime Street and discovered that what had become of the old coffeehouse would dazzle the human eye.

When the baseball major leagues insured themselves against the player strike, they insured through Lloyd's. When the Baltimore Orioles insured against rainout losses, they insured through Lloyd's. When Ted Turner said any losses that he might have in the suit brought by Bucky Woy were covered, they were insured through Lloyd's.

Hole-in-one prizes, Olympic telecasts, race cars, horses, and jockeys all are insured through the syndicates of Lloyd's. So, in a sense, Lime Street is on the sports beat.

How many times have you heard a figure in sports say, "It's covered by Lloyd's." Actually, Lloyd's is not an insurance company, it's a group of independent syndicate operators who pay dues to belong and take a piece of the action. When Lloyd's paid $46.8 million to the major leagues under their strike-insurance policy—on a premium of $3.25 million—this was the biggest Lloyd's payout in its years of doing business in sports. But no insuror suffered severely. The coverage was parceled out in small percentages among those of the 417 syndicates that participated, none at gunpoint. All syndicates have a right of refusal, many times exercised.

A few days before the second Cassius Clay–Sonny Liston bout in 1965, a caller from Lewiston, Maine, asked Lloyd's if he might get insurance against a postponement. He offered a premium of 20 percent of the loss, which is excessive. The man on the end of the line at Lloyd's smelled a rat and turned it down. The next day, it came out that Clay had a hernia and the fight was delayed.

On the other hand, policies against self-styled daredevils, such as Evel Knievel and "The Human Fly," are coveted. "We know they are going to take every precaution in the world," said Stanley John. "We know they want to live."

So Lloyd's joyfully covered Knievel at Snake River Canyon. "The Human Fly," a Canadian named Rogatte, got coverage for $70,000 on a series of three stunts, including a leap off a fifty-story building into a pool of water.

Stanley John also is Welsh, son of a miner, someone who spent enough time in a colliery to know he wanted something else in life. He followed the trail of his countryman to London and from Fleet Street worked his way into public relations. Just the day before, Stanley John had performed the loathsome duty of announcing that Lloyd's was giving up on Shergar, the kidnapped racehorse. Underwriters were paying up on $10.6 million worth of the coverage relating to loss by theft.

"We're sure he's dead," Mr. Stanley John said, though those insured against death only wouldn't profit by that private verdict, yet.

When the United States pulled its teams out of the Moscow Olympics, wrecking NBC's television plans, Lloyd's paid off the sum of $15 million, another of its sports whoppers. However, it turned out that, in a sense, Lloyd's loss was also its gain. Its underwriters are expected to pick up over $200 million of coverage on various nervous associates of the 1984 games in Los Angeles. Another spinoff of the Moscow payout was about $70 million worth of insurance against the collapse of the World Cup soccer kickout in Spain last year.

Three years ago, an American golf magazine put up prizes of $50,000 to any player breaking the current U.S. Open record score, and $25,000 to any female player breaking the women's record. The magazine was struck by a landslide. Both Jack

Nicklaus and Isao Aoki broke the men's record, Amy Alcott broke the women's, and Lloyd's coughed up $125,000. The magazine's loss was $30,000, cost of the premium.

While baseball was happily covered with strike insurance, the National Football League took a look and turned it down last year. On the other hand, twenty-four of the major-league teams have their stars covered, and nearly every professional team in the United States. The misconception about individual coverage is that Nolan Ryan's right arm is covered, or Pele's knees, as were Betty Grable's legs. The coverage is against their loss of earnings, as is the case in nearly every individual athlete's insurance. Most all of this American business goes through a firm in Massachusetts.

While Lloyd's is reluctant to speak of insurance in force, it does include among its cast of celebrated subjects John Conteh, the boxer, Bjorn Borg, Leon Spinks, Steve Cauthen, and, as Stanley John says, "entire American basketball, baseball, hockey, and football teams."

Such insurance games cover a broad range. It's another form of gambling that comes under the heading of laying off your bet. An applicant comes to the floor of Lloyd's with a prospect to be insured, and among the din rising from the booths they call "boxes," the offer is called out, and in time usually covered, for around Lloyd's it is said, "There's no such thing as a bad risk, only a bad rate."

"OUR GANG" TAKES THE REDS

FEBRUARY 24, 1980

LAKE PLACID, New York—Calm yourself. This doesn't mean the Russians have pulled out of Afghanistan and called Jimmy to say they're sorry. The hostages haven't been told to get packed for home. The oil crisis hasn't improved a gallon's worth. We still have inflation as fat as Blue Boy. (A seat to watch this event costs $67.20, unscalped.) But something of considerable international significance took place in the Olympic Arena at the vesper hour Friday.

The Americans beat the Russians in hockey. Not a National League team. Not the pros. They lost two out of three to these Soviets last year. The best of the NHL. The All-Stars. Forget Bruce Jenner, who wore out his soles, then sold his soul. Forgive us, Eric Heiden. You're grand. But the greatest thing in American Olympics in many a year is the 1980 American hockey team.

Impossible, of course. American amateur hockey teams don't beat the Russians, who play eleven months and get one month off. But this "Our Gang" bunch of kids, downy cheeks barely familiar with the touch of the razor, some yet unpledged to a frat, not yet decided on an academic major, they turned international hockey upside down and inside out. The young shavers took the blackbeards.

The Russians hadn't lost a match in Olympic hockey since 1968 at Grenoble. It may turn out to be the first gold medal they haven't won since 1960 at Squaw Valley. There's another round yet in which that'll be determined as we approach the snuffing-out of the torch Sunday night.

You must understand that the Olympic Games are not political. Forget the flags that were waved from the first icing of the puck until the team mobbed its goalie, Jim Craig—who, they say, will sign with the Atlanta Flames ere this business is done. Forget the Ukrainians marching outside the arena in protest of the Kremlin they despise from afar. Forget the snarling banners that hung from the railing. Forget those willing to pay scalpers $200 to get in.

Of course the Olympics aren't political. Americans wanted to beat hell out of the Russians because they don't like the personality of Juri Lebedev, Boris Mikhailov, or Vladimir Krutov, whom they wouldn't know if they rode the same elevator. Americans wanted to beat the Russians because they're Russian.

Soften that a smidgen. They wanted to beat them because the Russians don't "play" at the game. They make a career of it. The lineup is the best of 265 million inhabitants of the largest nation in the world, 749,940 of them hockey players. They come from such mysterious affiliations as the Central Army Club, the Dynamo Society, and Spartak. If they play well, they get an apartment twenty square feet larger, a new television, and an automobile. What happens to them after they play, I don't know. Some of them seem to play forever.

Eight members of this team are over thirty. The oldest, the captain, Mikhailov, is thirty-five. Some are teachers. Some are military officers. The best are honored with the title "USSR Merited Master of Sport."

Some of the Russians were playing in Olympic matches while most of the Americans were still playing peewee down at the rink, the days their mom could drive them. Most are still in college, or are just out. Their "old man" is Mike Eurizone, a grizzled twenty-five, graduate of Boston U.

Exactly halfway through the third period, the score a tie to the amazement of all, especially the grim-faced rows of comrades sitting to my left, Eurizone came blowing down the ice, found the puck happily delivered to him off the sticks of Dave Silk and Dave Christian—whose father scored the goal that beat the Russians at Squaw Valley—and fired a line drive past Vladimir Myshkin, the Soviet goalie. Myshkin had replaced Vladislav Tretjak in the last second of the first period after the starter and recent star gave up his second goal, and presumably is on the train to Gorki.

Thus did the Americans assume the lead, and thus to their undying credit did they hold it to the end, not building a protective barricade around it, but by skating furiously trying to make it 5-3 instead of 4-3.

At the moment of Eurizone's goal, naturally the arena went instantly insane. In the press box, the darnedest thing happened.

Veterans of many an evening, an afternoon, even mornings at the routine pursuit of duty in press box or in the field, their emotional sacs barnacled with cynicism and their minds programed for sardonic wit, sprang to their feet. Violating the self-imposed code of nonpartisanship, they shouted with glee, slapped each other across the back, shook hands, thrust clinched fists into the charged air, and down parchment cheeks rutted with age in the cases of some of the more moved, tears trickled in salty rivulets.

Some had seen everything from Larsen's perfect game in the World Series to Secretariat winning the Triple Crown, saw Ali in Zaire and Watson take Nicklaus down the stretch at Turnberry, and there hadn't been a wet eye in the crowd. But in this nonpolitical event, against the team whose Summer Olympics will not be favored by America's presence, and in honor of those flags that waved throughout the stands, and this old land of ours, the Red, the White, and the Blue, the purple mountain majesty and the rugged ocean shores, the nonpartisan American press assumed the privilege of being partisan on this rare, historic occasion. And we don't give a damn who knows.

A MORNING JOG IN THE SMOG

AUGUST 6, 1984

LOS ANGELES—Greetings, girls, and welcome to Ladies Day at the Olympic Games. In the baseball park in another time, that meant skirts got in free. That has gone down the drain with dishwashing by hand, the Monday wash, and booths for ladies and gents.

It used to be dreadfully unfashionable for a lady to sweat. Skin exposed above the foot was galloping immorality. Then the line was raised to the thigh. She can show anything now, and name her price. And sweat until she smells like a linebacker.

Until this year of Olympiad XXIII, women had never been allowed to run more than 1,500 meters, a little less than a mile. It was, as they say, in their own best interest.

Back in 1928, in Amsterdam, the 800-meter run had been dubbed in for women. Two of the contestants collapsed on the track, and the geezers who run the IOC said, tsk, tsk, no more of this.

Once a woman had run the Olympic marathon—in four and a half hours—but without Olympic consent. It happened in Greece in 1896, the year of the resumption after the longest time-out in the history of sports—1,672 years.

This year the IOC boldly voted the marathon into the women's program, all twenty-six miles and change, from Santa Monica College into the Coliseum. The idea of a woman stripping down to her briefs and sweating publicly in such a show would have appalled ladies of the day of Stella Walsh, who it turned out was no lady at all, and Nellie Flagg, the filly. It has become commonplace now, and so the show went on.

In deference to their delicate construction, also cleaner and cooler air, they went off at 8 o'clock on a Sunday morning, while Angelenos are still sleeping it off. The course moved out toward the Pacific, down the beach, past pumping oil rigs, along the freeway, and along city streets into the Coliseum.

By the time they got to Beverly Hills, it was over. International handicappers had overwhelmingly gone into the gate with Grete Waitz, the Norwegian who has ruled the marathon from ocean to ocean. An upset was in the making here, as they say on the air.

Joan Benoit, who holds the world record, but who had never beaten Waitz, ran off out of sight of the rest of the fifty girls. She looked like a person out for a simple morning jog by herself. She put it on automatic pilot and let her computer take over. She made no visible change in form or stride, but just kept picking them up and putting them down until she hit the tunnel.

She was so far ahead it was a wonder they didn't make her show a ticket and frisk her. Security is such out here that they even make you show what's inside your sandwiches at the gate.

She crossed the finish line just as Waitz came through the tunnel, then she did a victory lap, waving a flag that somehow found its way into one hand, and with her little white cap in the other, her hair a black mop, looking as if she had just stepped out of the shower. Marathoning doesn't do a lot for a hairdo.

She found her folks, hugged them, found the energy to be affable on television, and was in the midst of making the day of the women's first Olympic marathon Joan Benoit Day when the scene focused off her and onto a semitragedy. Also semicomic in a sense that the clown brings comedy relief to the rodeo.

It was comic only in that Gabriela Andersen-Schiess's mind and her body were out of communication. She ran a staggering path into the Coliseum, then, running out of steam, slowed to a weaving, unsteady walk. She was so far gone, her head lay wobbling on her shoulder. She was some dazed creature trying to figure out where she was through all that commotion.

Her vision was blurred, for at the top of the stretch coming around for the finish, the intersection addled her. She paused and finally determined she should take a left turn. Through all of this, cheers and encouraging cries cascaded down upon her from the 60,000, who meant well, as when they cheered on the lagging walker, but knew not.

A humanitarian tracksider in uniform had made a move toward her when it was obvious she was in dire need, but she avoided him. She should have been hauled in in the interest of saving

174

her life or her health. Such exhaustion has caused brain damage. Prizefights are stopped when the referee decides a boxer is out of it. The boxer doesn't decide. Gabriela was in no condition to decide for herself. The doctor who didn't have her brought off the track is one I don't want for my family doctor. It took no Rosie Ruiz to turn this into a travesty, and take away from the glory of Benoit. Andersen-Schiess struggled across the finish into the arms of two attendants, there was treated, then rushed to a hospital. After injections and refurbishment, she was able to be delivered back to her quarters in the athletes' village, all of this for a thirty-seventh-place finish.

Gabriela is an American citizen living and coaching in Sun Valley, Idaho. She is no novice at the marathon—to the contrary, had won one at Minneapolis and another at Sacramento last year. She had been invited to the U.S. Olympic trials, but chose to go with Switzerland, where she was born, because there she was a cinch. She is, at her normal best, an attractive person of 39.

Meanwhile, Joan Benoit, of Freeport, Maine, and Bowdoin College, was telling the story of why she was in the Summer Games of Los Angeles and not the Winter Games of Sarajevo.

"I'd always had this ambition to qualify for the Olympic ski team," she said, "but I broke a leg on skis. While I was training to get back in shape, I started running a lot. I discovered that I could run anywhere, anytime, and it went from there.

"When you grow up in a family with three brothers, running is a matter of survival. What this has proven today is that women can go the distance in these events."

What the day had meant to Joan Benoit was victory; to Gabriela Andersen-Schiess, it was survival.

The
Aaron/Williams
File

AARON'S PURSUIT OF 714

Last day of the the season—September 30. The setting couldn't have been more perfect had it been contrived. Box offices opened at 9 A.M. Lines had been forming since early morning. There were 40,517 at the game, 32,000 of whom bought tickets that day. It was the busiest day in the history of the Braves's box office. It urged attendance over 800,000, a face-saving level.

By noon, two hours before the game, streets leading to the stadium seethed with scurrying people, fathers carrying small children and tugging others, mothers struggling to keep up. Traffic was stacked up in all directions and far beyond the state Capitol, whose gold dome glistened in a bright sun. That lasted only a short time. Clouds began moving in during batting practice. In the second inning, rain came, first in a drizzle, increasing the pace intermittently, never really ceasing.

Dave Roberts, who had served #711, started for Houston. Henry Aaron beat out a topper down the third-base line, driving in a run the first time up. He arched a single to center field the second time, and officially his batting average reached .300 for the first time during the season.

Rain was coming down harder. It was a dismal and a dangerous day for a thirty-nine-year-old immortal to be sloshing around in the outfield. "Why doesn't he get out of the game and let well enough alone!" I said to Eddie Robinson. We sat in the general manager's booth.

"I wish he would," Eddie said. "That's something we've left to Henry all season."

Settle for .300? Not on your life. Aaron showed his stuff. He dropped a single into left field. Three for three.

He popped out to Tommy Helms the last time up. His average stuck at .301.

It began to well up, gradually, as he jogged back out toward left field. It spread with each squishy step. It had become a crescendo by the time he reached his position, and Henry Aaron stood there in the rain, gloved hand and bare hand on his hips, as 40,517 people, now standing, cheered him for a full five minutes. He tipped his cap several times, then took it off and held it aloft, and the cheers cascaded down upon him.

It was, in all my time, the most moving ovation I'd ever seen for any man, not to mention one who had just popped out to second base.

Most of the spectators stayed to the bitter end (the Braves lost their eighty-fifth game of the season), though the rain had become a downpour by the time Frank Tepedino struck out, concluding the season. As a substitute for Aaron's 714th home run, they had seen Leo Durocher manage his last major-league game. The next day he retired as Houston's manager.

"I'm sorry I couldn't hit one for them, sitting in the rain and all," Aaron said in the big interview room. "I was going for the home run. I wasn't trying to hit singles.

"And that applause, I guess that's the biggest thrilling moment I've ever had in baseball. I guess I didn't realize the people cared that much."

There was one delicate moment during the interview session. A man with a tape recorder asked, "What have you done for baseball?"

Aaron looked puzzled for a moment. "I don't get what you mean."

"Well, when Babe Ruth hit his home runs, he saved baseball. He brought it back from the throes of trouble. He gave it a new face and it became stronger than ever. What have you done for baseball?"

Unfair a question as it was, tense as the moment became in the press room, Aaron paused for thought.

"Well, that's a new question," he began. "Maybe what I've done is create some new fans for baseball. At first there was a lot of mail from people, older people who didn't want me to break Babe Ruth's record. The younger generation took notice of that and came to my support. I think they wanted me to relate to, to see me have a record in their time, not somebody their granddaddies had seen play. That's about all I can say I've done for baseball, I guess."

There was a brief silence, then a short burst of applause.

Percival Wentworth Ford, a moon-faced little Bahamian who writes a column for a Nassau newspaper in the off-season, had been the Braves' starting pitcher that day. He was a rookie just in a few weeks from the farm club in Richmond. He had pitched more like a columnist than a pitcher. By the second inning, he was gone.

He stood in the crowd outside the interview room when it broke up. He carried a bag. He had been in the center of the field before the 40,000, pitching in front of Henry Aaron. Now he seemed lost, a face in a sea of faces. Aaron moved near him as he left. Wenty Ford looked into his face. He said nothing. He stood there a moment, holding his bag, in frozen idolatry. Then he turned and started walking—to Nassau, I guess.

Inside the locker room, Aaron pronounced his benediction to 1973. "I'm thankful it's over and that it came out as well as it did," he said. #714 was for 1974.

BOWIE KUHN PLAYS JUDGE LANDIS

MARCH 13, 1974

Well, I see Bowie Kuhn is trying to play baseball commissioner again. Who does he think he is, Judge Landis?

The Old Man had a few things to say about who *couldn't* play—like Jimmy O'Connell, Cozy Dolan, and Shufflin' Phil Douglas. Bad Boys. But he never dialed any manager to tell him, "You pitch the knuckleballer today, and play The Switcher in center field—bat him fourth—and I want the little guy at second base. It's good for the game."

Kuhn went to bat again in the Henry Aaron Cause the other day and popped up with the bases full. Would Pete Rozelle tell the Miami Dolphins that Earl Morrall *must* start the Super Bowl game if he needed two completions to break somebody's all-time passing record?

Kuhn apparently has made Aaron the object of his 1974 spring crusade. It hardly bears repeating that there is nothing in the contract of the commissioner of baseball that gives him the right to say who can and who can't play in any major-league game—so long as the player is legal and decent, and hasn't fixed any results lately. Lineup cards shall be made out in the dugout, not in an office on Fifth Avenue.

This is unadulterated meddling. There's a place in baseball for a commissioner if he'll just stick to counting All-Star votes and deciding if the field is dry enough to play the World Series. Since Happy Chandler, there has been little for a commissioner to do except be a butler for the owners.

I do hope that Kuhn doesn't have Aaron, Henry, confused with Aaron Burr. Patriotism is to be upheld at all costs.

After all, it isn't as if Bill Bartholomay is trying to sell out

181

to the Red menace. He is only an American businessman practicing free enterprise. Laissez-faire, the law of diminishing returns, and the bottom-line principle. McDonald's doesn't send business across the highway to Burger King.

Here is Bartholomay, whose major commodity is a man about to hit the two most-gabbed-about home runs in the history of ash meeting horsehide, to garble an old spring expression. He should package it and market it for Cincinnati? The Reds don't need the people. They've been making playoffs. Atlanta hasn't had this much to cheer about since Sherman ran out of matches.

The Braves have six more games to give Aaron to Cincinnati this season. Give the sons of Rhineland #s 726 and 727. Or 734 and 735. But #s 714 and 715? Okay, let 'em have #714. Hell, he may still be trying to hit #715 in the middle of May.

Poor guy, there's nothing private for him anymore. He must feel like a streaker in slow motion down here. He's being guarded like a threatened heiress. He got up to walk to the water cooler during a game the other day and a wave of applause broke out.

Now there's an ex-lawyer calling his boss from New York telling him when he ought to play and where he ought to play. Doesn't Henry have the constitutionally guaranteed freedom of choice and the right to the pursuit of his own happiness?

Is Sinatra ordered to play Wichita Falls? Does Jack Nicklaus have to play the Sertoma Classic? Did the Jockey Club order Secretariat to run at Latonia Park?

If you're puzzled by Kuhn's turnaround, count me in, too. The last I'd read was that he was assured "that the Braves would do their very best to win the opening three games in Cincinnati." One can only conclude that he was so unnerved by all the shrieking and the hollering, and the ravings on the subject of "insidious fix" out of Council Bluffs-on-the-Hudson that he suffered a severe attack of chicken fever.

But, if it be so, then I feel it only proper that Bartholomay should be given the reciprocal privilege of designating Cincinnati's pitcher. May I suggest Don Gullett or Tom Hall? Aaron leaves left field a rubble when they play.

HENRY AARON GETS 715

APRIL 9, 1974

The flower of American sporting journalism was caught with its tongue tied. With its fingers arthritic. Its brain turned into a glob of quivering gelatin. Its nervous system drawn as tight as a banjo's strings.

It had rehearsed every move, memorized every line. Then took the stage to perform and every word stuck in its throat!

Henry Louis Aaron hit the 715th home run in the 2,967th game of his major-league career, and nobody had anything left to say. I mean, there just aren't 715 ways to say that Henry Aaron hit a home run. Besides, they'd worn out all the others in a long winter's anticipation, and last week when he hit #714 in Cincinnati.

In fact, #715 was only a rerun of #693, also hit off Al Downing in Atlanta Stadium with a man on base. And it was nothing to compare with #400, which cleared everything in Philadelphia and came down somewhere near Trenton. Aaron's guest of honor that night was Bo Belinsky.

There is this to be said about it: It was the first home run he has ever hit after hearing Pearl Bailey sing the national anthem. It was also an occasion added to extensively, though witlessly, by the absence of Bowie Kuhn, riotously referred to as the Commissioner of Baseball.

It was a Louisville bat against a Spalding ball, which hit a BankAmerica sign over the left-field fence and was fielded by a left-handed pitcher named Tom House. Fifty-three thousand people saw it in person, but what they weren't going to appreciate so much was when they got home, they learned that with their tickets their sellout had bought free television for the other million and a half Atlantans who stayed at home.

The Braves had thrown open the show for local consumption just before the field was turned into a riot of color, Americana, teary-eyed emotionalism, political swashbuckling, and deafening fireworks.

Alphonse Erwin Downing has won a Babe Ruth World Series for Trenton, New Jersey, and pitched in a World Series for the New York Yankees. He has won 115 games, twenty in one season, and become known as a steady, reliable member of the Los Angeles Dodgers. But Monday night he carved his initials on America's memory.

He has a new cross to bear. He won't be remembered for the 115 games, but for the inside fast ball that Aaron hit over the fence.

At the same time, he assured several pitchers of a place in posterity, a little hall of notoriety of their own. They all belong to the "We Served Henry Aaron a Home Run Club," senior member Vic Raschi, then on the shady side of a substantial career and serving it out as a St. Louis Cardinal.

The lineup of Aaron's victims is a procession of extremes, from Sandy Koufax, who was on his way to the Hall of Fame, to Joe Trimble, a Pittsburgh rookie who never won a game in the majors.

He hit #10 off Corky Valentine, who now may be seen around town as a cop. Then, he was a Cincinnati Red.

He hit one off an infielder, Johnny O'Brien, one of a pair of famous college basketball twins trying to discover a new career with the Pirates. He hit one off a congressman, the Honorable Wilmer Mizell (R-North Carolina), then "Vinegar Bend," a bumpkin rookie with a bashful smile and the kind of "aw-shucks" personality that made sports reporters look him up.

He hit another off Faul and off Law, and another off a Brewer, a Boozer, and a Barr. One off Rabe and one off Mabe. And off Hook and Nye.

He hit 'em off Morehead and Moorhead. And R. Miller and R. L. Miller, three different Jacksons, and Veale and Lamb.

With #715 he assured permanent attention for handservants merely passing that way: Otherwise, Thornton Kipper, Herb Moford, John Andre, Rudy Minarcin, Tom Acker, Lino Dinoso, Art Ceccarelli, and the improbable Whammy Douglas would have passed on and been forgotten. They are now forever engraved on the marble of Aaron's record like the roll of the soldiers memorialized on a courthouse monument.

Naturally, one is supposed to feel that he has been witness to one of the monumental sports events of all history, if he were in the park. These things don't penetrate the perspective so soon. You're overprepared. It's not like sitting there watching this flippant youth, Cassius Clay, knock a bear like Sonny Liston out of the world heavyweight title. Or Centre College whip Harvard.

There's no shock to get your attention. Number 715 was anticipated, awaited like childbirth. Everybody's so thoroughly ready that nobody can appreciate the history of it all. Even the president sat in Washington with his dialing finger exercised for action.

"He invited me to the White House," Aaron said. It is suggested that he not loiter on the way.

"Magnavox gets the ball and the bat for five years, then they go to the Hall of Fame," he said. That covered several other loose ends.

I don't want to fuel still another fire, but as I depart I feel compelled to leave with you another record in the line of fire: Aaron is well ahead of Ruth's pace the year of his sixty home runs. The Babe didn't hit his second home run until the eleventh game.

THIS IS IT—
COOPERSTOWN

AUGUST 2, 1982

Usually, on a Sunday in Cooperstown, you can cause a commotion with a noise from just scratching yourself. It's as still as a millpond. You can hear a bird chirp at the upper end of Lake Otsego. Otesaga. Or Otasego—nobody spells it the same way twice in this town.

On this Sunday morning, there was much bustling along the streets. Dads were scurrying along, leading their kids down the street to the Otesaga (see above) Hotel to get in line on the lawn for autographs of the chorus of Hall of Fame players. The small fry clutched baseballs in their meaty little hands and they chattered like magpies.

It was early. Late-rising birds were still testing their chirps. Cars and vans with out-of-state licenses were coursing through the streets. Town kids were out early with their "Park Here" signs, and "$3 All Day."

This is typical American village life. The flag was draped out in front of houses with porches you can rock on. There's a typical small-town fifties American theater with a Saturday matinee tempting the street traffic with a nutty aroma of popping corn. The streets have healthy, woodsy names like Elm, Chestnut, Walnut, and Maple. There's a diner. A drugstore with a soda fountain and kids hanging around on the curb or in their runabouts, flirting with the town belles who are waiting around to be flirted with.

Cooperstown is "bush," as "bush" as Keokuk or Poplar Bluff. It's "hick." It's as unsophisticated as horseshoes. That's why it's right that baseball came here to make its nest for immortals. For Ruth and Cobb and Johnson and Speaker and Wagner and Grove and Frank Robinson. Henry Aaron and Travis Jackson. I don't know how immortal Happy Chandler is, but he will long be remembered for the ten-minute acceptance speech that he joyously ran into a half hour. Mrs. Chandler shall surely have a place reserved for her in heaven.

On baseball's annual day in Cooperstown, two of the greatest black players who ever slept in a fleabag hotel and thrilled a crowd in October went into the Hall of Fame with Jackson, John McGraw's old shortstop. He was sort of a touch of gray on a background of ebony, a contrast of the game as it is as against what it was.

The arrival of Henry Aaron in the baseball Hall of Fame is not news. It would have been only if he hadn't made it. He made it with the largest volume vote since they opened the doors and chartered it with Ruth, Cobb, Matthewson, Wagner, and Johnson.

Robinson said, "I've been chasing Hank all my life and now I've finally caught up with him." Actually, he passed him. He went in first, Aaron went in last, but only on the program. Robinson never really caught him, except in length of oratory.

Aaron was a jewel of brevity and conciseness. He got to the point. He didn't wander or indulge himself in the maudlin. He handled his duty of making his manners and his thank-yous, and sat down in a third of the time that Chandler and Robinson ran through.

The difference was, Aaron came prepared. He took no time rambling around Robin Hood's barn.

In the long run, I guess, it was Aaron the person as much as it was Aaron the player, Aaron and his style as against Robinson and his.

Robinson was a smoldering, tempestuous player. If trouble didn't find him, he looked it up when he was playing as a Cincinnati Red. Suddenly, he was traded. It shocked him. Baltimore? Orioles?

"That was the turning point in my life," he said. "I had something to prove to myself and to Bill DeWitt," the man who traded him, and who got mentioned otherwise during the day only as another one of baseball's people who died this year.

Robinson became another Frank Robinson by his own hand, the same who now manages not only himself but the San Francisco Giants.

Cooperstown returns to being old Cooperstown this week. But it has some new images, blessed with the dignity of Henry Aaron. He went into the Hall of Fame the way he played himself into it, quietly, with an economical use of verbiage and a record that will be a challenge for generations to come.

SEARS, ROEBUCK, AND WILLIAMS

JANUARY 4, 1961

A few days ago, an international mail-order house announced the employment of Ted Williams, rather widely known previously as tender of left field at Fenway Park in Boston. In the narrow mind of sports, it was assumed that since Sears, Roebuck and Company was approaching its seventy-fifth year in business, Williams was being retained as the diamond-anniversary attraction.

About Wednesday noon, a tall man wearing sports jacket, white shirt, and blue tie and walking with a loose-jointed gait stepped off an elevator at the Biltmore Hotel with a covey of executives. Only a fellow with a program and all the numbers of the players would have been able to pick Williams out of the crowd.

The former "Splendid Splinter" had been polished up to look like a piece of solid mahogany. He wore a name tag that said "Ted Williams, Sports Consultant."

He was cordial, gracious, accommodating, everything a Boston sports writer would ordinarily say he isn't. Such a mention caused him to bristle.

"Those cotton-picking cotton-pickers," he didn't exactly say. "One of those guys called my daughter the other day to find out what I'd given her for Christmas. Anything to stay on my back."

The elder tier of baseball oracles has contended that Williams has changed, mellowed to the state of a pure charmer in his latter days of baseball.

"I've got two words for that," he said. Neither of which I am able to print here.

He could tell that the shirt and tie were getting some special attention. His face broke into a smile, for 99 and 44/100ths percent of his waking life has been spent inside sport shirts.

"I'm wearing a shirt and a tie," he said, "and that's a change. But I told these people that was only in cold weather. When it's hot, I'll be in sport shirts."

Now he was serious. "Here's the way I look at myself," Ted Williams said, picking up the original drift.

"I'm the same guy I always was, except I'm a little older and maybe a little smarter. I still have the same moods and I can still fly off the handle when I feel like it."

You could tell this was true. The fire still burned inside him. His eyes snapped at times. When a question aroused him, he fairly leaped to an answer, like a bass rising to assault a top-water lure.

He was smarter, too. A high-level executive of Sears, Roebuck confirmed this.

"Let me tell you that this is a hardheaded business man," said Vice President L. E. Oliver. "We didn't hire Mr. Williams for window-dressing. We think he'll be of great value in assisting these men here in our approach to the sporting-goods field."

The retirement of Theodore Samuel Williams took place last fall. It almost took place a year earlier.

"Tom Yawkey didn't want me to play last season," he said.

"I'd dropped off to .254 in 1959. He thought I was over the hill. He knew I'd been having trouble with my neck. I couldn't face the pitcher the way I was accustomed to. He didn't want me to ruin my record.

"I told him I'd like to come to spring training and see how it worked out. The year before, I hadn't been able to play for the first month, then I got in one day against Herb Score.

"Now, I had always been able to hit Score pretty good. I went 0-for-five. I finally got my average up to .180, and then .274 at one time, but I dropped back.

"The neck was bothering me, but I thought I could still hit. I wanted one more chance at it, and I'm glad I stayed with it."

In spite of Sears, Roebuck and the nonexistent J. C. Higgins (their sporting line) et al., Williams will again appear at spring training with the Red Sox. This time he will be Professor Williams, dean of the science of hitting.

Tom Yawkey retained him first for this position. Sears, Roebuck and Higgins came second. The two jobs won't conflict. He and his two employers have agreed on this.

One of Professor Williams's first pupils will be his own successor at Fenway Park, a Long Island youth named Carl Yastrzemski, who played at Minneapolis. Last spring in Arizona, Williams became fascinated with Yastrzemski's manner with a bat.

"He'll take my place in left field," Ted said, "and he's liable to lead the league in hitting. He's that good. He's got an average build and hits to left center field. He's sort of a cross between Charlie Keller and Billy Goodman, and that's a pretty good combination."

Now, he was asked as the entourage moved toward the banquet hall downstairs, "Did you ever really have any serious interest in managing?"

"None," he said, emphatically. "Absolutely none. I couldn't stand all those newspaper writers around me after a game asking me why I pinch-hit so-and-so, or why I didn't relieve with some other pitcher. If I'm the manager, it's none of their damned business."

He has changed, too, for when he said that word, he smiled.

THE SPLINTER, MANAGER AND PARTNER

FEBRUARY 17, 1969

I trust that Robert Short is preparing himself for the eventualities of the day when he decides to tell Ted Williams that he ought to take the rest of his life off and let somebody else manage the Washington Senators.

That would be like Abercrombie telling Fitch to get lost, or Anheuser showing Busch to the door.

See, they are not doing things in sports by the old methods anymore. You don't just go out and hire a manager or a coach. You fit him out for a desk and a swivel chair, paint his name on a door, write it on several stock certificates, and call him "Partner."

In other words, Short won't be firing a manager. He'll be telling a partner his work isn't showing its old flair. Whereupon Williams, the partner, may reply, "And what about your blanken work, you blanken blank? Now get your blanken blank out of here and don't slam my door."

Assuming that his vocabulary hasn't lost any of its old livery-stable flavor.

That's one Ted Williams. The offer can charm the spots off a leopard. The Williams you write about one minute may be an entirely different Williams thirty seconds later.

His emotional transmission has an automatic shift, and you can say what you care to say about him, write what you will about him, and the mail will bring you a confusion of compassion and contempt.

Williams made it this way himself. He went through his playing career acting as if he despised the sound of praise, but couldn't live without it.

A few years ago, I wrote a column on the statistics that Williams might have had if he had not lost the better part of five seasons to military wars. He would have wiped out just about every worthwhile batting record in the game.

"Yeah," replied a cynic, "and how many pennants did he ever win for Boston? When a big hit counted, he never had it."

Then I wrote of my surprise when Stan Musial wasn't unanimously elected to the Hall of Fame, and indeed polled fewer votes than Williams.

"That's because you're biased," wrote another cynic. "Thank God there are enough professionals in the game to vote on record, not on a guy's personality."

"Why don't you give the bum what he's got coming to him?"

"Why do you hate Ted Williams?"

See? You cannot write of him but what you are whipped up in the same froth.

When he was flying for the Marine Corps at Bronson Field near Pensacola in World War II, I visited him.

The day he made his debut as a spitter, with one beautifully arched glob aimed at the stands in Tampa, I visited him.

When he came to Atlanta to push fishing gear, I spent time with him.

When he has made business appearances for Sears, Roebuck, I've had some good moments with him. But sometimes it's like walking on eggs.

Once I asked him, "Just who is J.C. Higgins, if there is one?"

"How the hell do I know?" he said. J.C. Higgins is the Sears, Roebuck sporting-goods line, and, as far as I know, is as fictitious as Ann Page or Sterling Silver.

As he aged, he appeared to mellow some. Surely, as he grew older, he acquired a mature handsomeness that blended with this impression.

Yet to the bitter, bitter end, which should have been one of his sweetest moments, he left Boston still not knowing what to make of him. Cab drivers, elevator operators, waiters, barbers, the plain people loved him. They separated him from themselves as an idol.

The average man who had to get along with him on a day-to-day basis of baseball or business never knew whether to smile or kneel.

He hit a home run his final time at bat in Fenway Park, and

here the confusion of reports fittingly marked his last act. Some depicted him as "calm, gracious." Others as refusing to take a last bow or tip his cap.

"He wanted the home run," one report read, "so he could sit there while the crowd yelled for him and tell them to go to hell."

He was asked if he didn't feel something as he ran in from left field for the last time. "No sentimentality? No gratitude? No sadness?"

"I felt nothing," Williams said, "nothing, nothing, nothing!"

Robert Short is a bold man to bring Ted Williams back to baseball as his manager. Maybe by this stage of life he has learned how to manage himself. This is the first man a manager must be able to manage.

Oh, it'll get attention. The Washington Senators will look like a war correspondents' press pool this spring. The confusion of reports will be no less than when he played, when Paul Gallico wrote, "You are not a nice fellow, Brother Williams." And when another wrote, "All the cab drivers love him." Maybe more cab drivers should own typewriters.

RUMINATIONS FROM AN OVERSTUFFED SOFA

FEBRUARY 17, 1987

Ted Williams was talking hitting, from a position of total comfort half-buried in an overstuffed sofa in his hotel suite. When Ted Williams talks hitting, it is advisable to listen, as it was when Bernard Baruch talked investing from a park bench.

Williams was not the greatest baseball player that ever lived. All he'd asked as a young man was that he could become the best hitter that ever lived. There was never one better.

"It's the hips," he said. "That's the key."

"Jim Rice came to me during the season last year and wanted to talk about hitting. I had never talked to Rice about hitting. Let him come to me. I told him the hips lead the hands through the swing. He was getting his hands too far in front of his hips trying to pull the ball, and it was causing him to hit ground balls. Pitchers and infielders love to see you hit ground balls."

It must have worked. In mid-August, Rice had hit only nine home runs. The last month and a half, he hit eleven.

"The best hitter in baseball today?" I asked him.

"The guy from the Yankees," he said, meaning Don Mattingly. "I have to go along with him, but I'm not sure the kid from California [Wally Joyner] isn't going to be as good as any of them.

"Wade Boggs is a good hitter, but he's the Rod Carew type, sprays it around. Oh, what a hitter I thought Dale Murphy was going to be. What a beautiful swing, but he goes after too many bad pitches, especially last season. What went wrong with him?"

"Trying to carry the whole team by himself," I said.

"I hear people say that, and I don't agree. I tried as hard as I could every time I went to bat. That's what you're supposed to do. I wanted to carry the team. No, I don't buy that."

One of the great running backs of this area, the legend named Charlie Justice, came up. The subjects were jumping from one game to another. Here Williams murmured, "If I coulda run. . .if I coulda only run, I could have had some fun."

Ground speed was not part of his game. In all his years, he stole only twenty-four bases, though why would you risk a lifetime .344 hitter stealing bases?

"Tell me some of the great athletes you saw or knew," he said, turning interviewer.

I told him that I'd seen Dempsey fight, saw Bill Tilden play tennis, saw Shoeless Joe Jackson play baseball (forty-six years old in a textile league), saw Cy Young pitch (sixty-seven years old and barnstorming), knew Red Grange, Bobby Jones and Ty Cobb, and saw Jim Londos wrestle.

"I knew Strangler Lewis," he said. "I asked him to try the stranglehold on me to see if it was really anything. He almost squeezed my head out of shape.

"I met Bobby Jones. I saw Rocky Marciano come out of a hotel and I said this can't really be the heavyweight champion of the world. He was so small. For my money, Joe Louis was the greatest fighter ever lived. Did you ever see Babe Ruth or Lou Gehrig?"

I didn't. I did see Babe Ruth in death. I happened to be in New York the day he died.

"I knew them both, but the Babe already was talking in a croak when I met him. I really didn't meet Gehrig, but I walked up the stairs behind him and I remember I had to slow down because he was already a sick man.

"I knew Ty Cobb well." Here he sat up and fire came with the voice. "Some guy wrote this story that we didn't get along very well. We got along just great. I never had any trouble with Ty Cobb. I think it bothered him that he lived in the shadow of Babe Ruth. He was bitter about that, I think.

"I met Judge Landis. I met Walter Johnson. He was a tall, rawboned kind of man. He was a congressman from Maryland then and I was nineteen years old. I never heard anybody speak an unkind word about Walter Johnson.

"I liked Happy Chandler. He was the players' commissioner.

What do you think of Ueberroth?" He paused for a minute for his own answer. "Peter Ueberroth, if he stays with it, I think will go down as the greatest commissioner of them all."

Other old heroic names flowed through his mind. "I knew Connie Mack, of course. I met Rube Marquard, the left-hander who won nineteen games in a row, and it's still the record. I spent a lot of time with Jim Thorpe when we both worked for Sears, Roebuck. I remember just watching him move made you know he was a special athlete. I think he liked baseball best because he was proud of his record in the big leagues. He played in a World Series, you know."

It was maybe two hours later, the sun was fading away leaving the horizon one long fiery streak, when the Hall of Fame came up. Williams is a member of the Old-timers Committee, and it meets shortly to vote on its 1987 favorites.

"What do you think about Roger Maris, and Babe Herman, and Wesley Ferrell?" he asked, but my answers are of no consequence here.

"Babe Herman was a great hitter," he said, and Williams has great respect for the batsman. ("Hitting a baseball is the hardest one thing there is to do in sports.") "What do you think his lifetime average was? .324. They talk about his fielding, but he said, 'You get a reputation early, it never fades.' And he could run.

"Ferrell won twenty games his first four seasons in the big leagues." And he won more than twenty twice more. "Then his arm went bad. And he was a fine hitter. He's a tough case. I think he belongs. So does Joe Gordon. Look at his record. He had power. He hit home runs, drove in runs, and there was no doubt about his glove. I helped Bobby Doerr get in last year, now it's Gordon's turn."

Mellowing factors have seeped into the Williams, who is two years away from seventy. He has taken up tennis with the kind of passion Williams takes up anything.

"I don't fish as much anymore," he said. "Tennis is great for condition. I'm about an average B-player, I guess."

The fiftieth reunion of his high-school class comes up in San Diego in March, and guess who's going to be there? TW.

"They've invited me for years and I've never gone. I'm going this time, and I'm looking forward to it, to see the guys I played baseball with. Yes, yes, I'm looking forward to it."

He lives well. He was the first big-league player favored with a deferred-payment contract. He has squirreled away his earnings carefully. Soon he'll take leave of the Florida Keys and establish residence at a development near Homasassa Springs. He has an 18-year-old son at Bates College, a fifteen-year-old daughter with her mother in Vermont, and the usual responsibilities of a concerned father, though at long distance. All of these serve to make mellow of a man who majored in swinging a bat and earned his doctorate.

A GOD
ANSWERING
LETTERS

FEBRUARY 15, 1987

RALEIGH, North Carolina—Almost every time Ted Williams's name crosses my mind, I am nudged back onto the gentle, nostalgic piece that John Updike wrote of the "Splendid Splinter's" last game at Fenway Park. Updike is making his explanation of why Williams does not tip his cap to acknowledge applause, and did not that same afternoon after he had struck the 521st home run of his life in the American League off a journeyman pitcher named Jack Fisher.

"Gods do not answer letters," Updike wrote, which clearly and coldly established Ted Williams among those of sporting immortality.

That in mind, this was an event, twenty-seven years later. Ted Williams was going public, a rare occasion. He is puzzled yet that there should be such a clamor about him wherever he appears, not realizing that the precious little he allows of himself to be beheld only heightens the fascination of the curious.

He had come from his retreat in Islamorada, among the Florida Keys, to bestow upon the thirty-seventh annual Hot Stove League dinner the aura of his presence.

"First time I've done anything like this in five years," he said. He raised his voice and it came out like a trumpet.

The moment he walked into the McKimmon Center at North Carolina State University, the room tilted. Every live body was drawn to him like a magnet. For a man who had professed a high disdain for such sycophantics, he lightened up, turned on the charm, and was especially attentive to the small fry.

"Do you know who Ted Williams is?" one bright-eyed chap of about twelve years was asked. He was standing in line waiting for an autograph.

"Yessir, he plays for the Boston Red Sox," he said. You could forgive the present tense.

"What position?"

"Outfield."

"What was his lifetime batting average?"

".341," he said. It was .344, but you allow three points for the generation gap.

The room was oversold. An ancient secretary of state, Thad Eure, fifty-one years at the post, said it was the biggest crowd that hall had ever seen. Old players and old Marine Corps pilots came to him—some timorously, some brashly.

Old players, like Tommy Byrne, a left-handed pitcher with the Yankees, now the mayor of nearby Wake Forest, traded friendly barbs.

Williams addressed them all: "Nice to see yuh." He took up extra time with an old pilot from his squadron in Korea, his hair white, his eyes magnified by thick spectacles.

Wars were not kind to Williams. The military took almost five seasons out of the tenderloin of his baseball career. When this traveler first came across him, he was an instructor at Bronson Field, an outlying Marine Corps base near Pensacola. He did a tour in the Pacific after Hiroshima, but when the shooting broke out in Korea, he was called again in 1952. He was thirty-three years old. This time it was for show. He was an example. No politician had the guts to intervene.

Williams never complained. Stretch the kind of record he built over twenty-three seasons instead of eighteen, some major-league history would have to be rewritten. There was no reason, on performance, to go when he went, except that he was ready to go.

"I was forty-three years old, and I'd come back from the bad season," he said. The year before he kissed the game good-bye, he had hit under .300 the only time in his life. The .254 could be blamed on a cranky neck that kept him under treatment most of the season.

He batted .316 the final year of 1960, but it is the home runs that are still alive in his mind. "I hit twenty-nine that season, and I only went to bat 310 times," he said. "That's a home run almost every eleven times at bat."

He was proud of that at sixty-eight, sprawled across a plump sofa in his suite in the Sheraton Imperial. For a couple of hours or more, we'd enjoyed small talk in this refuge, waiting for the evening. An old-time minor-league slugger named Willie Duke, who had been a teammate when Williams played at Minneapolis, and whose trail crossed this country back and forth when there was pride in the bush leagues, was responsible for breaking Williams out of his seclusion.

Willie is an elf, a living cartoon of a community doer whose leading forte is persistence. This isn't the first time he has leaned on Williams, but the fifth, and something in the little man's perseverance brings the great man in response in a day of players made indifferent by exaggerated wealth.

"An old pitcher named Howard Craghead once talked to me when I was starting out in 1936," Williams said. "He was a scholarly man, a teacher, one you listened to. He was telling me that I had a future in the game.

" 'Ted,' he said, 'you've got a chance to make $250,000 in this game.' "

Williams paused for the laugh, then joined in the laugh himself. "Now there are guys who make $2,500 each time they go to bat, and some making that much sitting on the bench."

That was only the beginning.

Some Dear, Departed Friends and Others

A DEATH IN THE FAMILY

NOVEMBER 19, 1968

He had a hide the rich brown color of the glow from a dying autumn fire. Don't ask me why an autumn fire. I guess that's just a personal assumption that all things are browner, redder, yellower, oranger, or whatever color they may be, at that time of year. And so is the glow from a fireplace.

He had a tail that never stopped wagging. Never. Even when he was on guard against a suspected menace, one end barked while the other end wagged.

He never could quite make up his mind if he wanted to be inside the house or outside. When he was outside, he wanted inside, and when he was inside, there always seemed to be some little matter of business he had to attend to outside.

He was always prompt at mealtime. If you forgot it, he had a habit of reminding you. He did everything but show up carrying his bowl in his mouth and pointing.

He had personality. *Really,* personality. His eyes burned out at you like two little dark coals. If you didn't have time to be bothered, he still managed to get your attention. He just turned those two little eyes on.

And when you brought him home from the veterinarian. . . well, you never saw such appreciation. He would either sit serenely in the middle of the back seat, ears at attention, so that the public would notice that he'd been sprung again. Or he'd snuggle his little head in your lap and gaze up at you with deep affection.

His name was Dean, a peculiar name for a dog. It came from the man who gave him to us. But he was too much like people to have a common dog name like Bowser, or Rover, or Frisky, or Spot.

Dean suggested a superior intellect. We all thought it was appropriate, for he was naturally smarter than the average dog.

Honestly, we'd finally reached the conclusion that he had

achieved indestructibility. You know, by the time a kid has grown up to dancing age, he has outlived two or three dogs, each of whom seemed absolutely irreplaceable at the time of demise.

Dean had had two previous encounters with automobiles, each of which he won. After one of them, he did have to get about on an aluminum "crutch" for several weeks, but it never seemed to slow him down.

He had a streak going, in other words.

Well, his streak ended in the afternoon traffic. He took a shot at the field, *almost* made it, but one of the cars brought him down. The driver didn't have a chance. He looked up and there was a bundle of autumn-brown dog in front of him and no place to go.

At least Dean could say that he left this earth a winner. His record was 2-and-1.

Funeral services were simple. Brief. Tender.

We didn't allow his body to grow cold and stiff. We wrapped him in an old shirt and put him away while he was still warm. That way we can think of him as just having a nap.

Two little boys sobbed and snubbed and their bodies shook uncontrollably. A smaller one stood with a stark look on his baby face. He still doesn't quite understand about death. Where the dead go and that it's really final.

The next morning, the little one seemed to be grasping the meaning. He had taken down the portrait of Dean he had drawn at school. He folded it and put it on a chair arm.

"I won't need it anymore," he said. "Dean's dead."

It's still lying on the chair arm.

I wouldn't say it's an exact likeness. In some places it looks a little more like a lamb. But Dean wasn't like just every kind of dog. It's not easy to draw a very special kind of dog.

He was an amalgamation of the Irish setter and the cocker spaniel. He was registered only in our hearts. But a prettier dog you just don't see. He looked, if I had to brand him, more like a Gordon setter than any of the pedigreed. I recommend that more setters and more spaniels amalgamate.

How that dog liked to roam! The city wasn't right for him, anyway. A dog shouldn't have to worry about automobiles. Only jaywalkers and halfbacks should be dodging human projectiles.

Give Dean an open field and he'd run until nightfall. One week on vacation, I thought he was going to free Hilton Head

Island of the seagull menace. No bird dared land within his range.

All dogs are irreplaceable at the moment of death, but most of them are eventually replaced. Dean is the exception. Dean, I don't believe, can ever be replaced. We'll have another dog. He may be with us another seven or eight years. But he won't replace Dean.

I can see his little grave from where I'm sitting. A few brown leaves from a maple tree have drifted down and fallen on it. I didn't cry yesterday. I couldn't afford to. It upsets little boys to see their daddy cry. It's my turn now when nobody else can see.

One of them said last night, wistfully, "I bet I get up in the morning and go to let Dean out, and then I'll remember."

I wish Dean were here right now. I'd gladly give him his choice. Inside or out? And I wouldn't complain one bit.

"THE CURE" COMES TO BOBBY JONES

DECEMBER 20, 1971

The final decisive humbling of man is death. It comes to each and all in various manners, and sometimes the lowly are redeemed in the end by dying heroically, and sometimes those of highest dignity are brought to their passing by the most excruciating of forms.

Several years ago—and I am not certain of the year for it is unimportant now—Robert Tyre Jones, Jr., and I sat and talked of life and philosophy and great moments until we finally arrived at a discussion of the ailment that had so viciously disabled him.

"What is the nature of it?" I asked him.

"The medical name for it is syringomyelia," he said. "I call it pure hell."

"Is there any cure for it?"

"Oh, yes," he said.

"What is it?" I asked.

There was a brief pause. Then he said, "Death."

Saturday morning, while I was heading toward Swainsboro for a dove shoot with Governor Jimmy Carter, Bob Jones finally got "the cure." In the most devastating, excruciating of forms. Drawn, withered, shrunken, cruelly stripped of all the dramatic coordinations that created of him the most celebrated player of golf in all these centuries, death finally mercifully arrived.

The one faculty spared him to the final stroke was his brilliance of mind. Never, ever, during the siege that seized upon him and never relented, did that great man lose one ounce of his mental presence, for which some great power unknown to us all is to be given grateful thanks.

Any attempt to describe Bob Jones to a world whose people

respond to the name is squandered effort. There is no vouching for this story, and frankly I doubt the authenticity of it, but many years ago it was related to me.

Some great hunter invading darkest Africa supposedly came upon this tribe and was confronted by the chieftain. This hunter, being from Atlanta, discovered to his relief that the chieftain was conversant in English and explained to him that he came from the United States. "Atlanta, Georgia," he said.

"Ot-lawnta, Geo-ghia?" said the chieftain, and a light flashed on in the dark man's face. "Ah, Bobby Jones and Coca-Cola."

Of all the athletes who have competed on the face of this globe, regardless of the game or the continent, the one untarnishable image was that of Bob Jones. The one supreme player, whether he struck golf balls, punted footballs, pitched baseballs, smote tennis balls, kicked soccer balls, attacked wild animals, or climbed mountain peaks, was Bob Jones.

The one ultimate ambition of every athlete, also regardless of his game, was to be regarded in that game as Bob Jones was in his.

I have no accounting for the number of columns and magazine stories I have written on other golfers. But to a man, all of them appear to have been inspired to be another Bob Jones.

Arnold Palmer, as he stood across that creek that coursed through the grounds where his father was the professional, said to himself as a boy, "I am Bobby Jones, and this shot is for the national championship."

When Jack Nicklaus set a goal for himself, it was to exceed Jones's record of thirteen major championships. And that's only skimming the cream off the top.

The most fascinating story was that of Bob Jones's first exposure to golf. It was bound to have happened one way or another, I'm certain, but to my mind, one of life's most unrewarded men was the anonymous fellow who took the cleek out of his bag at old East Lake Country Club and bestowed it upon the child Jones.

East Lake in those times was a summer colony to which Atlanta families repaired in the hot season. It was ten miles from downtown and a long streetcar ride. The Jones family lived in a boardinghouse operated by a Mrs. Meador.

"One of the tenants," Bob once told me, "was a man named Fulton Colville, a member of the club who played golf. I followed him about a good deal, as children will, but I had no interest in golf. I was only six or seven years old.

"One day he gave me an old cleek out of his bag. It was much too long for me. My father took it over to Jimmy Maiden at the pro shop and Jimmy sawed it off and put a grip on it for me. I dug a hole in the top of a little hill and began playing up and down the street with it. Those were the days when you could turn a child loose in the streets, and that was how I was introduced to golf."

He was born in an old residence across from Grant Park, delivered by a family doctor named Kendrick. In those days, nobody was born in hospitals. He was an only child, sickly in the early years, but obviously the object around which his father orbited, for they came to enjoy a remarkable relationship.

He was bred to good manners and gracious living. Throughout his life, he successfully depicted the term *gentleman*. He was, in truth, *the* gentleman athlete as the term originated.

WHEN SINGLE WING WAS KING

OCTOBER 8, 1986

When old men die, only old men are left to speak of them in their prime. The years often take the sharp edge off the memories and soften the harsher tones. The stubborn and the humorless will have been graduated into the class of the revered by the very extension of their stay in life.

This is not to say that Wallace Wade was humorless, but one had to be alert to catch his wit. It had a bite to it. He could smile, but he never filled a room with laughter.

Stubbornness once cost him the most humiliating beating of his life. Don Faurot brought a Missouri team using his split-T formation to play Duke. Scouting was not a science in 1948, and Wade was not on speaking terms with the split-T, but even if he had been, he'd have played it his way. He crashed his ends all day and Missouri backs kept breezing by the bewildered lads until the quarterback himself had gained more than 200 yards on foot.

Stubborn was the theme of football in the era of Wade. It wore the mantle of the single-wing formation. Play defense, kick the ball, and wear the other team down with power. The single-wing offense pointed where it was going and went there.

William Wallace Wade belonged to the age of Bob Neyland, Jock Sutherland, Lou Little, Knute Rockne, Carl Snavely, and other greats. The football coach was not today's public figure, who visits our parlors by television with his game film. He was a private, often aloof person, approached with trepidation.

Wallace Wade laid the foundation for his legend at Alabama. He continued and enlarged upon it at Duke. Between the two campuses, his teams won 171 games. He took five teams to the Rose Bowl. He'd played as a guard at Brown and became the first player to come back to Pasadena as a coach.

He lost four years to World War II, not swiveling behind a

desk, but as a lieutenant colonel in the infantry. He lost more, as it turned out. When he came back, he found the game changed. The most shocking score of the early postwar years was "N.C. State 13, Duke 6."

N.C. State didn't *beat* Duke. It was the old soldier's welcome back from war, and more defeats than he had been accustomed to would follow.

He was the winning coach in one of the greatest games these old eyes ever saw. Both Duke and Pitt were powers in 1938. Neither offense scored. Eric Tipton kept punting out of bounds near Pitt's goal line until Bolo Perdue, a crashing end, finally blocked a punt and Duke won, 7-0. In a snowstorm. In Pitt's kind of weather. In Durham.

Some said all Wade had to do was raise his hand and he controlled the weather. But a snowstorm in Durham?

He was kind to at least one sprig of a writer, in days when coaches spent little time with such types, except on joyous journeys by train. He spent many a Sunday hour patiently explaining the intricacies of the game to this fledgling, who later became president of the American Football Writers, prompting the then-retired coach to say, "What has this game come to?"

Wade retired to thirty-six more years as a rancher near Durham in 1950. He lived to sit in the stadium Duke University thoughtfully renamed for him, and when he wasn't on hand at some sporting event, his door was always open at Creedmoor. Wherever he served, he served with distinction, whether the serious matter of war or the serious matter of games.

This has been a season of mourning for Duke University. First, Bill Murray, who followed Wallace Wade and restored some of the glory, took his leave. In the summer, Ted Mann, who covered the flanks of both from the press office, passed on. Now, ninety-four years after he was born into the family of a Tennessee farmer, Wallace Wade has joined them. It takes a stubborn man to persist in life ninety-four years.

HE TOOK
ON GIANTS

JUNE 6, 1986

Bryan M. Grant, Jr. was only a name on a marker by the side of Northside Drive to thousands who passed on the way to work each day. All they knew was that it announced the proximity of some tennis courts. Not many knew whether there was a Bryan M. Grant, Jr.—probably the precinct councilman—and fewer still realized that the one and the same might be out there playing his game.

Rare is the athlete, no matter how celebrated, who has been privileged to play on grounds bearing his own name. Old Atlanta was pretty thoughtful about ennobling its own. Right next door is the Bobby Jones Golf Course, a glorious name squandered on a trifling municipal project. If it ever was Jones's misfortune to play a round on it, it escaped me.

Bryan M. Grant, Jr. was "Bitsy," for the reason that there wasn't much of him. He was so small that his father, quite a player himself, passed him over and dwelt upon trying to make the big-time player out of his bigger brother, Berry. It was left to Mama if the runt of the litter was to get any training, and so we score another victory for the lady of the house.

Bitsy was impossibly undersized for international tennis, a destroyer among battleships, a Volkswagen against Packards. If any athlete ever inspired the word *competitor*, it was this 125-pound package of grit.

He took on Donald Budge, who was tall and strong. He took on Ellsworth Vines, who was tall and had the wingspan of a bomber. Each was the finest player in the world in his prime. It is duly recorded in the history of tennis that Bitsy Grant laid upon them the worst defeats of their careers—Vines at Forest Hills in 1933, Budge in Miami in 1937.

Bitsy had a way of leaving a big hurt on some big men. I'd guess the high moment of his long career, fought as a bantamweight among Goliaths, was the Davis Cup matches of

210

1937. He had been bypassed for the U.S. team so many times the South had worked up a strong hate toward the stiffbacks who ran the USLTA. There was one man up there who liked him, Walter Pate, Davis Cup captain that year. Against the better judgment of all, Pate appointed Grant as Budge's singles partner against the Australians in a challenge match.

He knocked off Jack Bromwich one day and Jack Crawford the next, at a time when the Aussies were two of the finest players in the world. As smashing as that was, when it came to picking the team to play the British in the finals, Bitsy was put down again, and Atlanta bared its saber.

When it was all summed up, though, the day he beat Vines, such a versatile fellow that he later became a winning player on the golf tour, was the day of deepest satisfaction.

"That was my greatest thrill in tennis," he said some years ago. He had beaten Vines on grass. Dirt was his surface—good old Georgia red dirt upon which Mama had taught him.

"That wasn't the best I ever played on grass, though. That was when I beat von Cramm at Forest Hills in 1937."

That match ran out to five sets and into the darkness, "brilliantly and fiercely fought," as was written in those days. Bitsy had to win the last two sets to beat the German baron, upon which the West Side Tennis Club erupted into a frenzied ovation.

Bitsy led the nation in retiring, and as many times as he retired, he unretired. The doggedness in him wouldn't let him quit. Small as he was, he even tried basketball at North Carolina and made the freshman team. It was there that he came upon his doubles partner of long years' standing, Wilmer Hines, a South Carolinian, later followed by Russell Bobbitt, an Atlanta comrade.

Those were the days of long white ducks, tournaments at the club, and restrictive behavior. John McEnroe would have been sent to the woodshed. Bitsy lived close enough to censure. He had a temper as large as his body was small. He could scorch a pasture with his venom, but usually his severe remarks were addressed to himself, not some courtly gentleman in the chair.

He was my insurance consultant for years, meticulously dealing with the most insignificant item. He spoke with a nervous delivery and punctuated conversation with a matching laugh. Rarely did he ever speak of the game. Yet it was his life to the point that as recently as two months ago, he was still on the court at the center they named for him.

The last time we talked, he called about a stolen dog. Some thief had purloined his car and inside the car, which Bitsy had left running to keep his animal cool on a hot summer's day, was his beloved pet. The car had been stolen, too, but all Bitsy wanted back was his pooch. The hell with the car.

That was Bitsy loyalty for you, the wee fellow who died yesterday of cancer. Strangely, you might say, his big brother Berry died just a few weeks ago in Charlotte. Both cut down by the same killer.

A PLAIN AND SIMPLE MAN

DECEMBER 8, 1951

Shoeless Joe Jackson was a plain and simple man who thought in plain and simple ways. He stood out from his kind only by a remarkable athletic instinct, and an extra sense that made him one of baseball's great hitters. They say he was the greatest natural hitter that ever lived.

But without a bat in his hands, he had a weakness. He relied heavily on his friends for guidance. Any person kind to him got in return warmth and trust, and it has since been proven that Joe's trust was in bad hands.

I'm sure that he went to his death the other night in Greenville, South Carolina, still clear of conscience. I'm sure that when and if he did accept a spot of cash for an intended part in fixing the scandalous World Series of 1919 between his Chicago White Sox and the Cincinnati Reds he did so without realizing that he was committing a wrong. He was that simple a man, and that trusting in the teammates he thought he knew so well.

I know his own story because I spent several days with him a couple of years ago recording it for a magazine. It was published "by Joe Jackson as told to," etc., though Joe to his death had never learned to read or write.

He began in plain and simple manner one August day as we sat under a small tree on the lawn of his neat little home.

"I'm not what you call a Christian," he said, "but I believe in that Good Book. What you sow, so shall you reap. I asked the Lord for guidance and I'm sure he gave it to me.

"Baseball failed to keep faith with me. When I got notice of my suspension, three days before the 1920 season ended, it said that if I was found innocent, I would be reinstated. If found guilty, I would be banned for life.

"I was found innocent. I walked out of Judge Dever's courtroom in Chicago in 1921 a free man. I had been acquitted by a twelve-man jury in a civil court. I thought when my trial was over, Judge

Landis would restore me to good standing. But he never did. And to this day I have never gone before him, sent a representative before him, or placed any written matter before him pleading my case. I gave baseball my best, and if the game didn't care enough to see me get a square deal, then I wouldn't go out of my way to get back in it.

"It was never explained to me officially, but I was told that Judge Landis said I was banned because of the company I kept. I roomed with Claude Williams the pitcher, one of the ringleaders. But I had to take whoever they assigned me on the road. I had no power over that."

Didn't he know something was going on?

"Sure, I'd heard talk. I even had a fellow come to me one day and proposition me. It was on the sixteenth floor of a hotel and there were four other people there, two men and their wives. I told him, 'Why, you cheap so-and-so, either me or you, one is going out that window!' I started for him, but he ran and I never saw him again.

"I went to Mr. Charles Comiskey [White Sox owner] before the World Series and asked him to keep me out of the lineup. He refused, and I begged him to tell the newspapers he suspended me for being drunk, or anything, but leave me out of the series and then there could be no question.

"I went out and played my heart out against Cincinnati. I set a record that still stands for the most hits in a series. It has been tied, I think. I made thirteen hits, but after all the trouble came out, they took one away from me. Maurice Rath went over in the hole and knocked down a hot grounder, but he couldn't make a throw on it. They scored it a hit then, but changed it later. I led both teams in hitting with .375. I hit our only home run of the series. I handled thirty balls without an error. I came all the way home from first and scored the winning run in a 5-4 game.

"That's my record in the series, and I was responsible only for Joe Jackson. There was just one thing that didn't seem quite right now as I think back over it. Eddie Cicotte seemed to let up on a pitch to Pat Duncan and Pat hit it over my head. Duncan didn't have enough power to hit the ball that far if Cicotte had been bearing down."

Joe strengthened his case of conscience by pointing to the good fortune that followed him after his banishment.

"Everything I touched seemed to turn out good for me. I've got a nice home and a seventeen-acre farm. See that lot across the street over there? I paid $240 for it and sold it for $800 in twenty-four hours."

What you sow, so shall you reap. . . .

Joe always did say that "Say it ain't so, Joe" story was a hoax.

He charged it to a Chicago sportswriter named Charley Owens, who at least must be given a stout hurrah for his imagination.

"It was supposed to have happened the day I was arrested in September 1920, when I came out of the courtroom hearing. There weren't any words passed between anybody, except me and a deputy sheriff. He asked for a ride to the South Side and we got into the car together and left. Charley Owens just made up a good story and wrote it. Oh, I'd have said it wasn't so, all right, just like I'm saying it now."

Joe lived his last years in quiet and comfort, a man who dressed well, drove a Packard, and doted on the respect of his South Carolina neighbors. It is perhaps odd, but when he died, he was chairman of the protest committee of a semipro league around Greenville. Someone else was always delegated to read the protests and write the committee reports, it should be added.

THE ROOKIE NOBODY WOULD BELIEVE

APRIL 22, 1958

George P. Howard, Jr. died the other day, and with him went not only one of the world's most gentle and lovable souls, but also one of the last of the few untold truths of the most famous college football game ever played, and the worst.

He had an early brush with journalism, and it was his debut that is this story. It happened on October 7, 1916, when he was a freshman at Georgia Tech.

The Howard family had connections through which he was able to line up a job as campus sports correspondent for the *Atlanta Journal.* His first assignment was to cover this football game, walking the sidelines reporting a telephone play-by-play account to a rewrite man on the *Journal* desk.

Freshman Howard began with a report on the weather (fair and hot) and the crowd (about 1,000). He reported, too, that Tech won the toss but chose to kick off, which seemed somewhat radical, for John Heisman was a man greedy about his offense.

"Preas kicks off to Carney," George P., the freshman reporter, began, "who is downed in his tracks. Gouger goes over tackle for three yards. McDonald makes no gain in the center of the line. McDonald punts and Preas runs back to the Cumberland 20.

"Strupper sweeps right end for a touchdown. Preas kicks the extra point. Tech 7, Cumberland 0.

"Spence kicks off and Gouger returns to the Cumberland 10. Murphy fumbles, Guill recovers for Tech and scores a touchdown. Preas kicks the extra point. Tech 14, Cumberland 0."

All of this action had consumed something like ninety seconds of playing time.

"Preas bucks the line for a touchdown. . . . Strupper runs for a touchdown. . . . Shaver returns a punt seventy yards for a touchdown. . . . Strupper sweeps end for sixty yards and a touchdown. . . ." And this went on until Georgia Tech had a lead of 63-0 at the end of the first quarter.

"Boy, what's going on out there?" the suspicious rewrite man asked George Howard, the freshman. "Are you sure you know what you're doing?"

"Yes, sir," George said, "I'm giving it to you the way it happens."

"But no football team scores every time it gets its hands on the ball," the rewrite man protested.

"Maybe not," George Howard said, "but Georgia Tech's doing it."

About the middle of the second quarter, George felt a yank at his sleeve. "Here, boy," said the yanker, "let me have that telephone."

The rewrite man had been ordered to the football field by the managing editor. George protested. "If you don't believe I've got it right," he said, "check with the scorekeeper."

In those days, the scorer sat at a table on the sidelines and he was an official of some stature. The rewrite man checked the scorer. To his disgruntlement, he found Tech's score was approaching 100 points, whereupon he mumbled an apology to George Howard and caught a trolley back to the *Journal* office.

It was something less than a mere coincidence that a freshman reporter was breaking in on one of sporting history's most incredible events. Georgia Tech beat Cumberland, 222-0.

STORMY WENT OUT LIKE HIS NAME

JUNE 28, 1970

Stormy Winters died in Macon the other day, but the flags didn't fly at half-mast and the post office stayed open. The mayor didn't declare a day of mourning. Even the garbage trucks went on collecting garbage.

You had to look all over town to find anybody who really cared, and she was in jail. She was charged with the shooting.

It was all right for Stormy to beat up people in a prizefight ring. That was his game. But she wasn't going to take any more of it. That was the story—the drab, sordid, real-life story that you find under the fictional title of *Fat City.*

Fat City is the grimy, sweat-stained, seamy account of the prizefight life at its lowest level. Basement training quarters with exposed plumbing, plodding stiffs who try to make it in tank-town prelims, anything to have a dressing robe with their name stitched on the back. Any kind of booking for forty bucks a night—before the manager's cut.

It was written by a young writer named Leonard Gardner out of California, and it may be as fine a novel of sport as I have ever read. One of its characters is a Stormy Winters, but only because there is a Stormy Winters in every town where boxing still survives, trying to make it out of the basement to Madison Square Garden. Or even the Miami Beach Auditorium.

This was where Stormy Winters made it, the Miami Beach Auditorium. He reached Miami on a bus from Georgia at 3 o'clock in the morning, and as Edwin Pope tells it in his column in the *Miami Herald,* he arrived wearing blue jeans, a T-shirt, and a "pair of round-toed farmer's shoes."

He wasn't "Stormy" yet. His name was Melvin Eugene. I think

the fighting name of "Stormy" came from that industrious promotor of world renown, Chris Dundee. Chris liked his style and called him the meanest fighter he'd seen since Jake LaMotta.

Dundee had never seen Stormy until he got off that bus and came to the 5th Street Gym on Miami Beach. Stormy wanted to be a prizefight champion, and that was why he was in Miami, recommended by a former heavyweight who was a friend of the Dundees.

I stood in the 5th Street Gym with Dundee one day and watched the kid work out. He was still in the prelim stage, but his time was coming. The question, as it inevitable does, came up—why a kid from a small town wants to be a boxer.

"I asked him that," Dundee said, "and he gave me a classic answer.

"He said, 'Mr. Dundee, have you ever poured tar on a roof in Macon, Georgia, in the summer time?' "

Stormy was a roofer by trade, and back to the rooftops he had gone when the bullet caught up with him in Macon.

There was a time when it seemed he was on his way. He fought, Pope says, about thirty-five times. He lost only four, and when he won, it was almost always by knockout, for Stormy was a man of dispatch when set loose in the ring.

Apparently Stormy was somewhat less diligent between fights, giving off in his search for thrills and sensual pleasures the kind of dull, brown, alcoholic morning-after odor of the debauchery of Billy Tully, the middleweight of *Fat City*.

Tully was a promising "scrapper," a term lifted directly from the handbills. He was on his way, unquestionably, to the top, when women intercepted him, followed in swift order by booze. The opening of *Fat City* finds him on his way to hell, downhill on a handcar. It's just a question of which upstairs dump of a hotel he'll find it in.

He works intermittently, long enough to keep in a supply of booze, in the walnut fields and on the truck farms in northern California. Always in his mind is the plan—ultimately he will find the wife who divorced him, and his world will be glued back together again, and he will straighten out, and the ring lights will come on again, and they will be introducing, in this corner, Billy Tully, "worthy adversary going for the championship of the world."

But the plan is only a mental mirage. He is finally found

sleeping in a trash-burner in the end—broke, hungry, penniless, with only the clothes on his back. Victim of a vagrant dream, alive but not living.

Stormy Winters never hit such depths. He worked the fourth-rate hotel circuit. Worked in amusement arcades between fights, obviously denying himself little of life's lust.

His weight went from 130 to 150, and some of his condition went with it. Pope says that Stormy's dream blacked out the night he fought a junior middleweight named Art Hernandez in 1965. Stormy was 24-for-25 until that bout. That was his big one. The ring lights came up and there he stood in his robe—with his name stitched on the back—ready to revise the history of prizefighting.

Hernandez took him easily. Everything else after that was downgrade. Life in a print shop, a halfhearted attempt at a comeback, a few matches, but his heart wasn't in it, and eventually, back to Macon, close to the farm where he grew up, and where his daddy had tried to scratch a few crops out of barren ground.

He was only twenty-six years old, too young for a kid to die. That's still young enough for dreams, and Stormy had one as he went out. He dreamed of being a country music singer. Some friends gave him a guitar last Christmas, but he never got around to lessons. He'd played that dream game before and lost.

HE BROKE HIS RECORD— AND NINETY- NINE BONES

AUGUST 6, 1974

The shill blew in with such a gust I barely noticed the little wisp of a fellow standing shyly outside. Almost with the obedience of a child waiting to be signaled that it was all right to come in.

It was about this same hour of the day, late in the afternoon. Office cleared of everyone but me. Streets outside still strangled with traffic of homebound cars. Quiet. Peace. Tranquility in here. A mass of congestion and fumes out there.

"I'm Bob Somebody," the advance man said. I can't recall his name. He was from Prattville, Alabama, I remember that.

He put some material on my desk and began talking. Almost as an afterthought, he brought in the little man standing outside. Who was going for the world's distance record in the motorcycle jump at Phenix City, Alabama, on August 4, Bob said.

"This is Bob Pleso," he said. "He has already done things Evel Knievel hasn't done."

On August 4 at Phenix City, Alabama, he did another. He died.

When Bob Pleso stepped inside the door, there was one thing that was impressive about him—there was so little of him. I doubt if he weighed 150, if his waist was as large as Tommy Nobis's thigh, or if he was strong enough to lift Paul Anderson's right arm. He had a wistful little face, pitch black eyes, and a very calm manner for a young man who was so eager to keep an appointment with self-destruction.

221

"I'm going to jump thirty cars and go for 200 feet, and that'll break the world record," Bob Pleso said.

He said the distance record was held by Bob Gill, who had jumped 171 feet and twenty-three cars.

"Knievel has never jumped as far as 150 feet," he said. "He's all talk and showmanship. I want to get there by doing something, not with my mouth. When I make this jump, I'm on my way."

What should have been the prime indicator to Bob Pleso was the widespread obscurity of Bob Gill. Here was the man who held the world record for jumping a motorcycle over obstacles and he was a stranger.

There was none of the braggart in Bob Pleso. He was as orderly as an altar boy. There was a firmness in his face, but none of the fiery intensity that marks a fanatic. He didn't pound on my desk or stamp his little feet and make demands. He was the guy who was going to break the world record for motorcycle jumping at Phenix Dragway on August 4, and the world was invited—if it didn't want to miss seeing Bob Pleso make it big. Bob Pleso was on his way.

The story said that the crowd was probably 2,500. More people used to come out and watch wing-walkers over country airfields in Iowa. Or gather around North Carolina pastures and watch the first of the parachute daredevils. Friday-night wrestling draws more. Not only is death not involved there, but all the participants know how they're going to come out in advance.

It was a large crowd for a funeral, though. Bob Pleso had said he wanted to go big. His brother was pleased with the coverage.

My God, pleased with the coverage!

Here was a little fellow who hadn't made more than thirty motorcycle jumps. Only two years at it. Only twenty-two years old. Not willing to wait it out, but forcing it. Throwing himself like a piece of beef on a bonfire and expecting to come away unscathed.

Taking a chance in an occult area. Beyond the limit of exploration. You throw it out there and if you see there's no way back, there's no way to call time!

Knievel jumped from ramp to ramp. Bob Pleso was showing him up. He wanted nothing but the ground to catch him. No ramp on the other end. "Everybody does that," he said. "To get attention, you've got to go beyond what the other guys do."

He came out of the Midwest—Wisconsin, I think it was. He settled in Ocala, Florida. He hadn't made much money. The 200-foot jump at Phenix City was supposed to open doors for him. There wasn't too much money in it. Probably 2,000 bucks or so. The big stuff was later.

His personal record was 161 feet and sixteen cars. Had four crack-ups. "But never a broken bone," he said, never once laying it on.

Funny thing, there wasn't an ounce of upstart or swagger in him. While he discounted Knievel, whose jump isn't a motorcycle jump at all, but a rocket shot ("He'll reach the peak of flight, pull the ripcord, and he'll float down with his machine and say something went wrong that caused the bailout"), he still gave him credit for creating a sensation in which such as Bob Pleso could share.

Well, Bob broke his own personal record Sunday. He cleared twenty-eight cars and about 185 feet. He also broke his first bone— and about ninety-nine others.

"This young fellow is on his way," Bob S. had said that day. "We just want the people to know about it."

They gathered up what remained of his little body and hauled it off to the hospital, and what part of him wasn't dead at the time soon was. One human being thought he saw a slither of fame through the forest of oblivion and it was only the wraith of death. God, what a waste of man.

But he got good coverage.

WALTER WELLESLEY SMITH

JANUARY 14, 1982

He was seventy-six when he died Friday. The shock wave the news spread through our industry was like the emptiness felt across the country when Bing Crosby died. A young sportswriter without Red Smith as his ideal was on a primrose course.

He was showing disturbing traces of age at the World Series, but each day, and night, he made his route faithfully in the discomfort that baseball inflicts on even one of his stature. Despite physically draining night flights, and cramped, jerry-built "press boxes," he still faithfully delivered his day's work to *The New York Times.*

When I last heard his voice, sometime in November, coming from his study in Connecticut, he said, "I'm sitting here groping." The column was his life and breath down to the very Monday of the week he died, and that beautiful mind of his never lost any wattage.

Red Smith started life in Green Bay, started newspapering in Milwaukee, then went to the *St. Louis Star-Times,* to the *Philadelphia Record,* the *New York Herald-Tribune,* the *World-Tribune-Journal,* and—if you can believe it—*Women's Wear Daily* before the ultimate marriage to *The Times.* Indictment of the Pulitzer Prize process is that his work wasn't recognized properly until he reached *The Times.* If ever there was a star of a more brilliant show in sports journalism than Red Smith when he played the lead on the old *Herald-Tribune,* I've never known it.

He grew up in Green Bay's football atmosphere. He waited tables in the players' dining hall at Notre Dame, then began newspapering as a city reporter. In later years, he moved to sports, and his affection switched to the more healthful surroundings of horse racing, fishing, and the outdoors. Those were his loves at the end, baseball's imbecilism having long since lost him.

His closest friend was Frank Graham, Sr., the *Journal-American* columnist. They traveled so many miles together they became known as "1" and "1A." After Graham died, Red took up with Jack Murphy of San Diego, drawn together as they were by fishing and horses. He outlasted them both, for Jack died of cancer before his time.

What Red Smith did most impressively was make a reader feel the scene he was writing from, delicately selecting only those relevancies that transmitted the mood of the event. And on deadline. Some of his choicest lines linger in my mind, such as his description of Cookie Lavagetto in the coaching box: "He clapped his hands intelligently," Red wrote from spring training.

Harry Truman came through in this humanizing vignette from an Army-Navy game: "A slight four-eyed man stood teetering on his tiptoes near the 40-yard line."

And when the British had to give back the only gold medal won in the Olympics of 1948, a track victory repealed by committee, he wrote: "The Royal Air Force band must now return to the desolate, forsaked field of Wembley and unplay 'God Save the King.' "

As lovely and gentle a man as he was, he could sting the ball. No one has felt it more than Bowie Kuhn, and the rapacious owners who have violated baseball in his eyes. He came along in a time when the game was a mistress to be cared for and adored. He unhappily saw it turned prostitute. It grieved him.

He lived well. He had his high times, sang many a night into the dawning hours harmonizing with misguided tenors, encouraged by strong potion. He had a taste for aged Scotch.

Red Smith was the last of the heavy hitters, all gone now: Grantland Rice, Bill Corum, John Kieran, Dan Parker, Joe Williams, Jimmy Cannon, Frank Graham, Arthur Daley, all who lived through their columns. Red Smith was the newspaperman's columnist, the consummate craftsman, a loss our trade can ill afford.

SOMETHING VERY PERSONAL

DECEMBER 31, 1986

Standing on the curb looking down upon the flickering lights of the modest business center of my hometown, the municipal Christmas ornaments still in place, it finally descended upon me, the desolate feeling that after all these years I must now face life without a parent.

Behind me, in the funeral parlor, the lighting reverently dimmed, the conversation descreetly hushed, lay my mother, free of pain at last. Ninety-four years seemed such a short time now.

"The end of an era in this town," the minister said in his eulogy. He was a young man whose sermonics had pleased my mother. Such godliness in youth appealed to her, and she wanted no ancient orator intoning her last rites.

"As close to a saint as I shall ever know," one of her adoring grandsons had said.

I hasten to declare her free of old-revival stodginess. She was of hearty spirit, she could laugh, listen well, resist with quiet stubbornness, enjoyed eating, and her kitchen was famed in its province. Testimonial to that was an embroidered verse framed on the wall:

"No matter where I serve my guests,

"It seems they like my kitchen best."

Just a month ago, I walked into her room and she was upright in bed crocheting an afghan one of her granddaughters had been working on for a year.

"I told Ann she was never going to finish that thing," she said, "bring it to me and I'd finish it for her."

She did. Just in time.

She was sick in bed the day my dad drove me off to college. When I sent my first batch of laundry home, she returned it with some of her cookies. I was reassured.

When I discovered journalism had been dropped at Furman,

and asked to switch to North Carolina, there was never a pause, though I had finally reached a scholarship state that eased the financial pain. Journalism was as foreign to them as Tibet. There wasn't even a newspaper in town. They felt confident that I was worth a further investment of their faith.

For all the wrath that I have directed at television, it nurtured her belated interest in sports, bringing Atlantic Coast Conference basketball. Her devotion centered on N.C. State, the Wolfpack. Her brother had been superintendent of the physical plant at State for more than three decades, and a building on the campus is named for him. She thought this was worthy of partiality. Besides, "I don't like the way Dean Smith acts at the games. Is he ever happy?"

When she broke into the big time as a spectator, it was at the top. She came to Atlanta for the Final Four in 1978, and then went home content to leave it to TV, glorying when N.C. State startled the world at Albuquerque. Someone even asked Jim Valvano to send her a note; she wasn't greatly impressed.

She would have rankled at being identified in death as "Mamie M. Bisher." Let the moderns go in their own style; she was "Mrs. C. Bisher" in her eyes. Her life was her man.

Forgive me if I have intruded on your good nature with something so heavily personal. But my heart is heavy. My loss is great. The hurt runs deep. Somehow, no matter how prepared I thought I was, I came up short.

Beyond that, those of you who care have the right to know something more about what lies behind that cragginess that peers out at you daily from the top of this pillar of piffle. The important things. To know that whatever may have gone wrong with this creature could not be traced to the hearth.

It was the morning of December 30, 1986, 8 o'clock, a layer of frost coating the brown leaves, that I drove out of the yard for the last time. No longer will it ever be home again. Without parent, without mother, home is no more.

Few of My Favorite Things

THE WORLD'S STRONGEST MAN

MAY 27, 1983

Downtown Toccoa had come to a halt, stock-still. It would be the afternoon rush hour back in Atlanta, but the streets here were silent and barren, except for an occasional car.

Out on Tugalo Street, at #912, a reason became apparent. Police had blocked off the area. Cars lined streets, poking in any which way. People stood quietly and listened, clustered in front of a house built of stone. In front of the house was a sixteen-ton monument of the finest granite Elberton could supply.

"Paul Anderson Day" was in full force, and thus the story moved forward with a plot as old as the granite itself, and now so Americanized we sometimes think we created it: Native son leaves home, native son gains great fame, native son returns and old hometown works up a lather doing him honor—in this case, long after the parade has passed.

Where Paul Anderson is known, he is known as "the world's strongest man." He brought Russians cheering to their feet in the rain in Moscow in 1955. He brought home a gold medal from the Olympic Games in Australia in 1956. He broke every world record a man could break lifting weights. He came home to Toccoa for his *coup de théâtre,* and on June 12, 1957, hoisted on his broad back a platform bearing 6,170 pounds, more than the weight of a Rolls-Royce. He didn't simply break the existing record for the human weight-lift, he shattered it by 2,270 pounds, or the weight of two horses!

The record is in the Guinness book, and now chiseled in the granite monument standing at 912 Tugalo Street that proclaims him "The World's Strongest Man." It was so dedicated Wednesday afternoon by the Toccoa–Stephens County Chamber of Commerce at the inspiration of a lady named Eletha Matuch.

This is only the surface Paul Anderson. The real Paul Anderson took up partnership with God in the midst of his pursuit of the gold medal in Melbourne, and has remained true to his pact. To him, this was recognition not for weights lifted, medals won, glory brought to his hometown, but of Paul Anderson, the humanitarian. This could never have been, though, without the sweaty, exhausting labor of lifting, more agony than sport, for this brought his name forth and gave him human leverage. Now he is dangerously ill. Before the week is out one of his sister's kidneys will have replaced a diseased kidney in his fifty-year-old body in an operation in Minnesota. Greater love hath no sister than Mrs. Julius Johnson, the donor.

From Tugalo Street, "Paul Anderson Day" moved out to the bank of Lake Louise, where in the Georgia Baptist Assembly hall, banqueting and speechmaking then took place. At the head table sat Paul Anderson, pale and drawn, the body that once weighed 375 pounds now wasted away by Bright's disease, his daughter and wife, Glenda, beside him.

Tom Landry, better known as coach of the Dallas Cowboys, had come to praise him—"a great man to honor a great man," as Jerry Campbell introduced him. Landry and Anderson came to know each other as directors of the Fellowship of Christian Athletes nearly twenty years ago.

"You may not recognize me without my hat on," Landry said, his baldness glistening under the glare of podium lights, and from there firmly and openly dealt with the consecrations they share. "We both love the Lord Jesus Christ, we believe in America, and we believe in the free-enterprise system," he said.

Beyond all the weights he has lifted, Paul Anderson's benchmark in life is the homes he has established for young people without caring parents or a base in life, troubled and neglected. The first was located in Vidalia because of a friendship struck and the sponsorship of Gerry Achenbach, now retired president of a supermarket system located there, and now two more homes serve Texas, which Landry and Don Carter, who owns the Dallas Mavericks, and friends have underwritten in spirit and financing.

Paul once made as many as 500 public appearances a year to finance his philanthropy. He wrestled professionally for a short time, giving himself a financial underpinning, and I never saw a more uncomfortable athlete than Paul Anderson doing combat with such as Masked Marvels I and II.

It was done now in the assembly hall, and time for Paul

Anderson to approach the rostrum. It had seemed he could not possibly have the strength, but yes, he stood, wavering somewhat, and he responded.

Out of that weakened body came the old Paul Anderson voice that boomed again with feeling and vibrance, and as he spoke his voice filled that huge hall.

"Don't weep for me," he told Toccoa, "don't weep for Paul Anderson, for I have been blessed. There was a time when I didn't think I could make it through the night, but I may make it now. While I once stood there the world's strongest man, I think I have been more effective these last few weeks while I've been weak."

Thomas Wolfe was wrong, he told his townspeople. "You can go home. You have brought me home, and I thank you for bringing me home."

He walks unsteadily, with the help of a cane. The exit was a scene from a movie not yet made, the once-mighty man, once huge of bulk and strength, plodding heavily along, leaning on the cane on one side, and on his beautiful wife, angelic in white, on the other. The people who had come to honor him sat in their chairs at the rows of long tables until he had disappeared through the doors, a broad smile on his wan face. Toccoa and Paul Anderson had their peace.

YOUNG MEN
AFLAME WITH
PROMISE

JUNE 7, 1978

You've seen the pilot for the scene from old movies in which John Wayne or Wayne Morris, dressed out in whites and starched shirts, salute briskly and get their wings, then march off to fight some war on film. The girl rushes up, Teresa Wright or Jane Wyman, and they embrace, thus accepting an indefinite future with their man.

I'd seen the caps tossed into the air, that final unleashing of four years of "sir-ing" and stiff backs. But only the newsreels, as far back as Fox Movietone. This was my first time seeing it in real life, at the Air Force Academy at Colorado Springs, which even Cecil B. DeMille, who was famed for what Hollywood came to call "extravaganzas," wouldn't have dared try to improve. The campus sits in symmetrical glory against a backdrop framed by the Rampart Range. The bladelike spires of the chapel, the most photographed and most visited of the buildings, symbolically posed above them all. Before the week was out, seventy-nine former cadets and brides would march to the altar there and become second lieutenant and missus.

Four years ago, 1,600 "Doolies"—"freshmen" to you and me—checked in at the academy, and last week 973 of them were rewarded with degrees. This is more than simply a graduation. It's a front-page news event in Colorado Springs and Denver, a full-hour television show, a week-long series of ceremonials, an emotional experience in which a great sigh of relief seems to rise from 973 gentlemen that says, "We survived."

I had seen graduations before, and have been graduated, but I had seen nothing such as this. Two days in a row, several thousands had come to the parade grounds to witness the awarding of honors and the last inspection of squadrons. The mornings were bright and crisp and the air crackling with the pealing brass of the drum and bugle corps. It made you want to go someplace and enlist.

Then the cadets came marching down the ramp, forty squadrons of them, from beneath that challenging slogan, "Bring Me Men." The white-trousered legs moving in a precise synchrony, and oh, the stirring sounds of a military band.

On graduation day, the scene transfers to Falcon Stadium. Little of consequence has taken place in the stadium the past four years, for the Falcon football team won barely a dozen games for the class of 1978. I hadn't run into such a jam of traffic, though. A mile from the parking lots, cars were queued up. There was a fermenting air that usually erupts into a big game.

This was no local ceremony. They come from across the country for June Week—not simply parents, but aunts and uncles, brothers and sisters, cousins and in-laws. By the time the seniors came marching down through the Talbot Portal, 20,000 spectators were in place.

I've known emotion, but this brought tears surging through your eye ducts. To know that it was over, that #162 was yours. "Hey, dad," he said later, "did you recognize me? I was in white pants with a blue jacket."

Chaplain James C. Townsend poured more fuel over the emotional coals. "These young men," he intoned, "aflame with the promise of America. . . ."

It was no occasion restricted to heavy solemnity. Some families brought out banners. HERE'S TO GARY. WE'RE PROUD OF CHRIS. And when graduates' names were called out, balloons, confetti, and streamers sometimes flew into the air, accompanied by cheers. It was in recognition of a triumph in academics.

One legend of the Air Force Academy has been dispensed with. "Tail-end Charlie" has been drummed out of the wing. "Charlie" was the cadet who brought up the rear in academics. The administration has come to decide that this was reflecting too much glamour on mediocrity, not to mention the fact that #973 would have collected a dollar from each of the other cadets. So this was the first year that nobody will ever know who finished last. Instead, a young fellow named Vincent Stewart Wilcox received the 973rd degree purely because he was the last man in the last squadron.

A Rick Searfoss was graduated as #1, but it wasn't all fun and glory. This is no place for the social bird. "At any other college you can go down and get a pizza on Friday night," Searfoss said, "but not here. On some of those Friday nights, I wondered if I belonged here."

There were few compensations in athletic excitement. A football coach who should have moved on stayed over after talking his way into a new contract when the superintendent intended to fire him. The coach was in line to become president of the national association of coaches.

The grand conclusion was the hurling of caps, a kind of safety-valve eruption. Urchins gather along the field, and as the caps go up, they bore in, and if you've ever really wondered, many of the hurled caps never make it back to the heads of the cadets who wore them.

AH, THE ENLIGHTENED AGE

JUNE 28, 1985

Two fellows who wrote in jointly a while ago under the name of Smith asked when I was going to join the twentieth century. They had been sorely put out by my view on college athletes and academics—in their eyes, most archaic. The very idea that any athlete should have to clutter up his life with reading, writing, and homework when he's busily engaged with the playbook, trying to nail down a bowl bid or a place in the Final Four!

I found the first half of the century to be right useful. Apparently, in the eyes of the two Smiths, my clock stopped in 1950 or 1960 and I took to my cave.

Well, let's take an inventory of what this side of the century has brought us in the sporting life. What exciting advances, what contributions to society:

- The sports strike. Not to be confused with a pitch over the plate or the football "bomb." This takes place like in any blue-collar union, except here we have guys under contract, making in a season what would have been a career's wages for Babe Ruth, walking off the job. Not many know what the issues are. (Issues? What's an issue?)

- The agent. This is the fellow who makes up a list of grievances for his bobo, sacks him for a fat percentage, and of whom a recent headline said it best: "Reputable Agents Few and Far Between."

- John McEnroe, Jimmy Connors, Ilie Nastase, and the tennis boor. Once the money came out from under the table, so did their manners. Two of the above may be without challenge called the epitomization of the American jerk.

- The drug life. I haven't kept a box score on the number

of athletes who have been through rehabilitation, jailed, put on probation, or committed suicide from addiction, but give the Smiths and their half of the twentieth century all the credit they want.

• Sports litigation. Little Leaguers sue. Girls sue to play ball with boys. Athletes sue agents. Agents sue athletes. Schools sue the NCAA, which is like suing themselves. Owners sue their league.

• The specialist. We have the baseball player who never goes to bat, the placekicker who never plays football, the relief pitcher, the career pinch-runner and pinch-hitter, the kick returner, the pass rusher, the third-down player, the tight end, split end, holder, long snapper, the hatchet man in basketball and the brawler in hockey. Laugh, if you will, but you never knew a real hero unless you saw a four-letter man, the athlete who could play any game—and make it in class, too.

• Television. The game has been delivered to the living room. The kickoff, the tee time, the first pitch or first serve available at any hour. We aim to please for the right price. It is our policy to oblige the network, the hell with the bloke who buys the ticket.

• The professional "amateur." Check the wage scale of the Olympian, the William Simon–pures like Carl Lewis, Edwin Moses, Mary Lou Retton, Mary Decker Whoeversheis, et al.

• The boycott. Americans boycott the Russian Olympics. Russians boycott the American Olympics. Argentines boycott the British. Red China boycotts the other China and everybody boycotts South Africa.

• The soccer hooligan. This is mainly an innovation of the extremely cultured British.

• The leapfrog franchise. Two baseball teams, the A's and the Braves, are now operating at their third stop. Washington gave birth to two teams and both took flight. And a toast here to two of the pioneer leapfroggers of the National Football League, Al Davis and Robert Irsay.

• The nonstudent athlete. This is a category for the musclehead who has an allergy to learning. He doesn't know how to form a declarative sentence, can't tell a participle from a pronoun, or find the square root of anything. Nor does he care. He was recruited to put the team on national television and hone his game for the pros.

- The NCAA Bureau of Investigation. In 1950 it was a staff of one. It is now up to the size of a herd. Walter Byers can't give you an accurate count, so many are off staking out campus felons.

- The dollar god. With which you try to buy tradition with a fat purse.

Then there are the torn rotator cuff, the pulled hamstring, the ruptured bursa, tendinitis, and all those other ailments of parts we didn't even know we had until we came into the enlightened age of rock music.

THE MARAVICHES, IN PRIME TIME

MARCH 27, 1970

Some forget that as a player he set scoring records at Davis and Elkins College in West Virginia. And that he played professional basketball for a few seasons when the living was primitive. And that he coached a championship team in the Atlantic Coast Conference, toughest basketball league in the South.

They think of him only in terms of a sire, as if he were Adios or Bull Lea. They think of him as Press Maravich, Pete Maravich's daddy, then as Press Maravich, basketball coach at Louisiana State University.

Press Maravich is a volatile man. He has a temper that goes off as if it were set for a certain time and temperature. Perhaps this relates to the origin of his name, for he is the only man I know who's named for a newspaper. When he was a kid, he carried the *Pittsburgh Press* in Aliquippa, Pennsylvania, where he was born, and so he became the "Press" kid around town. His real name is Peter.

Friends who know him well enough to take such a liberty refer to him as "The Screaming Serb." Men who officiate basketball games in the South will testify that it's appropriate. So will the son who played for him and broke every scoring record worth breaking in the colleges.

"Dammit!" Press Maravich screamed at Pete Maravich during a time-out once, "I'm the coach here and don't you forget it!"

On the other hand, he is capable of turning absolutely aglow in adulation of the son he has coached. Somebody suggested once that "he's a lot like Bob Cousy, isn't he, coach?"

"Cousy never saw the day he had moves like that," Press snapped back, almost offended at the comparison.

He has taken—with the accomplished aid of his son—basketball out of a "cow barn" and moved it into a coliseum at LSU. It was on its way before Pete Maravich was out of high school, but that doesn't stop them from referring to it around Baton Rouge as "The House that Pete Built."

Before he reached LSU, Press Maravich never knew what it was to make more than $10,000 a year. When Jim Corbett, the late athletic director, telephoned him and said, "This is Jim Corbett, the athletic director at LSU, and I'd like to talk to you about our basketball coaching job," Press was skeptical of the caller and fired back:

"Yeah, and this is Adolph Hitler, and war is hell when you finish second."

Now, basketball has become a means of wealth. Not altogether, but largely because of a son who can play this game like no man has ever played it before, salary is bigger. Opportunities arise in bunches. He has some broadcasting accounts, and "Press Maravich's Maryland Fried Chicken" places around Baton Rouge.

Illogical as it may seem, Pete Maravich has signed a contract with the Hawks for exactly two-thirds of the price that the whole franchise cost when Tom Cousins and Carl Sanders transported it from St. Louis. The buying price was $3 million.

Illogical, I say, because you can't pay such a price with a house that has only 7,000 seats in it. Therefore, Pete Maravich's influence may again be reflected architecturally at another address in the South. The demand to see him and his act may at last make the addition of a coliseum to the muscular culture of Atlanta feasible.

The explanation of Pete Maravich and his genius at basketball goes beyond human perception, even after an evening of attempt at same during the annual gathering of the Atlanta Tipoff Club for the purpose of bestowing upon him the Naismith Award. He did not take to the game naturally, even though he was surrounded by it as he grew up.

Press used every ruse a father could use but couldn't stimulate the interest with a basketball. "Wherever we have lived, we have had a backboard in the backyard," Press said. "When I'd see Pete coming down the street from school, I'd get the basketball and run out in the backyard and start shooting, but he never took the bait."

What did get him was a game played indoors with paper wads and a wastebasket. "When he needed movie money, we'd toss paper wads across the room at the wastebasket. At first, I let him win some. Then it got to the point I didn't have to let him win anymore."

Eventually, this led to the backyard and the backboard. The only time Pete's accuracy ever became embarrassing was when he was a scrawny high-school kid, weighing about ninety pounds, all eyes, as big as Eddie Cantor's, and bones. He would go down to the gym at Clemson and beat Press's own players at "21" and take their money.

FIREBALL
FIRES OFF

NOVEMBER 3, 1980

In the parlance of the track, I'm known as "Fireball." In my heart I know I'm "Chicken Paté," with a slash over the "e." The sound of a stock car revving up causes me to blanch and my neck to shrivel. If I was running at Indianapolis, I'd be delighted when my engine blew on the parade lap.

Nevertheless, on this glistening autumn Sunday afternoon, when a fellow could have been enjoying croquet on the lawn or bird-watching, here I was on the asphalt of Atlanta International Raceway looking into the steely-eyed challenge of four apostles of speed from the local tube. Art ("Ace") Eckman was there, his name etched in the lore of Laguna Seca; Bill ("The Bomb") Hartman, whose tire prints have left their mark on every dirt track in North Georgia; Dave ("Leadfoot") DeSpain, more commonly associated with two wheels than four, a whiz on bikes; and John ("Right Turn") Buren, who has been over more walls than Willie Sutton.

But in reality, they are the "Four Horsepowermen," Eckman of Channel 11, Hartman of Channel 5, DeSpain of Channel 17, and Buren of Channel 2, men of the spoken word and the videotape.

We were having a little speed party at AIR, laughingly called (and I blush) "*Atlanta Journal* 500 Furman Bisher Challenge Race." In the first place, I want it known that I challenged nobody. It was done by proxy. Old goats of my vintage have no business challenging anybody but older goats. I had these kids by several laps on the calendar.

All these years I've talked to race drivers who insisted they go to the track without fear. They never think of dying. They tell death to sit in the corner and shut up, they're doing the driving.

Ho, ho, ho, don't let them kid you. They're scared. They're

so scared they won't be home for dinner they tell their wives not to cook until the race is over.

Death Rides Beside Me was the title of some race driver's drivel, about how he accepted death as just another passenger in the car. I've been there now and I know. The driver was scared to death. Well, that isn't exactly how I meant to say it, but you get the idea.

I didn't sleep well Saturday night. I laughed my way through breakfast. Every little phrase I dropped was to let the family know that I fully expected to be home for dinner. I wish I could have convinced myself.

Then I got to church, and would you believe what was printed in the sermon program? "The State's All-Purpose Will May Not Fit Your Needs. Now Show Your Interest in Your Church." Also, being the week of my birthday, that was in the program too. What an irony!

I hurried home and called my lawyer to make sure my church was remembered in my will, and he said, "What will?" I said, "Make one out right now and put the church in it, and I'll get back to you tomorrow—if I'm still alive."

Sunday night he called and said, "Now, about the church, you forgot to tell me which one."

"What church?" I said.

Speed is a relative thing. The car we raced in was an RX7. I know, it reads like a prescription, but it was a Mazda. Inside, you felt like you were Craig Breedlove at Bonneville Flats. Outside, it sounded like a cat purring. Inside, you felt like you were in orbit. Outside, it looked like another obstacle in freeway traffic.

I wanted it to sound like the blast-off of Apollo 14. Instead, it cooed like a dove. I wanted it to sound like Darrell Waltrip. Instead, it sounded like Woody Allen.

When all the laps had been driven, when all the wordsmiths of the air had been matched against this graying old head, not a drop of blood had been spilt. All lived. Art Eckman, judged by a spurious clock as the fastest, immediately announced his retirement.

Me, I wanted to know why NASCAR doesn't have a Senior Division. And if not that, then how about going over Niagara Falls in a barrel? Courage is cheap when the sun is going down across the bar.

by a spurious clock as the fastest, immediately announced his retirement.

Me, I wanted to know why NASCAR doesn't have a Senior Division. And if not that, then how about going over Niagara Falls in a barrel? Courage is cheap when the sun is going down across the bar.

REDNECK YANKEESE

DECEMBER 11, 1976

I don't know if we can ever forgive Jimmy Carter for this, but because of him the North has discovered the South.

"Hey, Mac," they're saying, "there're really peepul down there, and they tok funny."

Since that electoral Tuesday in November, it has been as if some dark continent has been opened, the savages calmed, and the missionaries sent in to see that we stop boiling our own for dinner. Analytical dudes have been infiltrating our magnolias, dallying about our barbecue havens, eavesdropping at our filling stations and on our elevators—shocked to learn we have them— trying to find out what on earth kind of civilization has spawned our next leader.

The rush would be described as "mad." Each leaps over the other trying to be the first to arrive at the next outlandish revelation. They've made an international celebrity out of a plain man who talks too much, drinks Pabst Blue Ribbon, and pumps gas.

They're taking a cram course in Southern I. And flunking it.

I suppose you noticed *The New York Times* had sent some fellow named B. Drummond Ayres—not just "Drummond Ayres," but "B. Drummond Ayres," if you please—to mix and mingle and reproduce our idiom. (No, that's not the native tongue of idiots.)

First, he arrived at the conclusion that there was a certain element of the "red-neck" about. They have them in the North, except they're "blue-necks," derived from the mixture of clothing, the dust, and the smoke from the factories.

In just a few minutes, he figured he had the South pegged, especially as to how they spoke and how damned-awful, dawgoned, downright rib-tickling it is, and took off.

"Co-Coler," my bicycle seat! And "Lanter?" Hasty Southern

analysis is that Mr. Ayres, Esq., got hold of a bad manuscript written by a resident of Lon Guyland—a land mass lying east of Manhattan and south of Yale—for a low-budget movie set in East Tennessee.

In order to clear the Ayres, and better prepare our various tribes to cope with this influx of Yankee explorers, I shall undertake now to acquaint you with *their* native lingo, how it comes out, and what it means, such as:

"Hawaii?" (Inquiring as to your condition, as in "How's yer healt'?)"

"Noo Yok" (The Large Apple, or Gotham.)

"Caw" (What you drive to work in.)

"Pock" (What you pay $5 a day or $175 a month to do with your caw.)

"Ecks" (What you order scrambled or over light.)

"Berl" (Or sometimes about three minutes.)

"Beckon" (What goes with ecks.)

"Chez" (You. I mean, actually, you yourself, as in "Whatch-chez up tuh?")

"Youse" (Also you, especially if you came from Brooklyn.)

"Cheese" (An old Brooklyn expression, the equivalent of "aloha" to the Hawaiian, ranging anywhere in meaning from "ye gods!" to (censored).)

"Brod" (A woman of dubious reputation in most cases, but in others, any kind of dame.)

"Doc" (Commonly known as man's best friend. Or, as in "Call off yer docs.")

"Kert" (Where you go to get justice, or what has become loosely known as justice.)

"Jawr" (As in "I'm going to give you a bust in the. . . .")

"Lawr" (What you obsoive, unless somebody's watching.)

"Hot" (An organ that beats for nobody else but youse.)

"Coil" (As in the song, "Cause my hair is coily. . . .")

"Goil" (As in the song, "The bells are ringing, for me and my. . . .")

"My-YAMMY" (Where they all hope they go to when they die, provided they can get double-occupancy rate.)

"Sperl" (What happens to the kid if you spare the rod.)

"Joisy" (Either a state or an article of clothing.)

"Bahs" (The guy you work for, or, out of her earshot, the old lady.)

246

"Fuzz" (You know, the mink's gift to womanhood.)

And now to move a little nearer the sporting vernacular:

"Scar" (Like who's ahead, and in what inning.)

"Cause" (The direction you plan to take, as in yachting.)

"Yachtage" (What a running back gains and O.J. Simpson leads the NFL in.)

"Soopah" (As in Bowl.)

"Hoit" (Injury, or as the Brooklyn newspaper hawker once cried out on the street when Waite Hoyt, the pitcher, was wounded, "Hurt's Hoit.")

"Cock-a-Calla" (The drink of the pock.)

"Herd" (First name of a verbose party to Monday Night Football.)

"Bok" (What a pitcher does when his pickoff move doesn't work.)

"Pernt" (As in "Do you get it?)

END OF AN OLD RELATIONSHIP

JULY 1, 1985

The origin of the publicist hasn't been documented, but this story will do as well as any. Moses was standing by the Red Sea with the Egyptian army bearing down on his rear, and he said, "I think I will raise this rod and command the waters to part. Then we can walk through to the other side."

The original publicist, standing at his side, said, "Do it, Moses, and I'll get you two chapters in the Old Testament."

Who created what we know as the columnist, or where or when, is a matter of even murkier nature. It may have been Addison and Steele in *The Spectator,* although they chose to address themselves more elegantly as essayists. On this side of the water, it may have been Ben Franklin, but he came forth rather tentatively under the pen name of Richard Saunders.

The American press seems to have broken out with columnists in the age of Westbrook Pegler, Damon Runyon, and Ring Lardner. But it remained for Grantland Rice to bring glory and some kind of dignity to the sports columnist, soon followed by John Kieran, Henry McLemore, Dan Parker, and, as the broadcasters say, a host of others, some good, some not so good.

The columnist sometimes has been described as one owning a typewriter, an expense account, and an opinion. The early columnists indeed lived lavishly, for they had their audience where television has the audience today. They were dramatic people, given to bulky fedoras, the tailored look, tweeds, neckwear, and scarves. Some flew their own planes, lived in villas, and enjoyed the celebrity of the heroes they wrote about.

They wrote in flowery tones, sentimentally, exaggeratedly, and with worshipful flattery. If he came back today—and that was twenty years ago when he said it—Paul Gallico admitted he would have had to change his style.

Gallico was a chronicler of what a self-flattering age chose to call the "Golden Twenties," of Jones, Ruth, Tilden, Tunney, Dempsey, Sarazen, the rise of radio, the million-dollar fight gate, the first major quest for speed. The era, Gallico wrote, of "the adulation of sports heroes to the point of near hysteria."

Gallico would need a guide to hysteria in sports today, and armor to shield him against it. He took flight of games and heroes, leaving the *New York Daily News* behind in 1936 and settling in a castle in Spain. It was from that refuge that he wrote his somewhat critical but still sentimental "Farewell to Sport." He turned to writing novels, documentary history, and film scripts, moving into the loftier world of letters.

Column writing has not. Gallico would suffer in the world of chipmunkism today, under the hooves of television and its herd and the loss of the national audience. Television has done a lot to the press, none of it good. It has its blood upon its conscience, if it has a conscience.

Even so, the columnist has one last word left, for he has a wide choice of subjects and freedom of opinion. The poor reporter is left with only the result, which is already across the continent by the time he writes.

Writing a column in these times becomes more deploring than adoring, as in Gallico's time. That siphons the cream off the pleasure. You find yourself sitting in the cynic's seat more often than you would choose, instead of writing cheerfully of happy times.

Character in the athlete has been washed away, both in color and in the real sense. Ring Lardner would have no chance in these times for a "You Know Me, Al" kind of series. There's an agent, the pursuit of gold, a players' union, and a clubhouse rule that would stifle such a personality—not to mention the chasm between players and press.

So it is that I take my leave of you, deploring instead of adoring. I came along half a lifetime too late. *The Sporting News* has decided to put this space to other use, and thus I depart. It's time to go. In the bungled phrasing of Primo Carnera, when he was the heavyweight champ no more, "It has been many fun."

The Magazine Field

SOME OF
LIFE'S
MEMORABLE
MOMENTS

SEPTEMBER 1985

Usually, in an article such as this, the reader expects the great, the famous, and the shocking. There is some of each here, but the great are not necessarily shocking, the famous are not necessarily great, and there are as many noncelebrated adventures as events. These are happenings that took place before the eyes of one now a veteran, and there was something about them that had an adhesive effect. They became locked in memory, the ten most memorable moments I have known in sports.

Rather immodestly, more as a form of identifying vintage, let it be said that this veteran saw Jack Dempsey fight, Bill Tilden play tennis, Dazzy Vance pitch, Shoeless Joe Jackson play baseball—long after the parade had passed—Eddie Arcaro ride, had lunch with Pop Warner, sipped bourbon with Ty Cobb, watched a sundown with Red Grange, sat at the bedside of Bobby Jones, and saw Cy Young pilot—at the age of sixty-seven. Some of these will cause one to wonder and question. Where are the Super Bowl, the Indianapolis 500, the Olympic Games, the World Series? Some of these are here, but not what you might expect. Some are here because somebody didn't win. So read on and be your own judge.

In the first World Series I ever covered, the Yankees and the Dodgers were playing the fourth game in Brooklyn. 1947. The Yankees started a journeyman pitcher named Floyd ("Bill") Bevens, and, twenty-six outs later, the Dodgers still had not made a hit off him. Poor fellow, he never got the twenty-seventh out.

Not only did his no-hitter go a-glimmering, but the one hit that Bevens surrendered cost him the ball game. Cookie Lavagetto, a pinch-hitter, rapped a double off the right-field wall at Ebbets Field, two Dodgers scored, and the game was decided by a score of 2-1. Bevens turned to watch the flight of the ball, then, looking neither left nor right, walked straight for the Yankee dugout and into oblivion. It was a scene I'll never forget.

It was probably the most extraordinary heavyweight title fight of all time, forgiving some of the travesties of the present day. Pete Rademacher was the Olympic heavyweight champion, a college graduate and an entrepreneur who organized his own match. He was an amateur who turned pro fighting Floyd Patterson for the championship in Seattle, in an open baseball park called Sicks Stadium. Emil Sick owned a brewery and the Seattle team of the Pacific Coast League. Rademacher floored Patterson in the second round, but the fight ended in the sixth after he had been down seven times for a total count of fifty-three. But he had stayed with the champion of the world. They said he was too old to be coming out as a pro, but, later, Rademacher beat such heavyweights as Zora Folley and Eddie Machen. Today, he is a successful businessman in Medina, Ohio.

On Friday morning before the Kentucky Derby in 1953, my car became stuck in the mud of the barn area at Churchill Downs. A small man said he would be glad to give me a push. Once the car was out of the mush, I got out to shake his hand and thank him. He said his name was Hank Moreno. He also said, "I'll be riding Dark Star in the Derby tomorrow. Be sure to bet on me."

The heavy favorite was Native Dancer, one of the classic Thoroughbreds. Bet against Native Dancer? Of course not. Dark Star broke on top. Dark Star led at the mile. Dark Star led down the stretch. Dark Star won, though fading, by a nose. Dark Star never won a stakes race again. I never had even two bucks on him. It was the only race Native Dancer ever lost.

He was forty-five years old. Refereeing wrestling matches in Atlanta had led to a brawl, then a challenge by a wrestler, and the old boy felt the urge to kill returning. He gave in to bookings that led him to Charlotte on July 29, 1941, to box a former

Oklahoma A&M football player-turned-wrestler named Ellis Bashara in a football stadium. Before the fight, Bashara, who was twenty years younger, told Jack Dempsey, "I hate to knock you out, Mr. Dempsey, but I've always had an ambition to be heavyweight champion of the world. I just hope I don't hurt you." A thunderstorm struck about the hour the fight began, and Dempsey struck as well. Bashara was led back to his corner, then sent out again, whereupon Dempsey left him crumpled and bloody. It was the last bout Jack Dempsey ever fought. Bashara had lasted less than two rounds.

Everybody in Georgia had eyes only for the Georgia-Florida game in Jacksonville in 1980. Georgia Tech had won only one game that season. Notre Dame, ranked #1 in the country, was the opponent in Atlanta. A walkover. A rout. The crowd was sparse. The game rolled on scorelessly. One Georgia Tech quarterback went down, then another, then another. Coach Bill Curry was down to a freshman who had never taken a snap in college. The freshman, Ken Whisenhunt, ran and passed Georgia Tech into field-goal range. The kick was good. Only late in the fourth quarter was Notre Dame able to tie with a line-drive field goal that barely cleared the crossbar. The lowly Yellow Jackets had tied and unseated the #1 team in the nation. The next day, the *Atlanta Journal and Constitution* appeared with a story that began, "Georgia Tech crushed Notre Dame here yesterday, 3-3."

I remember so little of it now. It became a hazy fantasy, so unreal that even today Americans look back upon what they saw coming from Lake Placid with disbelief. A team of American hockey players, mostly college kids, amazed their own people, shocked the rest of the world, defeated the Soviet team in the Olympic Winter Games of 1980. So vivid is the memory that few realize even yet that it was not for the gold medal. After the Russians, they still had to beat Finland for that, which they did. I remember standing at the end, tears rolling down my crusty cheeks, cheering without shame, unprofessional as such behavior is for denizens of the press box.

Hardly a sport can become more hysterical about a threatened record than baseball. The buildup to Henry Aaron's assault on

Babe Ruth's record of 714 home runs reached such a frenzy in 1974 that even the commissioner, Bowie Kuhn, became involved to the point of helping the Atlanta Braves make out their lineup. He ordered Aaron included in the batting order on opening day in Cincinnati. The Braves had preferred to hold him out for fear he might break the record away from his own ballpark. He hit #714 in Cincinnati, retired to the bench, then on opening night in Atlanta, as if by the manuscript, struck #715 off Al Downing of Los Angeles before a full house, both in the stands and in the press box. It was Atlanta's richest moment in major-league baseball.

After five games of the football season of 1948, Wofford College was unbeaten. Also winless. Wofford and Hampden-Sydney tied 6-6. Wofford and Northwest Louisiana tied 0-0. Wofford and Catawba tied 7-7. Wofford and Furman tied 7-7. The fifth opponent was Davidson College, and, sensing an aroma of history, I drove to Spartanburg for the game. Davidson scored a touchdown. Wofford tied the score, and the game ended, 7-7. Wofford is a small Methodist college with no great claim to fame, but in the record book of American football, it is the only team with a string of five ties in a row. The Terriers were still unbeaten at season's end, with the most unusual tally sheet imaginable, 4-0-5. The coach, Phil Dickens, gave all his friends the same gift that Christmas. Ties.

Ben Hogan was fifty-five years old in 1967. He had won his last Masters fourteen years earlier. It was Saturday at Augusta National and he turned the front nine in thirty-six, even par. He was no threat to the leaders, only an old craftsman trying not to embarrass himself. He birdied the tenth hole to a standing ovation, and doffed his white cap. By the time he reached the eighteenth green, he had birdied five more holes and had been received at each green by standing ovations. He played the back nine in thirty strokes, and no player, older or younger, had ever played it in fewer. He checked in with a round of sixty-six. "I think I played the best golf of my life on those last nine holes," he said. "I'd had standing ovations before, but not nine holes in a row." It was one of the richest emotional moments I've ever known in golf. The next day he shot a seventy-seven. It was his last Masters.

The Scots are considered to be the world's most exacting judges of golf. The game has been wrested from them and the power structure is in the United States. In 1977, two Americans brought the auld gyme back to the Scots, and on the seaside acreage of Turnberry, an RAF base during World War II, Tom Watson and Jack Nicklaus put on a dogfight that had the natives of Ayrshire in such a dither they could hardly handle it. The two Yanks were paired the last two days of the British Open. It was two days of match play. Warfare with golf clubs. First Nicklaus, then Watson. Then Nicklaus again, as dramatic a finish to any golf tournament as I have ever seen. The Scots became so unruly that on the last round, both Nicklaus and Watson sat down on their bags in the middle of the ninth fairway and told the officials of the Royal & Ancient, "We're not playing again until you get this gallery under control." A long, winding birdie putt on a par-three hole set it up for Watson, and he came out from under a gorse bush on the eighteenth hole and saved his championship. It was the Scots' game. They gave it to us. It was only proper that this should be their show, romping over the hummocks, through gorse and whin, and going berserk along the Firth of Clyde.

THE MAN PETE ROSE CHASED —AND CAUGHT

DECEMBER 1985

Ty Cobb spent the last few years of his life like "The Flying Dutchman," not to be confused with Honus Wagner, the late great shortstop, but the legendary ship that sailed the seas without ever making port. Cobb tried to find peace in Nevada, in California; he made nostalgic trips to places where major-league teams were in spring training; and, in the most poignant gesture, made an attempt to relocate traces of the youth he had left behind in Georgia.

This is a story of some of that, of the man Pete Rose chased and caught in September 1985—Tyrus Raymond Cobb, sometimes called the greatest baseball player of all time.

Ty Cobb had decided to come home to Georgia to live out his days. He had first gone to Royston, the village in which he had grown up, but found all his old friends either dead or gone and himself an outsider to be pointed out and whispered about, like an expatriate returned. A ghost out of a dim past. So he searched about until he came to a mountaintop near Cornelia, about thirty miles from Royston, which he proclaimed "the highest point between here and Key West."

Cornelia, a town of about 3,500, called that hillside on which Cobb chose to settle Chenocetah Mountain. Cobb stood on the crest of it one February afternoon. There was a chill in the air. His breath fogged up.

"I've used myself up since I was seventeen," he said. He was seventy-one then. "I'm old and I'm tired. I don't like to say that I'm old, but I am. It has been a tough life, twenty-four years of fighting off Nap Lajoie, Joe Jackson, Eddie Collins, Tris Speaker,

257

and Babe Ruth, trying to stay ahead of them. I don't believe any player had any tougher time of it in baseball than I did.

"I want to get out of circulation. I'm going to be hard to find on my mountain."

He was in a mellow mood. His moods could run the full range from fury to sentimental in a matter of a moment.

"Do you see that little valley down there?" he asked. An open field lay between another rise to the east and a clump of forested hills at the foot of the mountain. "Just on the other side of those rises, in that little valley, is the house where I was born. Nobody lives in it now, but it is still standing.

"There is something sacred to a man about the place he was born, and I've come to feel something about this view I get from my mountain."

At the foot of that mountain, on December 18, 1886, Tyrus Raymond Cobb had been born to Herschel and Amanda Cobb, she still in her teens. His birthplace is listed in *The Baseball Encyclopedia* as Narrows, in Banks County. It was a settlement of Confederate Army officers, including Captain Caleb Chitwood, Amanda's father. There is no trace of Narrows today.

Cobb had been led to Cornelia by an automobile dealer who claimed to be a second cousin, but whose kinship Cobb dismissed. The only man Cobb spent much time with in Cornelia was a truck line operator. They drank together, and this was about the only casual pleasure Cobb found in the town, once known for its production of apples.

"I'm going to build a house on Chenocetah Mountain. It will be built of crabapple stone and red brick, and it will sit crosswise of the plateau, and there will be plenty of windows for drinking in the view in all its fullness," he said.

He had an architect's rendering of the home he planned in the house he had rented. "I've never built a house before. I've waited until I'm seventy-one. Every man should build at least one house in his lifetime. I'm sorry that I've waited so late, but I've found the right spot at last. If a man understands the symphony of the winds, and sees the things his soul sees, he can enjoy living on that mountain."

Sadly, Cobb never took refuge on Chenocetah Mountain. He was restless. He crisscrossed the country two or three more times. He had lived too long in the West to feel at home in the area of his birth. There were no friends, no natural ties. An excavation was made for the house, but construction never began.

"There is a quality about the people where a fellow is born that makes him feel at home, like he belongs," he had said, but he was only trying to convince himself. He tried so hard. "Just let me move in and belong. That's all this fellow Cobb wants here."

About all that was left of Cobb in that part of Georgia was the hospital he had built in the name of his parents and the mausoleum he had already built for himself in the Royston cemetery, and in which he was put to rest in 1961.

Two of his sons had died before him—Ty, Jr. a doctor, and Herschel, a Coca-Cola bottler in California. Ty, Jr. was forty-two, Herschel only thirty-three. They, another son, and two daughters were the children of his first marriage. A second marriage lasted only a few years, and he spent his "evening years," as he called them, a loner.

The family tragedy that saw his father killed in his own home while Ty was still in his teens came to visit upon him again once his days as a player were done. His father, an educator, legislator, and county official in Royston, was his idol. He would have had his son be a doctor or a lawyer.

"If I had been a doctor," Cobb said, "I could have had the companionship of my son. I could have been the beacon that pointed him the way. But I was a baseball player, and neither of my sons had any inclination toward baseball, so I never had their companionship."

A barrister in a nearby town once invited Cobb into his office. "He wanted to acquaint me with Blackstone, surely the work of my father. I cracked those books three or four times. . . . I knew I didn't want to be a lawyer."

Once he reached the big leagues, Cobb fought his way through baseball as a man beset by the miseries. In the autumn of his years, he explained himself, made an admission he had never been expected to make. "I did it for my father, who was an exalted man," he said, explaining his lifelong rage. "He never got to see me play. But I knew he was watching me, and I never let him down."

His success as a player with the Detroit Tigers never was matched as a manager. He was released after six years, and while his own performance never suffered, he could never bring his team up to his own level.

The records he set as a player seemed at the time unapproachable. He had played twenty-four seasons—terrorizing pitchers, challenging fielders on the bases, always on the attack, looking for the edge, demanding to be #1. Against the incomparable Walter Johnson, his lifetime batting average was .335. He stole 892 bases, made 4,191 hits, scored 2,245 runs, and batted an almost unbelievable .367 from 1905 to 1928, when, as a forty-two-year-old active legend, he batted .323 playing for Connie Mack and the Philadelphia Athletics.

It was written that probably no other player would ever come close to stealing 892 bases or making 4,191 hits. Surely no one would ever average .367 for a lifetime. Lou Brock has since stolen 938 bases, 118 in one season, breaking Maury Wills's record of 104, which had broken Cobb's record of ninety-six. Now Pete Rose has left Cobb in second place in hits-per-career, but let it be said that by the time the 1985 season opened, the Cincinnati manager/first baseman had already been to bat nearly 2,000 times more than Cobb. His lifetime batting average more then sixty points lower.

Still, fascination with the man goes on, and will endure, for Cobb remains after all these passing years one of the perplexing subjects of sports. Don Honig, in a recently published book, *Baseball America,* sums him up thus:

"His talent for collecting base hits was equaled only by a perverted genius for alienating people. So to hear Cobb described by his peers as the game's greatest player is a most telling tribute, because most of the encomiasts despised him, usually with evidence in hand, because Ty at one time or another had spiked them, run them down, slugged them, bedeviled them, insulted them, intimidated them, humiliated them, or otherwise unsettled their digestive tracts.

". . . Like him or not, Cobb was a symbol of America on the go, unstoppable, audaciously self-confident, innovative."

Even this characterization by a devoted historian of baseball only scratches the surface of a man whose life was lived as if driven. The mystery goes back to the little house in Banks County, where Cobb was born the son of a mother still a child herself and a baronial father who died in a tragedy that marked Ty Cobb forever.

WHERE COACHES COME FROM

SEPTEMBER 1986

One of the nicest immortals I've ever known is Red Grange, old #7, "The Galloping Ghost" of Illinois, product of the Roaring Twenties, when hero consciousness first began to come alive in the mind of America. And one of the neatest stories I've ever read successfully depicting an admirable humbleness in such a man was of an incident that W.C ("Bill") Heinz, a literary craftsman of his time, shared with Grange on a cold night in Syracuse.

They were leaving a restaurant and Heinz asked Grange, "That jersey with the 77 on it that's preserved at Illinois, is that your last-game jersey?"

"I don't know," Grange said, "it's probably a new jersey."

"Do you have any piece of equipment that you wore on the football field?"

"No," Grange said, "I don't have anything. I don't even have an I-sweater."

There was silence for about three paces. "You know," Grange said, "I'd kind of like to have an I-sweater now."

Naturally, such a man as this with such a talent for carrying a football and scoring touchdowns would make a splendid coach, would he not? The answer is he would not, which was something he best explained himself.

"I can't take much credit for what I did running with a football, because I don't know what I did. Nobody ever taught me and I can't teach anyone," he said. "You can teach a man how to block or tackle or kick or pass. The ability to run is something you have or you haven't. . . . The sportswriters used to try to explain it, and they used to ask me. I couldn't tell them anything."

So Red Grange, when his running days were done, went into insurance and broadcasting and did well. What, then, does go into the making of a coach, and why is it that so often it's the little defensive back, the obscure lineman, or the benchwarmer who becomes the big-time success in the campus game? The question is no more easily answered than Red Grange trying to explain how he runs, but we shall, here, take a look at some coaches and how it came about.

It just so happens that the National Coach of the Year last season is a vivid example of those who have coached their way out of the boondocks. Fisher DeBerry grew up in the small town of Cheraw, South Carolina, played football at the small college of Wofford in Spartanburg, South Carolina, and was coaching in the obscurity of Appalachian State when he was hired to coach the offense at the Air Force Academy. Last year, DeBerry finished his third successful season as head coach, with the loss of only one game, and came to know the feeling of instant celebrity. With all the renowned names in American head coaching in the audience, DeBerry marched forward to be awarded the trophy as the best of them all at the annual national coaches' convention.

There have been coaches who managed to succeed though they hardly played the game. In fact, the man who brought the greatest fame to Marquette University before the school abandoned the game was Frank Murray, who never played football at all. Dick Crum, a professorial little man who was head coach at North Carolina, was only a junior varsity player at Mount Union, a small college in Ohio. When Lou Holtz pursued education at Kent State, he was listed as a third-string 158-pound linebacker. "And you can imagine how much a third-string 158-pound linebacker played, even at Kent State," he has said.

Always in his mind, though, was the ambition to coach the football team at Notre Dame, to the point that one of the clauses in his contract at Minnesota allowed for his escape should the Notre Dame job become open. It did, and now, after William and Mary, North Carolina State, Arkansas, and Minnesota, Lou Holtz is indeed head football coach at Notre Dame with his background as a 158-pound linebacker.

A man long before him at Notre Dame, Frank Leahy, was no more than a journeyman lineman for Knute Rockne. He spent more time recuperating from injury than performing, but made it up to the Irish as one of their most dynamic coaches.

A fate followed another legend at Ohio State. Earle Bruce came down injured as a freshman and spent the rest of his college days on the house, due in no small way to the generosity of Woody Hayes, the man in whose shoes he later walked.

A coach unusual in this day and time is Dick Sheridan, who

made the transfer from Furman University to North Carolina State. Like Frank Murray, Sheridan never played college football. He was bound for West Point but needed some preparatory courses, which led him to South Carolina for a year, at the end of which he had lost his military fervor. He spent the rest of his academic years looking over Paul Dietzel's shoulder and preparing himself for what he knew he wanted to be—a football coach.

Miami of Ohio has been a greenhouse for major college coaches. Young coaches would come there, coach a few years, enjoy some success, then be plucked from the vine by some larger school. At one time, there were four head coaches in the Big Ten who had done their apprenticeship at Miami: Hayes at Ohio State, Ara Parseghian at Northwestern (later Notre Dame), John Pont at Indiana, and Bo Schembechler at Michigan. Now a fifth, Bill Mallory at Indiana.

Schembechler is our subject here, an average tackle who did military duty, then began preparing himself for coaching at Presbyterian College in South Carolina, working with another head coach who never played college football, Bill Crutchfield. It worked. Soon he was head coach at Miami of Ohio and on his way to Big Ten championships and Rose Bowl appointments at Ann Arbor.

There has been a pipeline newly opened between the pro leagues and the campus, triggering a reverse flow, retiring players coming back to coach, and with better-than-average success. Joe Morrison, Bill Curry, Ray Perkins, and Joe Kapp all spent long careers as professionals, and defying the trend stressed above, all as stars of some caliber. Morrison left the bright lights of New York and broke into coaching off the fast lane at Chattanooga, followed by a stand at New Mexico, and since has brought new prosperity to South Carolina. Both Curry and Perkins returned to their alma maters, Georgia Tech and Alabama. For Curry, the transition was painful until he learned what coaching is about.

"Coaching is getting the right kind of people about you," he said.

Perkins followed Paul Bryant, whose legendary reputation made the burden no easier. Last season, though, both he and Curry had their teams in bowl games and were at ease at last.

Kapp came home to the old school to coach the California Bears, but all has not gone too well. Nor for Maxie Baughan, another Georgia Tech alum, who transferred his Alabama-bred lingo from the Detroit Lions staff to Cornell. Life in the Ivy League has left a few welts on his pelt.

This is not to say that greatness as a player stands in the way of greatness as a coach. Bud Wilkinson was All-American at Minnesota, later a coaching legend at Oklahoma. Bobby Dodd was All-American at Tennessee, later a coaching legend at Georgia Tech. Johnny Majors was a few votes away from winning the Heisman Trophy as a halfback at Tennessee in 1956, and since has coached a national champion—with an asterisk by it—back where he was Mr. Touchdown.

Of all Heisman winners, though, only two have been college football head coaches. John David Crow, who won the statue in 1957, later coached football at Northeast Louisiana, though not for long. Another, Steve Spurrier, Heisman winner of 1967, has been a head coach among the pros, in the USFL, and now is at Duke.

The most prolific winner of all college coaches came from farthest back in the pack, and has won all his 329 games on the same campus. Eddie Robinson played college football at Leland, a small school in Louisiana where football is no longer played. True, several of his victories have not been over recognizable names, but when he put his team on the field, they were presumed to be among equals. In fact, you would not recognize Grambling by its old name today, and a story goes with that.

While Robinson was still a young coach, the president went before the Louisiana state legislature pleading to have the school's name changed from Louisiana Normal Institute for Negroes. When he came to his major selling point, the gentleman told the assembly, "Gentlemen, last week we were playing an opponent who had our team backed up to our own 10-yard line. Our cheerleaders started to lead our student section in a cheer, begging our team to hold that line.

"Before they could get out the cheer, 'Hold that line, Louisiana Normal Institute for Negroes, hold that line,' the other team had already scored."

The compassionate legislature allowed the change, and that is why today Grambling is Grambling.

A FEW LAUGHS AND A FEW TEARS

OCTOBER 1985

This is mainly vintage material. The stories here in date back to a time in football when a certain natural, simple-hearted humor used to abound. The appeal may lean more toward the seniors among us, but the young are invited to join in for a few laughs, a few surprises, and a hint of what it was like in Dad's day. Old Dad had a few chuckles in his time, you know.

Rensselaer Poly never has been a big name in football, but once, to the campus in Troy, New York, came a physical giant who stood out above all those around him. Big Stan Gorzelnic made a difference in a ball game.

RPI was playing University of Buffalo and leading, 7-0, in a game in which Gorzelnic rose to new heights, when, in the third quarter, his left shoe was so badly ripped he had to leave the field. Equipment budgets being limited in such schools, the coach searched up and down the bench for a replacement shoe large enough.

"Take them off," he barked at the benchwarmers. "You don't know what size you're wearing, anyway."

It was a fruitless search. There wasn't a size 13 among them. Meantime, Buffalo was running the end vacated by Gorzelnic and having its way, and by the time the trainer performed a crude repair job with the damaged shoe and the big end returned to the game, RPI was behind, 14-7, and lost.

The locker room was still, and the players were somberly undressing when they heard an outrageous roar and a huge shoe came flying through the air—one of the coach's.

The player it narrowly missed picked up the shoe and looked inside. Size 13, it said.

Chubby Kirkland was a giant among small college coaches, and a patriotic man. But when the U.S. Military Academy came to Catawba College and recruited—"stole" was the word for it—his star back after the 1945 season, he carried his complaint all the way to President Truman.

Charlie Gabriel was an eighteen-year-old sophomore who had led the nation in offensive yardage the season before. Kirkland had two great seasons in mind for him at Catawba, which, as a matter of fact, went ahead without him and scored in ninety-one straight games, a new national record.

"All the West Point people are looking for is football talent, not some boy they can make into a soldier," Kirkland said in his rage. Colonel Earl Blaik's team was at its peak then, with Glenn Davis and Doc Blanchard in their prime.

Charlie Gabriel became a plebe in spite of Kirkland's protests, but his football career at West Point never became what it might have been. He was injured and his play was limited, but he plugged on and worked out his commission, graduating on schedule.

Chubby Kirkland has long been dead. What a shame he could not have lived until that day several months ago when the U.S. Air Force announced the name of its new chief of staff: General Charles A. Gabriel. Charlie, the kid from Lincolnton, North Carolina, who led the nation in offense at Catawba in 1945.

The field clock was a luxury late arriving on the campus of Greeley State in Colorado. Official game time was kept by a member of the officials' team at a table on the sideline.

One Saturday night, as Greeley State was locked in a ferocious battle with a traditional rival, the coach, John W. Hancock, as it were, called to a substitute and said, "Go check on the time, son." It was late in the game and seconds were precious.

The player raced toward the timer's table, and after what seemed an eternity, returned to the coach's side breathless and tongue-tied.

"Well," said the coach, impatient and anxious, "what about the time?"

"It's fifteen minutes to ten, coach," the substitute said.

Still one of the classic games in college football history was the Notre Dame victory over Ohio State in 1935, last time the two teams played. With seconds left to play, Bill Shakespeare threw a nineteen-yard touchdown pass to Wayne Millner in an hysterical 18-13 finish, but lost in time is the name of the quarterback who called the play.

It was the first, last, and only play Jim McKenna ever made for Notre Dame.

McKenna couldn't make the traveling squad, but he wanted to see the game so intensely that he showed up in Columbus with his uniform under his arm and asked Coach Elmer Layden if he might suit-up so he could sit on the sideline and watch. Layden agreed.

Those were before the days of free substitution. No player could reenter a game in the same quarter in which he had been removed. Layden had sent in so many players desperately trying to save the game that he had run out of quarterbacks when he suddenly remembered McKenna. He called the uninvited quarterback and sent him in to call the pass that Shakespeare threw to Millner.

McKenna dropped out of school a few weeks later and never played again.

Tom Nugent said that in all his years as football coach at VMI, Maryland, and Florida State, only one player ever came to his home, knocked on the door, and challenged his judgment. The player had been used as a running back and a defensive back at Florida State, but at neither position had he been overworked. He was rankling in stagnation, when one day Nugent heard a knock on his door in Tallahassee, answered it, and found himself confronted by a disgruntled athlete.

"Coach," the player began, "I want to know why I'm not playing more. I know I'm better than some of these guys playing in front of me."

It really didn't increase his playing time, but it did give a coach something to remember him by.

His name: Burt Reynolds.

This may have been the most remarkable blocked punt of all time. At least it was voted the oddity of the football season of 1945 by the Associated Press.

California was playing UCLA, and the Bruins were favored to make it to the Rose Bowl. The field was a quagmire. The first half had been scoreless. When California got the ball on its 34-yard line, the Golden Bears decided to play it safe. Jack

Lerond punted on first down, but his kick was blocked. The ball was deflected sideways across the field, picked up by the California quarterback, and he started running upfield. He was cornered about midfield, where, turning, he saw Lerond, the punter, coming behind him. He lateraled to Lerond, who went the rest of the way for the only touchdown of the game.

A blocked punt had turned into the winning score for the team whose punt was blocked!

Earl Henson was a third-string back who didn't play much and didn't sleep a lot. The night before Appalachian State's big game against Catawba, he showed up in the sports publicist's office about 1 A.M.

"Sort of late for a player to be up before the big game, isn't it?" Gene Wike, the publicist, said.

"Couldn't sleep," Henson said. "Besides, I've got a story for you."

While dozing, Henson had had a dream. With a minute left in the game against Catawba, he had taken the snap and run ninety-six yards for the winning touchdown. "Write it down just like I told you," Henson said.

The next day, the game was scoreless. Forty seconds were left to play when Henson was sent in at quarterback. The third-stringer took the snap, broke over left tackle, into the clear, and ran ninety-six yards for the touchdown that won the game— just as he had told it to the sports publicist. Hard to believe, but true.

Television arrived in football in 1939, when Fordham beat Waynesburg, 34-7, to the attention of almost no one. Nine thousand spectators came to the game at Randall's Island Stadium in New York.

It aroused so little interest that the first televised football game in history was passed off thusly in *The New York Times:* "The Rams [Fordham] tallied in every period and had the *televised* game in hand by halftime."

No other mention was made of television.

The game was covered by one camera set up about midfield. Coaches have always said that's the worst place in the world to watch a football game.

Index